Contributing Editors

Ava Ruth Baker

Daina Krumins

Jane Meyerding

Sola Shelly

Acknowledgments

I am profoundly, head over heals grateful: to the contributing editors—each an extraordinary woman, irrepressibly Aspie—for all the work, energy, focus, and imagination they gave to the project:

- to **Ava**, for her stunning dedication to creating the thread chapters;
- to **Sola**, for her intensity and commitment to getting things said;
- to **Jane**, for her sound judgment and the clarity of her perceptions;
- to **Daina** for her creative genius and her ready energy.

And this only touches the surface!

Special thanks also:

- to Judy Singer for her rich perspective on neurological culture and her capacity for jump-starting anything dormant;
- to the participants of WFAP, our e-mail list, for helping create the knowledge of who we are;
- to Mary Margaret Britton Yearwood for helping keep me sane, more or less, and for introducing me to Boston;
- to Martha Kate Downey for her friendship, constancy, and amazing example;
- to the adult autism support lists for an accumulated wealth of insight: they've nurtured and birthed: InLv, AS-GIRLS, ANI-L;
- to fellow neuroAtypicals, Charles Avinger, Martha Held, Max Gibson, Angela Meador, and Mary Bogart for making me feel less alone.

Endless gratitude:

- to my family for bearing with my book perseveration:
- to Bernie for his courage, brilliance, and faith in me;
- to Adrian for his wisdom and insight;
- to Cassie for accepting me as-is and keeping me grounded;
- to my boy cats, the late Luigi, and his successor Louie, for the delight and soft therapy of their company;
- to my parents, in particular, for the delight they took in me as "a character" when I was a little girl, and also for seeing to it that I got educated;

- to my students and colleagues at Washtenaw Community College for many daily reasons, and to the College's open door that even welcomes *me*.

Finally, abundant thanks to my three magnificent writing teachers:

- to Janice Lauer for being a loyal and loving teacher and friend over a lifetime, for introducing me to poetry, for encouraging my writing, and for seeing value in me at a time when I didn't think I had any;
- to Winston Weathers, who taught me so many enduring lessons about writing style;
- to the late British novelist, Paul Scott, especially for encouraging me to "risk all!" ([Gulp] Here goes, Scotty!)

Jean Kearns Miller, Dancing Mind Books, Milan, Michigan, USA, February, 2003

Dedicated to

Women in the universe of autism
everywhere:
officially diagnosed or self-diagnosed
living independently or with supports
low or high functioning
aware of their AS
or
still searching for their truth.

Preface

Removing the Tarnish

Schuyler

Some people are granted a silver platter. They take it for granted, and toss it around carelessly scratching the surface, throwing it at people, and not taking care of what it is and its beauty. Others are handed a dirty old stainless steel trashcan. They work with it carefully scrubbing away at the surface finding the small dints of shine. Over time, they clean the grunge off, knowing it really isn't a silver lining. They continue working for a good, strong stainless steel surface. As they clean the can they find the stainless steel surface and they make their dreams come true. Silver platters may look pretty but if you don't know what to do with one, it is just a toy that gets tossed around and scratched mercilessly. Stainless steel may not be as pretty but it's strong and durable, and if you work with it carefully it has a beautiful shine. Nothing is anything other than what you want it to be.

Foreword

Travels in Parallel Space:
An Invitation

Judy Singer

We invite you to join us on our journey of discovery into realms of inner space. This is not a book that will give you a list of pathologies and signs. Rather we ask you to admire our surprising gifts and our insights that push the boundaries of what the human mind can accomplish. But we also ask you to recognize the very real limitations that frustrate us.

- Think how it feels to face the world with inadequate filters against sensory overload.
- Think how it feels when the simplest motor skills, the actions that should be no more difficult than breathing, escape us and become a struggle for mastery over an unwieldy material world.
- Think how it feels that we, of all people, who have such powerfully single-minded vocations, who hunger more than most to fulfill our vocations, must everywhere seem to be prevented by those eagle-eyed gatekeepers, the networkers, the social police who will prevent us from accessing the resources we need because we fail an irrelevant eye-contact test, or the right-kind-of-smile-on-the-way-to-the-water-cooler test.
- Bear witness to the violations of human rights we have suffered; the teasing, the torment in the playground; the discrimination by employers on social grounds in jobs where social skills should not be part of the criteria; the pressure from families to act normal, to be more feminine, to have children. If this is hard enough for NT women, how much harder is it for us?

We invite you to travel in parallel with us for a while, and see how the world looks from our angle. We invite women, but welcome men too, for we are not *real* women according to any of the known guidebooks! And, just as women in other beleaguered minorities have found their primary identification with the men who share their excluded status, many of us will feel that we have more in common with men on the autistic spectrum than with Neurotypical, or what I would prefer to call Sociophile women. In fact, we may have more in common with NT men than we do with NT women, for it is women who are more often the social gatekeepers who scrutinize our manners, care more for them than for our minds, and want to keep us out of the club.

We may look female, but we are not feminine in so far as being feminine is a social construct (or *social delusion*, as Laura Tisoncik says) and not an innate property of the female sex. Consider how much of femininity is about taking a precise reading of all the social currents of a given moment and aligning (and if necessary, abnegating) oneself to serve the stability of the moment and the wellbeing of all those who inhabit it, whether this means sniffing out the exact social dress code that precisely fits the moment in history, the subculture, and the occasion, or reading all the social cues in a group and occupying the niche most guaranteed to soothe, nurture, and harmonize all who are in it. This is not the role our wiring has created us for.

On the whole, we do not behave as women are meant to. We are not there to smooth the social consensus. We are there to follow the beat of our different drum. In this sense we speak for and can be role models for all creative women who feel a conflict between their vocation and their compliant, nurturing instincts.

But at the same time, do not forget that the human rights of autistic people should not depend on our talents or our creative potential. Many of us have vocations or obsessions that do not further the cause of human kind, that have no practical use, that are not likely to produce anything of social value. Some of us will need to consume more social resources than we can ever produce or repay—except of course in generating jobs for health workers, carers, administrators, and the entire health and welfare social apparatus. In this way we do indeed become primary producers who add to the gross national product, if that is your concern in these economically dry and supposedly rational times.

This seems like a good place then to come clean. What it all boils down to is this. We are *not* from another planet. We tricked you. We made you look. We are from right here, Planet Earth. We are an integral part of this earth's ecosystems, its intricately inter-dependant network of niches and potentialities.

What we are is the first of a new wave of consciousness in a planet coming to awareness of its extraordinary diversity. We are the first wave of a new liberation movement, a very late wave, and a big one, just when you thought the storm of identity politics, with its different minorities jockeying for recognition, was surely over. We are part of the ground swell of what I want to call *Neurological Liberation*. It is my hope that this book will begin the task of adding a further intersection to the current framework of gender, class, ethnicity, race, sexual orientation, age, and disability. I hope it will add *neurological difference* to the existing set of social variables.

I hope this book will be a starting point for the kind of process that the women's movement went through of transforming the supposed pathologies of women into gold. Remember *dumb* blondes; *dried up* spinsters; *ugly* eggheads; *raging* nymphomaniacs; *smothering* mothers: *castrating* females; the choice between being madonnas or whores and little else in between?

Remember how the women's movement turned these stereotypes around to show how oppression based on gender had turned good women into monsters, first by existentially undermining them, then by pathologizing their attempts to fight back? May this book do the same for people who are neurologically different, who never fit into the neurological procrustean bed, who have a range of abilities and disabilities that, until the last few years, were never dreamed of in any therapeutic philosophy.

I hope this book will push the envelope for people on the autistic spectrum, going some way to recasting our so-called pathologies, and opening up new thinking, new ways of organizing society, new ways of being, so that all kinds of minds in all kinds of gender identities and bodies can flourish and feed their gifts to our waiting planet.

© Judy Singer

Table of Contents

Introduction

The title of this book is, among other things, a play on the title of an immensely popular book by John Gray called *Men Are from Mars, Women Are from Venus*. Gray's book typifies men and women with a set of characteristics associated with the warrior planet, Mars (men), and the amorous planet, Venus (women). So resonant is this taxonomy with the public that it has spawned a cottage industry of sorts, complete with novelties and training courses. People seem to find it a useful interpersonal tool. For me and the other women whose writings and conversations appear here, Gray's book can serve, at best, as a field guide to two subgroups of the same culture, a culture we find as bewildering as you may find us, and to which we belong only provisionally, as though on permanent visa. We are from neither Mars nor Venus, but—from another planet? Our planet may be as far away as Pluto or, as a number of us speculate, as near as Earth. We are women on the autism spectrum.

Autism: a Makeshift Definition

Before considering the concept of an autism spectrum, some basics. This may be oversimplifying, but I tend to see autism, at its roots, as a *significant information processing problem or difference* (depending on circumstance). Information comes in but the processing varies remarkably from the way normal people process, and resulting behaviors may differ as well, whether the incoming information is:

Sensory: extreme sensitivity or hyposensitivity to stimuli, which may be variable among the senses; sensory overload; the use of "stims" (self-stimulation routines) to get relief from sensory and social bombardment.

Social: asocial; inability to perceive others' intentions (i.e., poor *Theory of Mind (ToM)*); difficulty determining the rules for give-and-take interaction; inability to assume/recognize social roles; strong preference for inner world; gullible and tending to accept at face value; lacking common prejudice; poor eye contact, or its over correction, staring; little or no reciprocity.

Cognitive: weak, or faulty inference making; strong pattern recognition; visual memory; literal, concrete thinking; extreme difficulty with "multi-tasking"; unusual abilities in specific areas; focus on inner world; can be masterful over special interests but may have trouble mastering even simple information otherwise; may be well read, with large vocabulary, but may not grasp concepts well.

Kinesic: inability to draw common inferences from posture, facial expression, other body language; unusual mannerisms and expressions.

Emotional: incongruity between affect and felt emotion, or between affect, emotion, and trigger event; difficulty with modulation; lags in emotional development; thinking before feeling.

Executive: difficulty prioritizing needs, sequencing tasks, estimating time and resources; reliance on fixed routines; difficulty judging needs; able to approach problems intellectually that are considered emotion laden by the culture.

Sensorimotor/kinesthetic: large or fine motor coordination problems (or gifts); difficulty judging distances; unusual gait, posture; limited body awareness.

The Autism Spectrum and the Diagnostic Dilemma

The concept of an autism spectrum has arisen out of a diagnostic and discursive need, and the search to elucidate distinctions began in the infancy of the diagnosis. Autism was discovered by two geographically distant contemporaries: Leo Kanner in 1943 and Hans Asperger in 1944. This would have been merely an interesting coincidence but for the disparities between their descriptions of the condition. The subjects of Kanner's work, it seems, differed in some ways from Asperger's subjects, a historical accident that immediately sparked the search for a vocabulary adequate to describe the nuances of what they were seeking to define. That search continues today. Some autistics are said to have *Kanner type* traits. Some are said to have *Asperger's Syndrome*. But this binary classification has proved inadequate. Generally, Asperger's Syndrome is the label applied to those who lack some of the highly pronounced (usually sensory and cognitive) markers for autism, as the term was applied by Kanner. These people also may be told they have "mild" (or at least, "milder") autism. Some diagnosticians and other interested parties prefer to restrict the term *autism* to those seen as *Kanner type* in full, although Asperger used the term *autism* as well. Now comes another label, high-functioning autism (HFA), a multi-purpose term I have seen used to refer to those who are autistic without intellectual impairment (retardation), to Asperger people, and to those who have made such progress that their condition has been upgraded. However, some people who make that kind of progress have seen their diagnosis change from autism (*or* HFA) to Asperger's Syndrome. Confused? I thought so.

Adding to the confusion are the markers used to distinguish among autistics that raise more questions than they answer. For example, children (and adults) diagnosed Asperger often have motor skill deficits and difficulty with spatio-temporal orientation. The typical recipient of an Asperger diagnosis is quite clumsy. Those who receive an autism (or HFA) diagnosis are not. Also, *autistic* children have a significant delay in language acquisition. *Asperger* children do not; even when they do not speak until near their third birthday and then begin speaking in full sentences, this is not a statistically significant delay. What might account for such disparate differences?

Now we're up to three terms, but there's a fourth: Pervasive Developmental Disorder (PDD). PDD is the name for a larger category under which autism and Asperger's Syndrome fall, along with their versatile companion, PDD-NOS (not otherwise specified). This diagnosis can be given to children who are disqualified somehow from the other diagnoses. For example, any hint of hallucinations (possible schizophrenia) negates the Asperger diagnosis, even when all other criteria are met. And what to do about those with a smattering of autistic traits but no definitive match in the autistic alphabet soup dished up so far? Clearly, the diagnostic difficulty is rooted in the diversity of autism itself, which is neither unitary, nor binary, but plural.

The issue of diagnosis is also complicated by two other things, the first being likelihood of comorbidity. Many autism spectrum people have one or more other conditions, such as Attention Deficit Disorder (ADD), chronic or recurrent mood disorders, Tourette's Syndrome traits, learning disabilities, *Prosopagnosia* (the inability to read faces in an integrated way, and therefore inability to recognize people), and others. Whichever symptom the person presents as needing expert attention (which often implies consulting a medical specialist) tends to become the basis of a primary diagnosis, even though the autism spectrum designation may accommodate these seemingly comorbid conditions as well.

The second problem with diagnosis applies to those who are functioning well in the world: getting an education, holding down a job, maintaining relationships, raising children, or otherwise not needing or, at least, not getting social or medical intervention. The DSM-IV (Diagnostic and Statistical Manual of the American Psychological Association, fourth edition) checklist imposes the criterion of significant impairment in critical areas of the person's life. A number of people have been refused diagnosis on this basis. The professionals they consult tell them they cannot possibly have Asperger Syndrome, since they are functioning so well. Fair enough when it comes to psychologists and psychiatrists whose job it is to heal or treat the sick. (*If it ain't broke, don't fix it.*) Yet I wonder how completely professionals can understand AS without the bigger picture of those who live with AS every day but have not seen fit to show up at their doors. Indeed, one of the points most of us will make is that AS is a neurological difference that often *turns clinical* in a culture that doesn't value AS strengths. Much of our survival requires us not to become better functioning, but to better function according to the cultural hegemony of NTs, the neuro-typicals, who call the shots about what is valued in people.

An Autism Spectrum Phrase Book for This Book

I reckon it's time for a side trip into the terminological universe of this book. You will see both AC and AS used throughout. AC stands for autistics and "cousins," to include those with autistic traits insufficient for an autism diagnosis. Also considered cousins by many autistics are all those with neurological conditions such as those mentioned above: ADD, Tourette's, et al. AS is used for autism spectrum and for Asperger Syndrome; frequently the two meanings are functionally indistinguishable. Likewise, AC and AS often are used interchangeably, with some writers in this book using AC and others AS. A final term is *Aspie*, shorthand for someone with Asperger's Syndrome. This joins a growing number of diminutives, like *Addie* for someone with ADD, and *normie* for a person not included in a particular disability community—a term replaced by *NT*, neuro-typical, by many Aspies. We Aspies like *Aspie* just fine, although it's a bit grating—like a fingernail down a blackboard—when those who see us as clinical specimens appropriate the term. Kind of like a door-to-door salesman who calls you honey. Now, where were we? Oh, yes...)

Challenges of Life on the Spectrum

The fact that an Aspie is not requesting or receiving assistance does not mean his or her life is not significantly impaired by difficulties that come with AS. Life for most of us involves making peace with, and learning how to manage considerable limitations. It's harder than people might guess from our external presentation. Things NTs find easy often require elaborate compensatory tactics for us—and still we fall short. This may not show at all on the outside, though often there is a pattern of mishaps, ranging from simple gaffes to surprising (to others) failures, which no one connects with a pervasive neurological disorder. It is hard to imagine someone with AS for whom the condition does not impose significant challenges, however invisible her AS may be.

In this diagnostic context, *Women from Another Planet?* focuses on a particular AS population: AS women, whose existence further compounds diagnostic issues but also offers the hope of important insights.

There are a number of reasons why *Women from Another Planet?* needed to be written. The three major ones are: the under-diagnosis of AS in women; the socio-cultural expectations of society borne by all women and what that means to women with social deficits; and the need to discover and present our personal knowledge of how women manifest and experience being AS.

Under-diagnosis in Women

AS has long been considered a male condition, so great was the professional community's focus on boys. In recent years, the growing number of women seeking diagnosis has called into question not only the condition's prevalence in the female population, but its commonly accepted parameters as well. Professionals are beginning to speculate that AS often manifests differently in women. Empirical and clinical embellishments to the DSM-IV criteria have portrayed AS in the form of a *little professor* utterly absorbed in recounting factual information in a monotone. Yet this manifestation of AS, not always present in boys, is even rarer in AS girls, who may, for example, have the same passion for facts but less drive to exhibit that knowledge. Clinicians who default to this boyish profile engendered by their own diagnostic narrowness may have a blind spot that keeps them from seeing the whole autistic spectrum. At the same time, little professorial girls may be seen as a social anomaly (not acting like girls), and their perceived socio-sexual deviance may obscure their neurological difference.

In fact, a paradox has existed since Asperger first identified the syndrome. He was aware of the existence of AS girls but explained them away as having a post-puberty syndrome resulting from childhood encephalitis—as opposed to boys, who are born autistic and therefore have the more essential condition. In any case, his subjects were boys; girls were simply beyond his scope. Many years later, Uta Frith attributed the vast disproportion of AS boys over AS girls to genetic transmission that is sex-linked, making AS females sort of an abnormality or fluke. But are we really such an anomaly? Perhaps our invisibility skews the data. Like Attention Deficit Disorder, AS often is diagnosed in response to a series of events originating in a schoolteacher's observation of aberrant behavior. A child who is aggressive, noisy, exhibiting lack of motor inhibition (wild, acting out) is attended to, and this behavior is characteristic of boys. A child who is well behaved, quiet, and apparently compliant will often be overlooked, sometimes despite underachievement. Such a child is quite likely to be a girl. Consider the following scenario:

A schoolteacher tells students at the beginning of a lesson that they should be sure to ask for help whenever they need it to understand the lesson. A boy with AS has his hand raised from the outset and won't put it down. The subject matter is, after all, new and he has taken the teacher's words literally. A girl may have taken the teacher literally as well, but she resolutely keeps her hand down. She has known too many occasions when people's words did not represent their intention. She has been ridiculed or criticized for missing the point. So she keeps her questions to herself and, in this isolation, misunderstands a good many things, therefore failing the lesson. In this hypothetical example, observers would easily detect the literal-mindedness, with a touch of perseveration, in the boy's response, which so clearly manifests AS cognitive traits. The girl, though she has the same traits, handles them differently in her efforts to navigate through a confusing world. But she is AS—and her life challenges are rooted in AS—just the same.

Of crucial consequence is what un-, under-, and misdiagnosis in women mean in the lives of women who are AS and don't know it. One meaning is that they have no way of explaining themselves *to* themselves, thus no access to the support and positive sense of self they need. And, perhaps more important, more difficult, and more destructive than that, they accept the default explanations for the string of problems, setbacks, and oddities in their experiences and behavior: character weakness, resulting in a vague yet profoundly affecting belief in their own worthlessness. I hope this book will reach at least some of those women who will find resonance here.

Another factor in the diagnostic marginalization of adult AS females is the way some acceptable roles for women provide a cover for women's AS traits. Examples can be drawn from her choice of domestic circumstance. When an AS woman marries, she may be making a survival decision, i.e., marriage will afford her the support of a trustworthy (one hopes) significant other in navigating the world. She may be almost literally unable to live (function) without that support. If her husband were not there, her struggles would sooner or later become apparent and daunting. He leaves, and she contracts a virulent case of AS! Similarly, what's so unusual about a woman with children staying out of the work force? Stay-at-home mothering can be seen as a choice in favor of forming close bonds with one's children and raising them properly. With this cultural *permission*, a woman may be able to live in the kind of seclusion vital to her functioning. She doesn't have to deal with work she can't do efficiently, people who will shun her, difficulties with the simplest multi-tasking, or embarrassment and stress over routine matters like which bus to take. Similarly, a single woman living alone does not attract scrutiny. Many single women prefer this, but an AS woman may require it as a necessary condition of her ability to survive in the world. She must be able to escape to a place where she can recuperate from the exhausting demands social interaction makes on her system. Living with another means there is never a respite.

Socio-cultural Expectations of Women

Women are considered the socially adept gender, and this creates a raft of cultural expectations rooted in the presumption of social aptitude. As a result, AS imposes a heavy burden on the AS woman to perform socially useful functions for those around her and, thereby, demonstrate requisite femaleness. Women are expected to discern appropriate social responses, presumably out of inherent, sex-linked social strength. Lacking this capacity, AS women are perceived by themselves and others (especially other women) as defective and, well, not real women, so high is society's social requirement of our sex. This book, in toto, is an elaboration of this point.

The Making of the Knowledge of What and Who We Are

Given the relative inattention of the research community to women with AS and our own dismay at the inadequacy of diagnostic description, especially as it pertains to women, we began the process of self-definition through interaction with each other. In particular, we used an e-mail group to come to a rich understanding together through threaded discussion. We were, in effect, observer-participants in our own ethnography. As such, our research is qualitative, a metaphoric thick description intended to provoke thought and raise tantalizing questions. It is not quantitative. Though we have commonalties in experience and outlook, we defy reduction to those points of convergence.

The first two sections allow you to eavesdrop on some of our discussions: first, a description of the group and its evolution and dynamics, along with the discussion topic of how we perceive success and failure; second, a discussion of AS characteristics *as we see them* in our own experience.

The next section of the book is an invitation into our lives and minds and *who* we are as individual women with a diversity of circumstances, viewpoints, and experiences that may surprise you. You will find essays and creative pieces (perhaps a counter argument to our clinical depiction as lacking imagination) that disclose something of our distinct experiences as AS women in girlhood and adulthood, as women in the world and alone in our different womanliness. We want you to know us as the whole people we are.

The writings you will see are from writers who live at many different locations within the autism spectrum, either officially diagnosed or self-diagnosed, with varying degrees of autonomy and self-determination, living in a number of countries. AS and femaleness are all we necessarily have in common, and there is considerable diversity even given this point of convergence. But you will read accounts that resonate with each other as well.

Is this a tribute to the indomitable spirit of AS women? Self-advocacy for a victimized population? Life is far bigger than those categories, which confine and distort as they attempt to pin down the complexity of the women we are. We are women, living our ordinary lives, with joys and sorrows as our circumstances dictate/allow, doing many of the things non-autistic women do, feeling many of the same feelings, yet we are, in all of this, profoundly, astonishingly, and perfectly different.

Threading Our Lives

Beginnings

Sola Shelly
Ava Ruth Baker

This is the story of a book: why this book? But more than that, this chapter is about us, as individuals and as a group: What drives us to express ourselves? How do we create? What draws us together? How do we communicate? Cooperate? What is the role of this activity in our lives?

The Book List Begins

The idea to write a book about AS women came up on an email list whose members are mainly people on the autism spectrum.

Jean: When we very first started discussing the women's book on the list, it was upon a discussion of possible differences in the way AS manifests in women, and somewhere along the way, someone said, "It'd be great if we could put together a book of women's writings!"

I'm not sure whether I was the one to say, "Let's do it!" But I was the one to say, "I'll do it," assuming I would have company and for a while having it in Liane Holiday-Willey. She later had to drop out because of more pressing concerns, so the cheese stood alone.

Our group started when Jean sent a message to every e-mail list, and every AS woman she could think of:

Jean: The reason I'm e-mailing you (and a few others) is to tell you about a book proposal I'm in the process of putting together.

The book will be a collection of essays/creative works by Asperger(ish) women, edited and introduced by me, addressing the female experience with Asperger. How it will differ from the biographies done so far (practically all by women): pluralism and inclusion (many voices heard from in potentially several genres and styles); implicit or explicit attention to the issue of female under-diagnosis and the male diagnostic model; implicit or explicit acknowledgement of the way the elevated societal expectations of women impact AS women (nurturing, social lubrication, nesting, and the like.) My hunch is most of the submissions will be narrative or have a strong narrative component, but that most certainly doesn't preclude other approaches, say, poetry, advocacy, research review.

I thought you should know about it in case you'd like to write something for submission. I'm also wondering whether you would be interested in joining an informal e-mail list of contributing editors who are brainstorming with me.

This e-mail list of contributing editors became what we called the booklist. Early on, we knew that it was going to be more than a place to discuss how to put the book together. Email is our preferred mode of communication and socialization, because it is asynchronous, allowing us the freedom to process each other's ideas at our pace. There are many email lists for people on the autistic spectrum. In fact, most of us came to know each other in one or more of these forums. But for some of us, the book list was (and still is) the place where they felt most comfortable.

Ava: This is perhaps my favorite list. Maybe because the focus is more defined, so that even after six months of absence it's possible to chime in. Maybe because we're all AS women. Maybe because of the creative aspects of it.

So how did the book list go? A good way to give the feeling would be, to present here a thread, a discussion that starts with a topic and evolves in various directions.

Jean: I'm getting so much out of reading your submissions, even—and maybe especially in some ways—the dialogue posts, the longish things that respond to another's post. I'd love to see some of that exchange format in the book because it's so vibrant—even discussions of our fears of being misunderstood. If I had the nerve I'd propose a whole book as letters/conversations.

Success/Failure

An example of our interactions: a thread (a discussion that starts with a topic and evolves in various directions), is brought here in its entirety, with very minor editing. The thread titled "success/failure" was chosen as an example for several reasons. One reason is chronological: it was the first developed discussion in the beginning of the book list. Another reason is the variety of participants: a thread usually involves a few posters but this one drew responses from many. Finally, as the reader will observe in this book, the thread of success/failure runs through all stages of our lives, and touches all areas of our being and functioning.

The discussion stemmed from our concerns about the message that would be conveyed by the book:

Jean: If any of you need a topic to work on, here's what a potential contributor told me and why I find it compelling. This woman raised the issue of the marketing concept of "AS person makes good!" She is not by her estimation *making good*. (I think she's heroic, but that's probably irrelevant to her.) In the fray, all she feels are the extreme difficulties of her life and she perceives that the focus of the autobiographies so far has been "in spite of adversity, these *weirdos* went on to lead productive lives." I think this poses an open-ended ethical and philosophical question that bears thinking/posting about. There are successes. There are failures. There's also just AS, the good and the bad. Everything in life is *both/and*, not *either/or*.

Gail: People shouldn't be given the impression either that we could all be college graduates or that we are all so dysfunctional that we can'ttie our own shoes. If it comes off too *rah-rah* then people will think, "Then what's the problem?" If it comes across the other way then people might think we are hopeless or something. I say this from experience, having gotten both reactions from people over the years. There are times when I am more functional, and other times when I am less. Just the other day I got into it with hubby because he sees the times when I can do certain things. He then thinks I can do this all the time if I "try hard enough." That I am making excuses if I don't. I try to make him understand that there are times I can't, and he thinks I'm saying won't!

Jane: The "can't" versus "won't" or "won't try" dilemma!

Jean: Oh, Gail. I know the feeling. My home is where I feel most inadequate/least accepted.

Gail: I've run into this so much in my life. "You can do it Gail, I've seen you do it, you're just being lazy, selfish, etc." (Of course, there are the times I *am* being lazy and selfish, but I am one to admit it when I am.)

Jean: Yes. And I'm run ragged trying to compensate for all this and I still hate to be seen in my customary pose, staring into space, scratching away at my thumbs, chewing my tongue, looking like a total slug, yet my mind's in a frenzy, trying to process the deluge of information.

Gail: Then there are the people who think I am a complete basket case and they feel sorry for me and treat me like I'm two years old, or like I have half a brain. I hate that! The first reaction frustrates me; the second makes me totally irate. I hate pity! In real life, some of us do better than others, are more functional in this society. I consider myself pretty high functioning, but according to the view of some in society, I am lower functioning because I don't have this big career.

Sally: Mmm…Interesting point. Nowadays I meet people and they say "how come you don't have a degree," "never had a career," "you're obviously intelligent," etc. Gee thanks! So friggin patronising!

5

Jane: I sure can understand that viewpoint because the same is true for me. according to certain people like my high school guidance counselor, I should have whipped though college and professional school (probably law) and been a career person of some sort by the time I was 25. Instead, I've remained a low-level clerical worker.

Morgan: Jane, I admire you. I couldn't handle even working at a sheltered workshop as a VR [vocational rehabilitation] client. I had trouble with the work rate demanded, and the accuracy (I tend to transpose numbers sometimes). And as for the social rules, I asked my boss one day if I could come in 15 minutes early and leave 15 minutes early so I could catch the earlier bus and meet my family at the transfer stop, rather than having to wait 45 minutes out in the cold and then walk home. I could spend more time with my kids that way. She said, no problem. Then a week later it seemed she meant just for that day and was mad at me for repeatedly leaving early. I also don't hide my emotions well enough: if I am angry it exudes through every part of me, even when I keep my mouth shut and say nothing about it. So when I came in to work on my last day of that trial placement, it didn't last the whole day. She didn't like the look on my face (scowling), or the way I ended up setting the folders down too hard on the desk, or the attitude of my walk. She herself gathered my things and escorted me out of the building, though I never said one bad word.

Other problems I have with working: I desperately need approval and will seek it naggingly. I can't handle negative criticism or rejection. And I lack the "excellent communication skills" that most employers look for. Eye contact is a biggie. Comprehension is another. Most employers expect you to get it after one explanation and then leave you to your own resources. Me, I need to be hand held as I do it and talked through it, and that's no guarantee I'll remember it the next day. On once a month tasks? Geez, give me 6 months to learn them! I'll forget between now and the next time. I could never live on my own or support myself. That's why I stayed for 11 1/2 years with Alan and didn't leave when he abused me, because I knew I couldn't support myself.

Sally: I am pretty happy at the moment because no one is forcing me to do anything and I can do pretty much as I like, within the constraints of motherhood of course! I only realize I have problems when I get faced with something I cannot deal with, sudden situations in groups, etc where quick decisions are taken and I struggle to catch up, mostly don't, and end up wondering about it and trying to fill in the missing bits, or piece it all together. Or not being able to buy into group emotions unless they are plainly obvious.

Gail: I had absolutely no desire for further schooling! High school was enough of a nightmare! But especially if people see that you're smart, they think that there is something wrong with you not to want a career. How many times have I heard that? "There must be something wrong with you because…you don't have a boyfriend, you don't go to parties, you like to be alone too much." With the boyfriend thing, my father and stepmother were bothered by the fact that boys weren't calling me or I wasn't calling them. My step-mom once said, "You're a pretty girl. There must be something wrong with you not to have boys chasing you." Gee, that made me feel good.

Daina: Hello, Gail and everyone. Even those of us who have been to college (I have a masters in film) often haven't really been there for the same reasons, in the same way and with the same results as NTs [neuro-typicals, non-AS people]. They go to college for many reasons: networking, socializing, getting a good job afterwards, moving on in life. The actual learning is only maybe 10% of the deal, and the degree maybe another 20%. I went to study film as an extension of my inner creative needs, my desire to extend my various obsessions. Probably many Aspies do the same. Afterwards people said, "Why aren't you working in the film industry?" Well, 99.9999999% of all jobs in the film industry are closed. That is, they are open only to a select group of people and, as an Aspie, there is no way that I could get into that group.

Liane: The issue Jean raised is the very essence of one of my biggest struggles. I'm struck by how often I defend my AS, how often I exclaim (often rather emphatically) "I do have AS! You don't know what I go through at home! Must I *prove* it to you?" It dawns on me: I will be trapped in a very tight dichotomy if I am not careful. (I imagine it is the same for all of you?) I will be torn between proving I am AS and proving I can deal with AS.I cope with, I deal with, I struggle with, I live with, but I do not overcome AS. I do not want to have anyone think I've overcome some horrid issue, for that implies to me that AS is a tragedy!

Sally: The thing that so niggles me about the issue with AS is objectivity. I have no diagnosis, although I have a partner that swears I am, and a sister that does also. So, as has been said before, every time I mention any stuff to NT's they say, "Oh but I have that sometimes," and I myself am left wondering if I am just being a neurotic hypochondriac.

Jane: Well, I do have a diagnosis from an expert now, but I am not sure how much difference it makes. I haven't tested it out to see how well accepted it would be and by whom. I suspect that some people wouldn't consider AS any more legitimate with a diagnosis than without. That's one reason why we want to create this book, right? To help people understand.

Coa: My whole life has been a long series of surprising (to others) contradictions: success and failure, ability and disability, courage and fear. Everyday social life takes so much effort and courage just to manage to perform at a failure level, whereas doing well in non-social life (such as my exploring of erupting volcanoes) only takes 1% of the effort and courage. This is seen by NTs as not only contradictory but another proof of selfishness: if I am so capable, why then do I "refuse" to apply and share my capabilities in the group, as my silence is often taken to indicate? That's the worst consequence for me: the cruel moral judgments. If I were consistently poor at everything, at least "I couldn't help it," whereas given my demonstrated level of ability I "should be ashamed of myself" performing so ineptly socially. Not that people use those actual words, but that's how it comes across.

Elaine: Oh boy, you said it: the moral judgement applied to people who don't have the social skills! It's the worst! Also, I think this ties in with what Morgan said about getting or not getting scholarships based on how many extracurricular activities you are involved in. The kid who is in all kinds of clubs and social activities is going to have a better shot at scholarships, and later in the job market. It's like very social people are viewed as being better potential students, better potential employees, and better people in general. Even though it's not true. The worst part for me was when I bought into this nonsense. I thought I must be some kind of terrible person to be this way, and I was always looking for a way to get better. I ended up hating myself at times, and doing some really dumb things. I'm glad I don't have to do that anymore.

Gail: How well I know this! My lack of social skills and general cluelessness about it means I am a terrible person in the eyes of many. I've been accused of being deliberately rude and unfriendly when that has been the farthest thing from my mind. It is seen as a deliberate action because I do so well in other areas. If I failed at everything, then, like you said, my lack of social ability would be kind of understood. But because I can do well at other things, I am not believed when I try to explain my inability do to the social thing well. I am seen as making excuses, lying, and so on. Therefore, I am a bad person. How many times have I wanted to scream at people for not believing me when I say I can't, and they think I *won't*. I am a bad person because I am not a social butterfly…yeah, right.

Coa: It might seem a success that I work in a profession, but when one is capable of the work but lacks the expected image it's actually hell. Right now I'm so close to giving up and retiring early with a dismal sense of failure despite so much effort and surviving nearly five decades of living this *failed success* story. Do other people have this experience? Would this be a worthwhile thing to depict, the reverse twist of the success story?

Jane: Yes. Very much so. Although I'm not at as high a level professionally as you are, the same thing happens to me. Where I work, people have come to take my abilities/successes for granted, whereas my inabilities/failures continue to be very noticeable for them. Also, I have started to notice lately that my failure to build interpersonal relationships seems to be causing some hard feeling against me. It's like I do not have the same kind of cushion other people have. When things are going well, it's not much of a problem. But when anything goes wrong, or if there is any tension/conflict, then I am without the ties that bind. Nobody feels connected enough to me on a personal level, for example, to speak up for me if supervisors turned against me.

They don't have any kind of relationship with me that they recognize as requiring allegiance. No emotional bond of the kind they naturally/normally acquire with NT acquaintances/friends. I'm not blaming them for that. It's really, really hard for any NT to achieve/maintain with me a relationship that feels (to an NT) real enough to count. So I'm not complaining about their behavior, just pointing out a dilemma that can arise for an AS person in an NT workplace.

Coa: Jane, you describe so well the kind of social dilemmas that I too face at work. One factor for me, as for you, is limited connection with colleagues. (Though I do make much effort to attend meetings, my presence must seem a silent and rather odd one.) Another is that I don't make what others would judge socially prudent decisions/actions: I go by what I think right or wrong, not what the personal consequences might be of taking a stand, so any fallout is seen as my own silly fault. However, working in an NT workplace may for me be soon over, as I'm probably about to resign. I've had quite enough, after trying every approach I could think of over the years (ignoring the difficulties, or tackling them laboriously one by one, or disclosing my diagnosis to a few trusted persons in the hope of being better understood). I'll either give up work for good, or hopefully set up on my own in the AS-friendly conditions that suit *me* for once, so less of my energy goes into coping with overload and the social vs. work clash, and more into what I'm good at. I have a crazy plan for this but it's terrifying and risky in an era when others in my field are joining in bigger and bigger groups, for security. How could I, struggling so much more with stress than they, set up my own business? So I am indeed lurching wildly between a sense of failure and success, depressive despair and hypomanically intense planning. It may not seem very relevant to this booklist, but it's the dilemma I'm currently preoccupied with most of my waking hours that just happens to coincide with being invited onto this list.

Jane: Seems very relevant to me. You are struggling with issues that affect almost all ASers who are in the workforce, and you are contemplating a change to a work situation that would be AS-friendly. That's perfect for the book, and I hope to hear more about it as you go along.

Diane: I've been going through the same thing myself. I work as a software engineer and the hardest thing about my job is dealing with the social environment and dealing with being the odd-one-out with no social connections with any of my colleagues. I am 39. I've been thinking a lot lately about how I ended up in this career because that seemed like the thing to do, but I realize I've never been really happy in this field. Whereas community development and house design have always been really fascinating topics for me, it never clicked that I could go to school and learn how to have a career in these things. My guess is that it was due to how I was raised, with the idea that autism is bad, that I was bad due to my autism, and my special interests were bad. So I learned early on not to pay attention to things that interested me and just do what I thought others expected of me.

MM: "S-u-c-c-e-s-s:" I remember the cheer in high school that those bouncy cheerleaders did. "S-u-c-c-e-s-s, that's the way you spell success." Success in that case meant winning the football or basketball game. I didn't understand winning and losing, and I still don't today. It seems a rather odd idea. I just wanted to play. Because of my odd nature I was banished to the basketball bench. The coach didn't want me to embarrass her, so in many ways I was not successful as far as basketball goes. But if I look at the movie *Rudy,* in which a kid with great limitations makes it to the bench, to practice, well then success is determined differently. He overcame a great deal to just be there. As did I. Just to put on that brand new uniform, just to practice each day, just to deal with the verbal abuse from the coach, just to face my parents who thought ball was not intellectual and was ridiculous. I didn't miss a practice from 8th to 12th grade, didn't miss a game, and even though my coach was afraid of me and my lack of speech and my aggressive un-ladylike ways, well other coaches recognized my talent at basketball camp each summer and I could out-shoot the boys in our backyard. Was I successful in the limelight? I suppose not. Was I successful in my heart? Hell, yes. I got to play ball.

Success is when you follow your heart and do more than your limitations and your differences say you can do. Success is when my daughter finally sang her first solo in front of an audience, when she had melted in tears all the years before, and still has great obstacles to overcome every time she gets in front of an audience. Success was her mother in the back of the crowd (unable to handle being in the crowd) crying and saying in her heart of hearts, "That's my girl! That's my girl!" My neurological limits may never go away but I can at least try to be near the things and people that I love in my own way.

A long time ago, a little girl couldn't speak until she was four, and only said a word or two until she was eight, and though her vocabulary will always be quite limited, she is now a preacher and professional speaker. She has great limits in that the crowds overload her senses, and she must take care to take care of herself, but she has become a great preacher and speaker nonetheless. She is me, Mary Margaret.

Wendy: I like what MM wrote. Much to think on. In this society, success is measured by the kinds of things you surround yourself with. Things like what kind of car and how many, what kind of house, what neighborhood, what kind of clothes and how new they are, how much you travel and where, and how many of the latest fashion doohickies you can buy every month. But I'm learning that success is being able to live the lifestyle you feel the most at home in. And the kinds of people you are around, who tell you you're all right, you're great and unique, who still like you even after something upsetting happens. Being able to talk about things that you like, without them thinking you're weird and running away. Success to me is being content with what I have right now, and having a built-in, spiritual gyroscope that keeps me straight and level, even when things are falling apart in the outside world. And being salt of the earth. Helping people but not really noticed and glorified. Yes, now you all have seen my innermost want, my ultimate goal.

Jean: I hear ya Wendy. Though to me that's contentment rather than success. It's always struck me as odd that I, an asocial person, value so much the good people I know and love. I think I may treasure friends more consciously than many NTs because it never ceases to amaze me that: 1. They see the good in me as-is, and 2. They model so much for me about dealing with ambivalence and life's ambiguity. I celebrate them. I carry their insights next to my heart and I think about them (in pictures, of course) and feel their glow. And I never take them for granted. And in an odd way, I do, yes, thrive when I'm around them.

Ava: Likewise. I'm happy when I know I've put in maximum caring and effort along with whatever time and knowledge and experience I have, and when my clients find this helpful. But what upsets me is when others—not clients but more distant observers, who have had no one-to-one interaction with me—make judgments on my character, my ethics, or the quality of my work, based on social measurements, like whether I remember to smile at them if we pass in the corridor. Like you Wendy, I don't need to be noticed and glorified. But I also don't need to be put down as no good by inappropriate ways of measuring things, or feel pressured by that to give up my work. Not to do with money or status but because work is the one realm where I can usefully apply my unusual ways of thinking and problem-solving to help another person: a challenge and a satisfaction I would find hard to replace, a creative approach I've developed and refined over many years, the one place where I can actually draw on so many of the strange sidetracks and fixations of my life journey, and put them in the service of another person and their dilemma...

Carol: Thanks for saying that so well. It found a home. My work became unbearable long ago but that is the part I miss. My approach and outcomes were unique and valuable. Lately I have been reconceiving the idea that I could work again. I need to make a difference and at least struggle to apply what I have that they don't. In the midst of it, though, the misunderstanding and unappreciation feel more important than they do from this distance.

Wendy: That is where acceptance and self-forgiveness and forgiveness of others come in. People aren't going to make any fewer mistakes no matter how hard they try, but they *can* learn to be forgiving. And for those who can't forgive, but yell at a person for not being up to their standards, then the person being yelled at can look at the yelling person and see that their attitude is a weakness in itself, and yet the person being yelled at doesn't point it out, but just smiles inwardly and knows the yeller isn't really any closer to perfection than the person-getting-yelled-at-for-the-perceived-mistake is? Maybe self-

11

forgiveness, and forgiveness of others is a kind of perfection in itself? Maybe, just maybe, the whole act of growing and learning is an end in itself. Just being a human *being*.

Working Together

The book list served as a support group. It was also a working team. Working together was exciting, but complex, as our styles and needs are varied.

Jean: It struck me that we ASers are inwardly dichotomous, where NTs are usually integrated, whole. To get out of their internal homogeneity, NTs have to analyze experience for themselves—take it apart into bits of black and white and polarized thinking. (School is designed around this and so is standard psychotherapy.) While we're unimpressed with and skeptical of the analytical. NTs can learn from dichotomies like success and failure and so respond to marketing along those lines. To grow, we have to take the heterogeneous stuff inside, the bits and pieces, and synthesize them into something integrated and whole. And as Sola says, we live these dichotomies.

Jane: I read that and thought, huh? Then realized my confusion was due to lack of a word. I think we're not precisely *dichotomous*. We're more like *multichotomous*, right? Fragments rather than two neat halves.

Sally: Brilliant yes! Is that a word? If not official then it should be made so!

A few months later, Jean put together a detailed proposal for the book. The proposal discussed the concept of the book and its potential interest to readers. It also described the book structure as a series of sections covering topical areas, such as girlhood, adolescence, the workplace, and motherhood.

Ava had misgivings about the topical arrangement from the outset, because classification into topics opens the door to "the elephant man syndrome," with NTs in psychiatry showing us off as specimens and generalizing too readily.

Ava: Categorizing it in sections seems more like a textbook. Is that how we want to be read? I think that increases the risks again of faulty conclusions and misunderstanding. For me that's a major part of the point: there's an inner meaning and wholeness to the reality that each of us lives, and for an observer to have any comprehension of us more real than seizing upon our outward behaviors, it's vital that they *really listen and see* the threads. Both the thread that keeps each one of us whole despite attempts to pick us apart by focussing on isolated bits of us. And also the thread that connects us as a group. For the readers this would be more like an intriguing journey they would need to commit to in total, not something they could pick and choose from (just like we can't pick and choose which bits of our AS we live).

Jean: That is a consequence of book publishing as a market and the analytical mode of books. It's a highly unfortunate trade-off. Readers need sections to help them get at concepts. We AS folk find that not only unnecessary but destructive.

Anyway, for now, the book concept is and will remain a discomfiting trade-off. I took novel writing from Paul Scott (*The Jewel in the Crown, The Raj Quartet*) whose definition of a book was "a hard rectangular object," which always meant to me that it's finite and never all it could be. I always teach students that *essay* is from the French verb, *essayer*, to try, and that they've been lied to by being told there was such a thing as a perfect piece of writing. And that to write really well, they need to get rid of that idea and get down to the business of doing it, giving it a try.

Daina: I just saw an ad for a new book by some Latvian women writers— some in Latvia, some in the U.S. and other countries—writing about their experiences as Latvian women. It is organized by chapter, with each woman getting a chapter. This makes a great deal of sense, I think. The average NT mind needs a sense of other person to keep their interest. I think that for the purpose of the book, it might be a good idea to enable the NT reader to stay interested. How about this way of organizing the book?

Wendy: Just give each person a section, and they will write about some aspect of themselves that has to do with being a woman with AS. I think I was writing about being gifted in some areas, (such as art and creative writing) and yet struggling with doing the everyday things in life, yet because people saw my gifts, they thought I was quite capable in other areas of my life, and couldn't understand why I couldn't do them. I think a lot of people could relate to that, as well. I think that just relating our experiences and perceptions will help a lot of people who read the book. Make it an anthology. (Did we discuss this already? I have a very fragmented memory.)

Ava: I've been struggling with this idea since you posted it. First reaction, No! Partly a dislike of change (after I'd finally got accustomed to the topics idea) but more importantly, anonymity issues. Also a dislike of feeling spotlighted by a chapter being about me, instead of silently invisibly slipping into hidden corners of chapters which would be much more comfortable for me. But I guess I could do it the chapter way, if my biography bit focussed on where I regard myself on the spectrum, and my areas of functioning/nonfunctioning, ability/disability, without revealing my country or my work.

Jane: I'm not sure I understand the pros and cons of this option. It seems like probably the easiest way to do it (least editing work required). Is it automatic that individual chapters would be more revealing than some other format? Are pseudonyms an option? I don't remember the reasons why individual chapters are a problem, and need for anonymity is the only one I can think of at the moment.

Jean: My proposal emphasizes plurality of voices and counts on a thematic organization to support its notion of interplay: Voices on girlhood, voices on sexuality, and the like. That's what I'm committed to.

Ava: Maybe another solution, would be to just have one introduction (that includes what you would have written in the sectional ones), and to outline the different topics that will be covered within the book, and put it in a positive light that the reader will need to journey themselves, plunge right into our world, to have their questions answered, and not be able to look it up on page/section such-and-such and think they therefore know all about it.

Daina *summarized the dilemma and suggested a solution:*

Hello Jean and Everyone!

It's been a hot, toss-and-turn kind of night here in New Jersey, but I think all that tossing and turning resulted in a compromise. I think the book has to have *two* focuses:

1. To give the reader a concept of each of us as people. It seems to be important that the readers, AS and NT alike, come to understand that this book is about individual people with life-paths, life experiences, emotions that develop and expand, etc. A purely theoretical book would not accomplish that.

2. In order to make the book comprehensible and interesting to NTs, (the majority of potential book-buyers), there has to be interpretation and analysis that they can understand, in a general way—how we are similar to each other and different from NTs, particularly NT women.

A straight anthology of writing would certainly reveal each of us as people, but many NT readers might get confused and be unable to figure out what it is that we are writing about. In other words, "Here is a bunch of women, but why are they writing a book together?"

Maybe we could write a chapter all together about ourselves as a group. How are we alike? What difficulties do we share? How are we different from one another? Different from NTs?

MM: I shouldn't have assumed that everyone writes like me but I was thinking if there are more technical writers among us, what if those persons wrote comments about the autobiographical snap shots? Of course some folks are more than able to do both kinds of writing, but, though I can see and write technically, I really don't want to do it. For example, in my story, I wear red all the time and my parents insist I be a good girl every time I do anything autistic that doesn't fit the norm. Someone could pick out the female themes and talk about female dress codes and what the phrase *good girl* means.

Getting ourselves through

An important factor in our drive to write is the desire to be understood. Many of us already have had the painful experience of trying so hard to explain, and then being belittled or patronized. We are also familiar with the way some professionals analyze and misinterpret the AS experience, and with the wrong way some autobiographies by AS women were treated by professionals and the media. It might be even more painful if we expose our inner selves, which is very hard in itself, only to learn that we are again misunderstood.

Jane: I am not sure I can get across to anyone what my personal/private life is really like. I don't know if I dare try. There are things I have never laid out to anyone, not even to InLv [the Independent Living AS e-list] or Nancy or any relatives. My relationship with my bears, for example. There is a way in which nobody will ever understand what I'm *really* like unless they know about the stuff I hide. Should I be trying to reveal it, explain it, describe how it is part of autism? Would the result be that everybody would write me off as crazy?

Sola: How much you are ready to reveal is really a personal question, and you should not tell more than what you feel comfortable with. I can speak only for myself (as a reader), though as you say you kept some things to yourself, your writing has been very helpful for me (besides interesting and enjoyable).

Jane: I think we have talked a bit before about the problem of trying to write so that NTs will understand us and not just think, "Oh, I'm like that, too."

Sola: Maybe lots of examples of things that *look* the same with an explanation why they are *not* the same will help.

Jane: Added to that problem (and something I thought about while reading Sola) is the possibility that lots of readers might want to diagnose us on the basis of our writing. Not as autistic, but as something else. For example, they might think that everything Sola writes about is caused by depression. And that now she feels better because she has learned to cope with depression. Period.

Sola: There is always that risk. Look at what is said/written about the writing of Donna Williams, or Gunilla Gerland. There is no use fighting, at least, not through modifying our writing to prevent it. They can say that you have problems with your gender identity (%^&$%$ knows on what basis), that I am depressed, that Williams was abused, on and on. But not identifying with gender, and having depression (and anxiety) *are* more common among ASers but with reversed logic: *ASness is the cause, not the result.* Coming to think about it, who is the audience of this book? How hard will we try to make ourselves understood? It occurred to me that when I write, I do not think of the professional that would try to analyze me…but of my soulmate, who will finally find something that will make sense to her, as it did to me when I came across writings of ASers.

Jane: Might help (with the more NT readers) if the book has an intro by an *official* of some kind. An officially diagnosed person, perhaps. Or, if necessary, a Ph.D.

Sola: Might help, but there is no 100% insurance. Williams's and Gerland's books had a preface by a respected professional.

Daina: There is one very important thing. We mustn't worry about whether or not the book will ever be published. No one who writes a book and eventually gets it published knows ahead of time that it will be published. Of course, if a publisher had accepted a proposal before the book was written, that would have taken away the will-it-be-published? anxiety, but it also might have been a trap. We might have been afraid that what we were writing would not please them, thereby making our writing more tentative.

Ava: Great words, Daina! I think it's important to write the style of book *we* want and not feel constricted by the style and content publishers are perceived as wanting. That is part of maintaining our integrity, and expressing who we really are. It has long been my approach to life, to plough ahead with things that seem important or right, whether or not there is any model to follow, whether or not there is any interest or encouragement, and regardless of the hurdles. As long as the thing is not harmful to anyone. That way, not only am I fully and enthusiastically involved in the process, but I find it is usually, surprisingly, successful.

I find my NT acquaintances are not only very bound to doing things the proper way, but still insecure about the future outcome despite doing everything how society and organizations expect it, so I wonder what could be the point of trying to conform anyway? I've been a blatant nonconformist since my earliest memories, initially, of course, unaware of being different, then for quite a time trying oh-so-hard not to be so different, but eventually giving up feeling embarrassed or ashamed by it, and learning to live with insecurity about the future. (It's no worse than the insecurity of everyday social life).

The WFAP camp

Jean formed an editorial board. Not surprisingly, those of us who had been most involved in the discussion about book structure, expressed interest in contributing to the editing process. Jean also suggested some possible ways for the editors to have editorial meetings. One idea had been around for some time, since Judy told us about her planned trip to USA and we started to think about meeting in real-life at what we fondly called Camp WFAP, AKA the International Youth Hostel in Boston.

So, it looked like the book project entered a new stage, involving exciting plans for both finalizing the book and leading the connection among us from email to real-life encounter; at least, for those of us who could make it to Boston.

MM wrote: Judy coming to America pushes us to ask how we shall gather our persons and how we shall gather the book. We have (at least) two agendas for the book

1. what we hold in common, what themes appear in all of our lives;
2. how we have individually approached our neurological differences;

It sounds like Judy's trip to the U.S. will help to produce more of the book because it is pushing us to figure out how to continue to go forward.

Upon returning from Boston, **Jean** *wrote*: Going to Boston to work on the book (in a way independent of what actually got done) made the project *real* for me. Even though I'd always consciously thought the book would go, at some level I didn't believe it and felt it would fail because of my shortcomings. I no longer believe that and it feels good to have a positive frame of mind and some unblocked energy for it. I also now know the book *will* be published!

Differences

Ava Ruth Baker

As the reader will discover, we women on the autism spectrum experience self and world rather differently to neurotypical women.

This chapter illustrates and explores our differences, through online discussions that occurred during the writing of this book, linked by a commentary in which I attempt to relate our experiences to views from the wider autism community, professional thinking and popular stereotypes. This neither claims to be a complete list of differences, nor does it imply that these AS/NT differences apply only to women, or apply to all women: the emphasis is on perceived differences between AS women versus NT women as experienced in the lives of those AS women participating in the discussions.

So, how might our differences be characterized?

Hans Asperger in his original paper described the syndrome now bearing his name as (1994, p.37) "severe and characteristic difficulties of social integration...[which may be] so profound that they overshadow everything else...[or] compensated by a high level of original thought and experience." "Social adaptation has to proceed via the intellect" he wrote (p.58), due to (p.77) the inability "to pick up all those things that other children acquire naturally in unconscious imitation of adults." As a consequence (p.83) "A peculiar mixture of naivety and sophistication...they are full of surprising contradictions which make social adaptation extremely hard to achieve". His paper remains one of the most insightful professional characterizations.

Professionals since have defined autism spectrum conditions by a host of other features (most prominently "the triad of impairments: social, communication and imagination"), and attribute them to defects such as "theory of mind", "central coherence", and "executive function", arising from differences/damage/delayed maturation of the nervous system, and possibly other systems too, like the endocrine, digestive and immune systems. Popular stereotypes portray AS individuals as lacking feelings, empathy, imagination, and the ability to care and cooperate, and usually male. Such assumptions put us at risk of missed diagnosis, misdiagnosis, misunderstanding, inappropriate treatment, and restrictive advice about careers, marriage, parenting etc., as well as compounding the inner struggle for self-esteem and sense of identity.

While most observers, professional and lay, try to explain and define us by our behaviors, we are more aware of the hidden underlying differences that challenge us on many fronts and merely manifest in the behavioral differences that "outsiders" observe. Hopefully "insider" accounts here and elsewhere may help clarify which of our differences are primary and which secondary; which are fixed and which variable; which are "problems" and which may actually be ingenious coping or compensating strategies.

Processing Differences

Processing differences are regarded by many of us on the spectrum as perhaps the fundamental difference. Professionals call these executive function problems, but generally confine their attention to the cognitive and motor effects (difficulty with planning, organization, etc.), whereas we experience them as pervasive, impinging on most aspects of our lives. Typically, we process slowly, consciously, with difficulty managing more than one type of data or process at a time. Our systems are easily overloaded by sensory, social, emotional, cognitive or chemical stimuli, resulting in fatigue and shutdowns which may be transient or last for hours, weeks or even years. Which processes work best and which shut down when overloaded, varies among us. Our functioning also varies from occasion to occasion, depending on such things as the degree of overload, the response of others, and the effectiveness of our coping and compensatory strategies. How well we appear to function is often used to label us as higher or lower functioning. However this can be misleading and result in overlooking the abilities of those labeled low functioning while discounting the invisible stress faced by those labeled high functioning. We discuss some of these issues:

Wendy: Maybe high functioning only refers to those who have figured out how to put forth enough energy to work around their AS challenges. Because, believe you me, when I am mentally exhausted, and stressed, I'm not very high functioning at all.

Jean: Yes. I relate. And, under the right (er, wrong) conditions of temperature and pressure, I lose it. I think I put practically all of my high functioning into my job and stuff outside the home. My family has me at my most inept.

Morgan: Occasionally I have a high social functioning day regardless of the situation. But that's rare and only if I am well rested, well fed, and all systems go, so to speak.

Jean: Very much me. I liken my social skills to drumming. If I were a drummer in a band, I could keep the beat, well, more or less, as long as it was the only thing in my mind. Eventually, though, my concentration would shift, I'd be off in my head, and I'd eventually (or abruptly) just stop drumming.

Patty: That's the story of my entire life.

Coa: Of my life too! The reason, for example, why I might forget to look at someone because I'm so busy focussing on the problem they've come about. I can't do both social skills and problem solving at the same time.

Jean: I'd have to remember (and remind myself) to keep drumming. And in social settings, the *music* is not written down. It's all improvised so getting lost is all the easier to do and pretty disastrous, because everyone's part is supposed to be coming together in some kind of a composition. Someone I read in grad school made a distinction between *tacit* and *focal* knowledge. Focal knowledge is what you're doing as you learn to ride the bike. It's at the forefront of your consciousness. You have to focus. Tacit knowledge is what you have when riding a bike is old hat. It's knowledge that's there but not apparent to you. You don't have to think about the act of riding a bike and how it's done again because that knowledge is available to you without having to focus on it. I tend to think of my AS as simply an information processing disorder. When I look at its manifestations, cognitive processing problems seem to be the common thread. I think this may mean I/we have poor access to tacit knowledge (or very little of it) so everything has to be focal, hence, the fatigue?

Patty: I agree 100 percent. In fact, this is the first time I have seen a description that totally fits me. I can learn, and that makes it easier, and I have a lot of experience/learning. But everything new, everything directed to me orally or visually, is difficult to process, pay attention to, and deal with. I function well only inside my own mind, and sometimes even there I can't make the connections I need to!

Coa: And oh the fatigue! Again I risk criticism for using up my energy going off exploring volcanoes, etc (these days figurative ones, but real ones in my younger fitter days), but nobody sees that silently scaling volcanoes and such-like only expends 1% of the energy it takes to manage eye contact and thinking at the same time. (Well, actually volcano-climbing helps restore the energy that living in a social world depletes).

Development and Maturity

We tend to follow quite different developmental trajectories to NTs, for instance being more mature in some areas than others, and often late bloomers (not necessarily a bad thing, as research has shown (West, 1997, pp. 95-96) that those who mature slowly, and originally do worst, may on later testing be among the best!). As we discuss:

Daina: NT's see their lives in a linear time-line: babyhood, childhood, teenage years, adult years, etc. It seems that we ASers see our lives differently.

Jane: I certainly agree that at least some ASers (me, for instance) do not grow up by the same schedule as NT people do, and that it would be good to have that reality reflected in the book.

Ava: Just today I read something interesting Einstein wrote, about why he was the one to develop the theory of relativity: Because his "development was retarded", as an adult he asked questions that "only children ask…Naturally, I could go deeper into the problem than a child." (West, 1997, p.25). It seems many of us here have that interesting mix of child*like*ness and maturity, but if misunderstood as child*ish*ness, our maturity and insight on certain things risks being discredited.

Daina: That's interesting because it fits with some brain development stuff I read. It seems that as an NT grows up, something called *brain cell pruning* takes place—some areas of the brain atrophy in order to produce the normal NT adult. I don't think that happened with me, which is why some people think of me as childish because I still have pleasure in many of the things I had as a child. Perhaps people sometimes mistakenly think that because the childish parts of my mind have not atrophied, that the adult parts of my mind have not developed, which is incorrect.

Observant parents often notice differences in their AS child from infancy, particularly unusual fixations and reduced attention to mother's face (and therefore the focus of mother's attention and the wider social world). For whatever reason this initially occurs, it seems likely that this difference in focus profoundly alters the child's subsequent learning and developmental trajectory (Richer, 2001), perhaps becoming "hard-wired" as the nervous system develops. As we continue:

Ava: It's interesting what Daina writes in her essay: "Most NT children's way of organizing sensory information is either inherently similar to their parents' or, perhaps by watching and perceiving their parents' reactions to things, their mind wiring comes into line with that of their parents. This did not happen with me." I think our odd-maturing-schedule might explain many of our differences, and our tendency not to make the same assumptions and judgments NTs do. Also to be nonconformists, because of learning so much about the world for ourselves from first-hand experience, before learning about faces and the human-social-world attached to faces. So that by the time we did learn those, we didn't get so addicted to what other people think or do, because we'd already experienced such a lot for ourselves. And because we by then didn't easily fit in their social world, this became a self-perpetuating cycle. We ACs may have a real advantage in knowing things first-hand (though a disadvantage socially). Knowing things because someone tells us it's so is for us a secondary thing, coming later in our lives, and also shakier since it's based on opinions versus direct experience.

MM*:* I think that some of us not only have our five senses on high, but also our sixth sense: that we do not draw a line between inanimate and animate beings, that they all have soul to us.

Daina: As a child, everything was somewhat alive to me. Perhaps the face-processing tendency that most NTs have enables them early on to distinguish what is alive and what isn't, and what is human and what isn't.

Ava: Or maybe what is and isn't alive, is just another assumption that NTs make. So for the NT child, either because of the strength of those attachments to faces and the accompanying social world, or through some coincidental developmental process, the aliveness of the sensory world fades. Whereas we ACs retain more of the direct experience of the world and less of the face-addiction-belief thing.

Sola: This reminds me of a poem that I studied in high school, "The Pond" by Bjalik. The poem describes a secret place in the forest, where there is a little pond and a tree growing from it. When the poet was a little boy, he used to go there, alone, and listen to the "language of visions," an unmediated way for the child to communicate with the tree and the pond. The articles that I read about this poem discussed the role of spoken language, as adding the social aspect, separating the initially naive child from the true essence of the world. I was enchanted by the poem. For many months I perseverated on the meaning of communication and language, searching the library for more articles about this. However, unlike the conclusion of the poem, I did not feel that growing up and maturing inevitably meant losing this innocence and being expelled from nature. I felt that I was still that child in the forest. Now that I know that I am AS, I am not surprised that this poem had such influence on me.

Differences in Thinking

Differences in thinking may be among our fundamental differences, resulting in other secondary consequences. Though most professional writing about this confines itself to differences in central coherence or theory of mind (see below), we note other differences. For instance, whereas in the neurotypical world of contemporary western cultures, verbal thinkers predominate (West, 1997), many of us think nonverbally: visually (Grandin, 1995 & 1996), spatially (Baggs, 1999), or in other nonverbal modalities (for instance "visual images combined with emotions," as Daina describes in "Coming alive in a world of texture", this volume). Furthermore, our thinking may vary from typical linear thinking, as in branched thinking *and* helical thinking. *As we discuss:*

Ava: I think *spatially.* An advantage of this is that I readily detect the structure or patterns of not just objects but complex situations, which often helps solve problems that others with their more conventional thinking haven't. Spatial thinking has no limits, continually transforming and expanding to match any problem, contrasted with the limitations of words and categorical thinking. The disadvantage is that to express a spatial thought, I have to first translate the spatial experience into pictures, and then into words, a very slow process incompatible with group conversations where quick responses are needed. I simply can't keep up with the speed of conversation, or the shortness of the pauses, so may be considered bored, rude, shy or dumb because of my silence. Attempts to improve my speed don't work.

Sola: *Branched thinking* occurs when an idea bears several possibilities for development. It is hard for me to choose one and discard the others, till I have examined all of them. So, after dwelling some on one possibility, I have to go back to the original idea and do the same with the other possibilities. This way of thinking, known in computer science as *visiting a tree*, may be a disadvantage, as it is slower than purely linear thinking. Normally, a person would choose only one possibility, the most probable one, or the one commonly agreed among other people, and then follow only this one linearly and never come back to the others (or never even realize that there may be other possibilities). This is usually hard for me to do, as I do not always know what should be more probable, or if I do, then it is hard for me to prioritize and give up the other possibilities. This way of thinking can be very annoying to people if I try to employ it in a conversation, because it seems as if I am breaking the continuity of the subject. It also makes multiple-choice questions extremely annoying for me. But branched thinking makes me a very good programmer and is conducive to science. I use it for problem solving in my own life, as a scientific approach is my preferred way of making sense of my life.

Ava: In *helical thinking,* just as a helix comes back to the same place over and over again but at a different level, so we experience or learn something different, something more refined, each time round. To an observer, the topic or behavior may seem repetitive or monotonous, but inside, our thoughts are evolving.

Sola *Helical thinking* is my way of examining a set of related issues. Thinking of one issue leads me to another related one, which leads to another and so on, eventually leading back to the issue I started with. But then, after gaining insight about the related issues, I can understand the initial issue better, which in turn can lead to further understanding of the related ones. This way, I can examine each issue alone (as I can't focus on several at once), while simultaneously aware of the interplay of related issues. Helical thinking is linear in both senses: firstly, if we follow the helix curve, each topic leads continuously and naturally to the next; and secondly, looking at the vertical progression, each circle in the horizontal plane moves upwards linearly, as a whole. But someone looking downward into the helix may see only the motion in the plane, and think that I am moving in circles leading to nowhere.

Helical thinking is well known and recognized in education, where children are taught subjects several times, each time at the age-appropriate level and incorporating knowledge and skills that have been acquired in other subjects since the last time it was taught. Adults are usually assumed to think only linearly, thus repetition is discouraged, particularly when the context is not formal education but life experience. But for many of us, the only way to make sense of life experience is to apply formal thinking in a deliberate and intensive manner. There is a saying in the Talmud: "He who studies his lesson the hundredth time is not like he who studies his lesson a hundred and one times." How true for us, as our entire life is an ongoing lesson.

"Theory of Mind" (the ability to conceptualize or meta-represent other people's mental states) is viewed by some professionals as the basic defect in autism: however many on the spectrum disagree. At a recent autism congress, a group of AS presenters questioned both the theory and the testing methods, and put forward some alternative views (Blackburn, Gottschewski, George & Niki, 2000). They showed that though AS persons may have a different or slower or less mature theory of mind, this varies between individuals and may be secondary to other factors. Moreover, it seems that NTs may have even more difficulty reading our AS minds, than we have reading theirs! And though a more-considered-less-automatic theory of mind may be disabling in social situations, it may be better for complex problem solving (Baker, 2000), and perhaps has other advantages over NT thinking:

Daina: Simon Baron-Cohen's latest book has hilarious explanations of the NT mind (he thinks he's writing about deficits in the AS mind), how perception leads to representation to meta-representation to meta-meta-representation to meta-meta-meta-representation, which explains much of what NT's believe to be *reality*. They are totally alienated from their senses and perceptions.

"Central coherence" is cited by other professionals as the basic defect (though some are beginning to recognize the "asset" side of this, e.g. see Happe, 2001). According to this theory, autistic people have "weak central coherence" (focusing on details at the expense of overall meaning)—however the following discussion of ours (and "Scenes from a Car Wash" which arose in response to this thread) suggests that this may be over-simplistic:

Ava: Categorizing our writing in sections seems more like a textbook, more like an analytical left-brained way of doing it, while I think we are mostly more synthetic right-brained people.

Kalen: Are we? I'm really extremely left brained, linear, logical, analytical. I love textbook-like, categorized, defined, subdivided, hierarchies (of things, not people). I think I'm even impaired in some types of synthetic right-brained processes, or at least with using the left and right together (something typically considered a strength of the female brain). I've also heard that nonverbal learning disabilities (an impairment in right-brain functions) are extremely common in AS.

Jean: I just spoke at an English conference where I said university education was endlessly frustrating for me because my experience with the world was already broken and the analytical mode, which gave me baskets to put the bits in, which tidied up the bits, but offered no wisdom. I said that synthesis was the only way I learned.

Kalen: I wish I could learn by synthesis, but I can't seem to synthesize at all. I had to drop classes I otherwise could have managed because I was expected to draw things together and synthesize concepts and new ideas from all the things I'd been reading. I can't do that. I can put all the readings into categories, I can pull them apart and put them back together. I can find every symbol, every figure of speech, and every component of the characters and plot, and analyze them to death, but to know what it was about? To get a feeling or a concept about it, to make a whole from all the parts I can so easily distinguish? Completely and totally beyond me. After two dismal failures, I've decided I'm not cut out for studying English Literature after all. I can write in this language, but I can't understand it.

Jean: On the other hand, for NTs, unless they are in the presence of something completely new to their experience, their experience is unitary and integrated and synchronous to begin with, so to go beyond that ("to know anything requires contrast," says somebody important) they must analyze, break things down.

Kalen: This is so different from the way I thought NTs worked, based on my studies, experience, and discussions. I thought Gestalt processing (whole-to-part) was the exception, and a very right-brained approach. I thought NTs put the pieces together easily, not that the pieces were already together to start with.

Perhaps the tendency to focus on details, may be only the first part of our making sense of the world? If we are then able to build from those details into the whole ("bottom-up thinking"), then we may arrive at a more accurate whole than do those who begin with the whole ("top-down thinking") who have only an approximate idea of the component parts and underlying laws. Perhaps we can at times perceive the whole while retaining the details as well? This has been shown to be so in some situations, for instance (Hermelin, 2001, p. 73):"overall, within the domain where they are talented, autistic savants appear to use the strategy of taking a path from single units to a subsequent extraction of higher-order patterns and structures", "from parts to wholes". Perhaps a lack of "brain cell pruning" during development in autism (Happe, 1999) enables this? Whereas NTs, wired for "cognitive economy", must choose between whole and parts, typically choosing whole? As with theory of mind, the neurotypical style of (strong) central coherence has both advantages (making social life simpler) and disadvantages (being less conscious and detailed, it could in some situations be misleading or even dangerous).

Many on the spectrum study and deduce social meaning by reading and careful observation. Asperger noted (1944, p. 73): "Just as these children observe themselves to a high degree, so they also often have surprisingly accurate and mature observations about people in their environment." (Such insight, however, does not impart the ability to "act socially", which is more complex, as Richer (2001) explains). This has been said (Gilberg, 1999) to be particularly characteristic of higher-functioning females on the spectrum (another reason their AS diagnoses may be overlooked). The reader will find examples throughout our writing: in fact the very existence of this book is evidence of this!

Difficulty answering questions is another common experience of ours, and may arise for many reasons, such as comprehension or expression difficulties, concern for precise accuracy, branched thinking, or debating which perspective to answer from (own or questioner's? general or specific?). In the following thread, we discuss our difficulties answering the AQ test, a screening questionnaire for AS (Baron-Cohen, Wheelwright, Skinner, Martin and Clubley, 2001):

Jean: Sometimes I have to correct the question for myself. For example, the statement "I am fascinated by numbers." When I'm drawn over and over again to figure out how many miles it is between one place and another and how many minutes it takes to get there, I have trouble calling it fascination (in the common sense of the word) with numbers because I often detest it. Yet when the task presents itself it feels like a job that needs doing. I do, though, (along with my fascination with maps) end up a much better navigator on trips than most people even though, without the map memorization, I'd be panic-stricken and lost. Maybe the word *absorption* would have suited me better. Over my life, I've had trouble with tests because I'm always drawn to consider possible, however remote, situations of the opposite being true—extenuating circumstances, if you like.

Coa: Likewise. A question that was very hard for me to answer was "I enjoy doing things spontaneously." Does it mean my spontaneous idea or someone else's spontaneous idea? That makes all the difference in the world!

Jane: I have that trouble too. My brain immediately comes up with specific cases that would cause the question to be interpreted differently. And then I get irritated because I feel like the test is trying to manipulate me. I end up feeling cynical about such tests, because it seems like my brain is too quick for them. (Does that sound arrogant or egotistical?) I scan each question and know instantly what the right answer is from the viewpoint of the test-maker. And simultaneously my brain is analyzing why the creator of the test phrased the question that way, what he (or occasionally she) was trying to do to the test-taker, and examples of how the question could be interpreted differently in different circumstances. My frustration grows as I move from question to question. In this case, take the question, "I prefer to do things with others rather than on my own." OK, that's an obvious "definitely disagree" for me. And yet, if I have to go to a new place, such as a new store (or, especially, a new kind of store for me), I much prefer to have Nancy with me. So my response should be "definitely disagree," but it weighs on my mind that in some cases I really, really, want/need Nancy with me and therefore I do sometimes "prefer to do things with others" (or with "other," at least).

Other questions are too unspecific. For example "If I try to imagine something, I find it very easy to create a picture in my mind." This is something that we go over and over on the prosopagnosia list, so I've learned that it's not a simple issue. What does it mean to "create a picture in my mind"? What kind of picture? Some pictures are *more visual* than others, it turns out. Also, are you talking about a picture of a specific individual instance of something, or a generic picture? For example, if you ask me to think of a dog, I can/do form what it might be more accurate to call a "mental experience of dog-essence" rather than a picture in my mind of a specific individual dog. Creating a visual picture of a specific dog in my mind is extremely difficult for me. But creating a mental experience of the physical essence of dogness is easy. So how do I respond to this question? Can I assume that the person who created the question had any idea of how complex this topic is? I doubt it.

Communication Differences

Considering all the processes involved in social speech, it is not surprising we find this difficult. As Donna Williams (1996, p. 98) detailing these, concludes: "the concept of 'social', which requires simultaneous ability to process and monitor and access, becomes a shattered and intangible one and, at best, an evasive, undependable and inconsistent one." So for us there are huge advantages in writing as a means of communication. Most of the processing issues that impair live conversation recede when we can respond in our own time, manner and environment.

Toni: Email is a wonderful way to communicate! NT's complain that there is so much missing, like facial expression, body language, tone of voice, etc. This is exactly why I enjoy email. All those NT things confuse the heck out of me.

Among ourselves we can communicate well "live" too. Not bound by NT social protocol, we tend to talk very directly, relying on words (rather than nonverbal cues), and content (rather than personality), with a distinctive rhythm whereby we tend to say the whole of what we want to convey as a unit then wait for the other's response. Rather than smalltalk, either meaningful conversation or comfortable silence generally prevails.

It can be a sobering experience for an NT to attend an event where AS style prevails. Here, it might be the NT who seems odd or rude, with their characteristic interruptions, trivial remarks, constant changes of topic, bizarre habit of staring into the eyes, excessive face and body movements, and tedious NT difficulty appreciating and coping with silence or solitude. It might be the NT who appears to suffer a triad of impairments.

Sensorimotor Differences

Most of us experience coordination problems, some of us tics or catatonia, and many of us stereotyped or repetitive motor mannerisms (which we call "stims"), which may be unconscious or purposeful, for instance for sensory enjoyment or as a coping device to assist attention, learning, processing etc (Williams, 1996). Considering motor function in a broad sense to include the rhythms and intensity of output, one could speculate that motor differences could also account for difficulty in changing focus, stopping, starting, shifting modes and integrating components of processes, resulting in the processing differences, obsessions, compulsions, convulsions and even migraines common in autism; our tendency to lurch between inertia and hyperactivity; our intensity and hyperfocus, and therefore even our early failure to focus on the social realm, and the different developmental trajectories and consequences that ensued. Thus, motor differences seem to be another fundamental difference.

Sensory differences include synaesthesia, sensory agnosias such as prosopagnosia (face-blindness), and over-or under-sensitivity of any or all of our senses, including pain and temperature.

MM: I know about crying at the wrong times. I was called extra sensitive. On the other hand I never cried when playing tackle football (I always bumped into things). Not knowing the difference between pain that can injure and pain that comes with autistic skin has destroyed my knees.

As with other types of processing, it is usually difficult or impossible for us to process more than one sensory channel at a time.

Also common is a highly developed awareness, not only of the sensory world as NTs experience it, but of an essence that lies behind phenomena, experienced as a "resonance" (rather than discrete sense impressions) which may include emotional and other undercurrents. Donna Williams (1998) describes this in detail, suggesting that whereas NTs lose this awareness early in life, autistic folk may retain it to greater or lesser extent even after they acquire social capacities. Impossible to shut out, it may prove a useful guiding force in evaluating situations, but may also be deeply disturbing. As we describe:

MM: Autism is not being able to close the windows to everything around you.

Wendy: I might not always read faces or tones of voice correctly, but I can perceive peoples' emotions, through intuition. I'm sure the lot of you know what that is like.

Diane: I really do pick up on the attitudes of the people around me, and if they are negative attitudes (in my view), it really brings me down. I don't have the ability to voice my views and really be heard, or to change the mood of a crowd (some NT's definitely do have that ability).

MM: I have been accused of being self-absorbed and selfish, because I so desperately need quiet and time to myself. My autistic needs do not mix well with what is expected of a woman in the southern part of the USA. But I hate that people think that because I need more quiet that I am a selfish bitch. I'm not. If anything I feel so deeply for others that I ignore my need to protect my senses that overload so easily to be with another person in his/her pain. I bite this skin that won't let me do more, won't let me sacrifice myself unselfishly. For I need the quiet not because I have a cold heart but because I can hear every plea from every being in whatever space I stand or sit or lie down in. I need the quiet because I am too compassionate. I can only afford a certain amount of time among humans, and if I don't get to moving my senses will overload, and the rest of the day I will have to put myself in the quiet of my room, and miss out on the trees and rocks and streams that talk to me so much more gently than any human.

Feelings/Emotions

There are many misconceptions about feelings in autism. It is clear from within the autism community that we do usually know how we feel, though we may need time and space to identify this (especially in overloading situations). Our feelings may however be invisible to others, and even when we manage to verbalize them, others may not take our stated feelings seriously because they don't show in voice or body language, or seem so different to what an NT person would experience in the same situation, or how they might express it. As we discuss:

Jane: It often takes me a while to know how I feel. Physically and emotionally, both. Apparently I do not have a full time monitoring device that keeps me up-to-the-minute in touch with such things. I tend to be engrossed in (perseverating about) a particular thing—or else zoned out—and therefore don't pay attention to how I feel unless/until a feeling becomes acute or huge (gets in the way). On the other hand one thing I hate most about interactions with some NTs is the way they tell me what (they think) I feel. There are times when I need them to go away and let me figure out how I feel (i.e., I may be unable to articulate my feelings instantly), and often what I feel is not what they expect me to be feeling. But in no case is it true that I need them (or anyone) to tell me what/how I feel. I suspect I am perceived by some people as emotionally arid. And maybe they assume there are lots of emotions I'm hiding for some NT-type psychological reason. It would be awful to have NTs come to believe it's beneficial for them to handle our feelings for us.

Kimberly: Hello. I was wondering how everyone else feels about my friend's theory that it's not enough to have an emotion, because an emotion not expressed really doesn't exist. It came about because I said, "Of course I care about that person. Very much." The friend said, "I wouldn't have known. You don't really hug her, kiss her, that sort of thing." I said, "Yes but I do care, even if its not expressed, and the person knows me well enough to understand that's just my way. She knows I care." That's when my friend said, "Yeah but that's not enough. If it's not expressed, it doesn't exist to the other person."

I thought about this for years…thinking I was terrible, that I had no feelings simply because few were ever expressed so people could see them. But then, this: my friend greets her parents with a hug and kiss every time she sees them, even briefly. She said to me one day, "I'm not very close to my parents. Are you?" I said, "Yes I feel like we're very close." She said, "Isn't that strange to you? You consider yourself so close to your parents yet you never kiss or hug them, and I feel distant from mine yet I always hug and kiss them." Now this conversation seemed to contradict what the friend told me earlier and I ended up more confused than ever!

Gail: I really think it's a matter of communication. I've been accused of not caring for someone because I didn't express it in a way that they would recognize it. On the other hand, I have felt this way myself for the same reason. In my marriage, my DH and I have learned to ask questions and not make assumptions based on what we may or may not be doing. He might interpret my refusal to do something as lack of caring for him, when it just might be that as an AC I cannot do this thing. He has learned not to take that personally or as lack of concern for him. We make an effort to try to convey how we feel to each other in a way that we can both understand it. He learns my language, I learn his. We meet somewhere in the middle! He doesn't demand that I show love only in the way he thinks I should, and vice-versa. We learn to understand, accept, and live with the difference. So far this has worked, though there have been many people in my life that never bothered to learn my language and pushed me away as unloving and cold. After years of guilt, I have come to see the loss as theirs.

Kimberly: Warning! Warning! (Tongue in cheek.) Feeling about to be expressed! Thank you so much for your understanding. It sounds like what my husband and I have. He has an illness that is physically debilitating and I do care, and he knows it, but through the language you spoke of. The thing is, he cares enough to bother to learn my way, and some people don't. Thanks again. A little understanding goes so far!

Our emotional capacity clearly varies among us, and, like with sensory experience, we may be hypersensitive or hyposensitive to our own or others' emotions (Williams, 1996). As we continue:

Kalen: I have noticed two distinct types of AS—the emotionally hypersensitive ones and the extremely logical, un-emotional, excessively analytical types like me. Maybe the difference is partly whether we tend to be primarily left or right brained. I think I may have started out the opposite of how I am now, but changed as a defense mechanism.

Jane: Yes, emotional capacities do seem to differ among autistics, judging from this group and other such online venues. I wouldn't say I have "no emotions." I sure do get angry sometimes, and sad in various ways, and I feel affection.

How we access our feelings also varies, both in intrapersonal experience:

Jane: As I was walking home today, I was rejoicing in the beauty of the day (sunshine, flowering trees, blue sky) and began to chant a favorite poem to myself. It is a poem about loving the beauty of the world/earth, and it is like music for me, a way to access deep emotions that do not arise for me in inter-personal contexts. Certain poems help me reach that level, as do certain pieces of music. Also, mountains.

Kalen: Sailing does it for me. Real sailing on a tall ship with the engine off. There is no way to describe it. Even remembering it evokes something. I get very little out of flowers, poems, or other things that are typically considered beautiful. I enjoy music, but not in an emotional way unless it is connected to a significantly emotional event in my life.

and in interpersonal situations:

Kalen: I do feel connecting emotions, but I get the impression they are different than they are for NTs, at least in the way they start, e. g., I did not have an immediate, overwhelming feeling of love or pride when my daughter was born. Also, I considered things very logically before *allowing* myself to fall in love with my boyfriend, though I'm still not sure I'm in love in the same way as NTs. I sure haven't got that irrational thing they seem to get. On the other hand, I am quite sure I really do love both of them (and a couple of other people too).

Jane: Love is where I see a big difference between me and 99.9% of all NTs I know. Most NTs experience what I think of as sentimental love, whereas my version of romantic/sentimental love is based in intellect (as Ed Schneider describes in his book). For that matter, I guess all my love is based in intellect. I appreciate someone's qualities and therefore like, feel affection for, or love her or him. I do not experience the kind of emotions that people have expected from me in intimate relationships. I don't know how to describe it, since it is alien to me, but it always comes up. NTs who are in love want to discuss and agonize over things in their love relationships in a way that makes me feel like a robot in comparison. When they embark on these emotion-feasts and I am left standing there feeling lost, they first urge me to "open up" and "let my feelings show" and then, when I comply (and show them what my feelings are like), they either accuse me of lying or else conclude that I am deficient, insufficient, and boring.

In some instances our emotional experience may seem similar to that of NTs, in others quite different. As we discuss, for example, concerning grief:

Jane: As for grief, I'm not sure how my experience compares with what others feel. I loved my mother very much but didn't go into a grief-stricken decline when she died. Of course, she had been dying for a while and the death itself came into the category of blessed relief. I have gone through as much pain over the death of a cat, I think, and probably for the same reason. When I live with a cat, the cat becomes an important part of my life. The cat's death removes that portion of my daily life, and I got through the process of expecting to see the cat every minute (unconsciously) and then having to remember, "Oh, that's right. The cat died," over and over and over again until the new, cat-less reality takes over from the old cat-ful reality.

Patty: Same for me, except that when my father died (the most recent human) I felt a big hole in my life and my activities, and also in my ability to contact someone who could give me advice (when asked) and a feeling of stability in this wacky world. The day he died I instantly felt exactly biblical, and wanted to rub ashes on my face and run screaming out into the fields and hills and tear out my hair. I did scream and cry for about an hour, and then it was over. A couple of times since then I welled up with crying for just a minute or two. In fact I'm doing it right now, reading what I wrote. Now I drink coffee from his old coffee mug in the morning and feel his presence. I feel that his perceived responsibilities to me and to my stepmother are keeping him from getting on with his eternal business. I miss his physical presence, partly because he was a person I wanted to know better (he didn't interact with us when we were children), and I mourn for what I perceive as his failing to leave the things of this life and go on with his immortal existence.

Jane: Now that I think about it, however, it seems that my mother is not gone from my life to the same extent as the dead cat (perhaps because I have replaced that cat with two other cats). She was so important in my life, and we spent so much of my life together, that she seems quite present to me. Same as anyone else I care about who is not within reach. I feel as close to my dead friend Frank as I do to my live friend Liz who is arriving for a visit a week from today.

And anger:

April: Anger is one of my strong points, my best emotion. By my best I mean my most able emotion, the one I do not have to think about. It's not exactly my best point.

Jane: I used to think I never got angry, but I've since come to recognize in myself various kinds of anger, as well as despair that may look like anger (described in "AS Paradox: Rational Anger", this volume).

How we show distress, and what we need to ease it, may be very different to NTs, as we continue:

Jane: I very rarely cry. But when I do, people around me *invariably* assume a completely incorrect cause. Which makes me cry all the harder, of course, out of frustration!

Jean: When NTs cry, they generally prefer to be in the arms of someone they love. On the other hand, if you want to soothe us when we're upset, give us the information and ideas we need to understand our circumstances. Usually we're upset because we're in the dark about something and can't fathom a strategy, not because someone hurt us—in which case we'd probably rage if anything.

Sola: Yes. And be very clear, definite and unequivocal with that information! But if I am down, I want to be alone.

Sue: One of the questions my homeopathic doctor kept asking was "when you are upset do you seek others for comfort?" Each time I would look at her like she was crazy and answer, "absolutely not! How can I deal with others when I am trying to deal with my own emotions?" She looked at me like I was crazy and nothing more was said. I finally figured out that this must be the wrong answer! (i.e., not the typical response).

Our emotions do tend to change and develop in the course of our lives, through maturation and learning. For some this happened after giving birth:

Sally: Do any of you other mums here feel, like me, that they learnt loads in the emotional sense as a result of childrearing? That the process of childrearing has forcibly pushed them into places they wouldn't have otherwise gone to, mentally, I mean, and experience-wise?

Daina: From my year of breastfeeding my baby, I can personally vouch for the fact that Oxytocin (produced by women who are breastfeeding) works as a sociabilizer. Not only does it make the milk come down, but it makes the woman calm and passive and accepting of the situation, but only toward the baby. I was less interested in other people. Oxytocin seems to work on a primitive level and kind of forces you to be preoccupied with the baby. I could no longer remember what all the questions about existence and life were, but I knew the answer to all of them. The answer was baby! After I stopped breast-feeding, the questions came back and the answer disappeared (turned into a toddler).

Jane: I have not yet recognized any big changes of the sort described by Daina and Sally. Is this something that happens only to AS women who give birth?

Kim: This is an excellent observation, yet I can't help but wonder which is the cause and which is the effect? I find the insight remarkable!

Confusion about feelings has for some arisen from early caregivers teaching them to associate words that didn't match their inner experience (Baker, 1999), and for others from inappropriate psychotherapy (Baker, 1999 & 2002). Others again recall learning to suppress their feelings (as recounted elsewhere in this volume).

Depression, a common part of life on the spectrum, may also blunt our emotions:

Kalen: I have more range of feeling and expression now than I used to, but that is probably due at least in part to the fact that I am not depressed right now.

Self-esteem and Identity

Having difficulty with certain processes, does not necessarily mean the inner sense of self is impaired. Self-esteem and sense of identity do, however, vary widely among us. Hardly surprising, given the responses of others to our differences, such as dismissal of the reality of our feelings and even (as Daina recounts in "Coming alive in a world of texture", this volume) our perceptions! On top of this come society's default explanations for our difficulties: character weakness! As can be seen throughout this book and elsewhere (Baker, 2002), our social fumbling commonly earns us such judgments as selfish, lazy, stupid, rude, bad, aloof, etc. (Interestingly, research by the sociologist Garfinkel (1967) demonstrated the almost universal moral outrage engendered by seemingly innocuous breaches of social code, the perpetrator being interpreted as deliberately uncooperative or hostile). Even after correct diagnosis, misunderstanding may be compounded by the myths and stereotypes around autism such as "lacking imagination and empathy".

Thus, it can be a struggle to gain and maintain self-esteem, or even a sense of identity, as shown in our accounts. Depression and anxiety commonly accompany this struggle:

Jean: I do believe some of my ability to stick it out comes from a not very welcome gift, depression. It serves to blunt the anxiety so I don't completely crash but just struggle on hopelessly. I even have a hypothesis that what makes some of us AS-ers higher functioning is that this comorbidity with depression makes us able to function longer. (Thoughts?)

Wendy: The depression, yeah, it does blunt the anxiety, and I'm beginning to think that is why the antidepressants I took made me have such trouble with anxiety and panic attacks. It was doing away with the depression, which must have been buffering against the acute attacks.

Some of us sought (in vain) a sense of identity in religious, women's or other movements. While some maintained their unique identity by accepting the status of eccentric misfit, others coped by hiding, or by copying social gestures or even entire personas. As we discuss:

Wendy: The workplace, well, it's like I have to put on a coat when I go out. I kind of dull myself and sometimes am not able to perceive anything in particular. Have to put on a personality I've constructed, as though rehearsing for a play, then getting up on a stage. I can perform, but not for long periods of time, all day every day. It's rather odd at times, just how quickly I can change from one kind of thinking to another. It's like having more than one person living in this body, but each with the same consciousness, so I guess it's just I have a multifaceted personality. One of my masks is humor, being a clown, and being silly, because when I was serious about something, people wouldn't understand.

Jean: The clowning is another ability I have too, though sometimes these personalities don't come when they're bidden and they just pop up. I'm even called bubbly by some and few have any idea about the depression because all they see is this sudden surge of electricity that configures itself into a person in front of them. I'm also liable to find humor in wordplay or idea play, even when the topic is serious so I'm capable of appearing ridiculing or uncaring because I've just made fun with (not of) a name or concept.

Sue: I like the cloak analogy. I *was* surprised to discover my self beneath it. In fact I'm still uncovering it.

Toni: I too am still uncovering mine. I get confused because I often can't feel it. Part of what the cloak hides for me is access to my feelings. I ignored them for so long (I didn't start figuring this out till I was 47).

Sue: I learned to hide what I couldn't seem to explain about myself, and what seemed not to fit what was expected of me. When I finally decided that I couldn't take the pain of being emotionally hypersensitive in an environment that didn't support it (of course I didn't know I was any different from anyone else at the time), I decided to stop feeling.

Toni: Me too, I simply decided to stop feeling.

Sue: I did what others asked of me much as a robot would, and I hid what remained of *me* deep inside a world of my own, where no one else was allowed. I at least had some form of contentment this way. As the demands on me grew, I developed different characters that had specialized knowledge and skills to perform as others expected me to perform. I was so focused on surviving, I'd run all day on sheer tension (nervous energy) and didn't dare stop because then I'd collapsed in utter fatigue and be unable to get going again. I couldn't imagine how people could come home from work and go out grocery shopping. Or to a party. (Neither of which my nervous system tolerates even when I am rested.)

Coa: That sounds so much like me!

Sue: Suffice it to say, these past several years have been very difficult ones. I am *finally* learning to feel comfortable with myself without that cloak and even discover some of the good emotions I never knew existed as I interact with the world as myself. And I'm less exhausted. I've discovered that it's a whole lot easier being one's self than trying to pretend to be someone else. Thank goodness my husband of 30 years has stuck by me and accepted all these changes. He has said that he much prefers the real me (with all my weirdnesses) over the one that pretended to be normal all those years.

Coa: I sometimes wondered myself whether I suffered from multiple personality disorder.

Sue: I've wondered the same, but come to the conclusion, as I sense that you are too, that this fractioning off a part of myself to do what my whole self can't is just a coping mechanism to help me function. Because of the differently wired person that I am, not because of some clearly identified emotional trauma (as is generally the case in multiple personality disorder). I was not brought up in an emotionally nurturing environment, but if I had a normally wired brain, I think I would have handled it differently.

Coa: I discounted that too, as I had no major early life trauma (until the stresses of trying to fit began once I became self-aware and realized how different I was to other children). And my brothers and sisters, older and younger, brought up in same loving environment as me, all lead such normal, successful and happy lives. (Interestingly, my sister, though said to be much shyer than me, was much more socially adept.)

Gender

Many of us have a very different sense of gender compared to NT women, as well as different ways of expressing the qualities and roles traditionally regarded as female. As shown throughout our accounts, and in the following discussion:

MM: My gender came in question at that time—the boys would say, "You aren't like other girls. You don't cry whenyou get hurt, so you are better than other girls, but you aren't a boy, so you are a Mary Margaret." Of course it was lonely being given a category to myself and it taught me to hate my gender. It would take feminist readings many years later to move me out of my male-identified position.

Jean: For some of us here, our lives, outlook, and behavior don't have much of a sense of gender at all. I myself live a somewhat femme life but it feels in some sense detachable, like a costume. I was an androgynous kid and most clearly perceive the world in a non-gendered way.

Ava: There is so much misunderstanding about AS women, particularly concerning empathy, imagination and ability, illustrated well by what's been written in this group.

Jean: Yes, I agree completely. The point is, though, that this is a way of having gender. Also, that much of what we call gender is typical social presentation of the feminine. I think the importance of all this is the impact of others' assumptions that our sensitivity and caring are inadequate, which can be so painful for us. My dad thought I was a hateful person and pretty much convinced me too, because I'd see loving people and not be able to act like them.

Sola: Did you read Deborah Tannen's *You Just Don't Understand: Women and Men in Conversation*? I'm learning more how weird NTs are and how non-(NT) woman I am!

Jean: Never have but I've osmosed some of it from others. I guess what you're saying is why I'm still looking at *Women from Another Planet* as a working title. This addresses another book, to be sure—*Men Are from Mars, Women Are* *from Venus*—but it has the same premise, that of generalizing a female mindset from which we, um, vary.

Social Life

That individuals on the autism spectrum have difficulty mastering the social and communication skills that NTs pick up unconsciously, is well known. Some of these skills we gradually learn:

Jean: I now know how to tell if someone listening to me is getting bored. But this is a learned trait. Between not knowing at all, and now, there was a step when I'd notice signs of waning interest in others but it wouldn't connect with any means for shutting myself up. I'd just feel hurt. But now I can react more quickly to another's overload.

Gail: I have learned to read other peoples body language over the years, and think I am pretty good at it now. But I still am so clueless to my own body language. I have little to no idea how I come across to people.

April: When other kids criticized me for not looking them in the eye, I was shocked! So even though it was unpleasant I started doing it, but then they accused me of staring. Eventually I found by trial and error that a rhythm of three seconds looking at them then three seconds looking away, stopped the comments (but still didn't gain me anything except less criticism!)

However some of the subtler social challenges we face are not readily recognized by NT observers, and it is very doubtful that social skills courses could ever teach us to master these. For example, moderating the signals that cause others to approach, avoid or simply not notice us:

Gail: An acquaintance said that when I would be sitting at a table with other people, I had no presence. She described it as "empty air sitting in a chair." It was startling to her when I would say something, because it felt like to her the voice was coming out of nowhere. What do you think she meant by this? I find it intriguing.

Jane: I assume she was used to NT people who send (and receive) non-verbal communication signals all the time without even being aware of it. Since we don't do it (not automatically, anyway, though some have learned to fake it), it's no wonder we seem blank.

Jean: Amen, sister! Even my kids notice a syndrome where people get in line in front of me while I'm first in line and they get their needs met before mine. I guess my social face at rest is so passive that I'm virtually invisible.

Coa: Jane, I like the way you describe, in your essay, being a social dead-zone. You were referring to not being chased in the game, but I wonder if that's related to what happens when I suggest a new idea in a meeting? The idea is there, but devoid of social signals. A pure person-less idea. So after other people take it up and find it a very good idea, it is invariably recorded as someone else's idea! Never mine. This has always puzzled me. There are other situations too, where I seem to be invisible to other people. I think of the social signals as the fluff that surrounds and often obscures the real person. I myself try to see through this confusing fluff to the real core-person underneath. But for NTs set to detect fluff more easily than cores, we AS folk would indeed seem a dead-zone.

MM: Coa, the part of your story that is not like me, is that it doesn't seem to matter how much I crave to be alone and I look out the window or go to the back of the bus or attempt to sit by myself in the park, apparently I am an approachable person, I don't look mean enough even when I glare like a monster, everywhere I go people stop to talk to me.

Diane: People don't ever sit next to me either. Even at meetings at work, the seats next to me are always the last to be filled.

Coa: It would be interesting to find out why this happens, what sort of body language signals, make nobody sit next to Jane, Diane or me (even on the occasions I hope someone will) whereas people pester you even when you glare.

Jane: I wish I knew! I know a man (diagnosed-only-by-me-Aspie) who is like MM: everyone talks to him. I am like Coa and Diane: nobody wants to sit by me. I think it must have something to do with the signals we emit without knowing what we are doing, and with NT (mis)interpretation of those signals. One funny thing: Although my peers in normal NT society seem to steer away from me instinctively, I've often been seen as childlike (in need of protection) by kind individuals in non-normal environments.

Coa: Maybe it has something to do with speed of connections? I am slow. But some people with AS seem extra-quick (which doesn't necessarily mean they process things any better). Or maybe MM and Jane's acquaintance do something different in the first moments? One of the unspoken rules seems to me to be, that whatever signals one puts out at first contact are vital to what happens subsequently. If I arrive too overloaded to make some initial contact (eye contact and/or immediate comments), there tends to be no contact throughout the event, no matter how I try. I feel like either a social judgment has been made in those first moments, or a social dead-zone perceived, which is unchangeable regardless of what I try subsequently. (This happened most poignantly some years ago when I had traveled halfway across the world "to make some connections", arriving a mess due to disastrous trip, then after sitting through 3 days of non-interaction, tried so hard, even gazing at people's faces and eyes trying to catch their attention, to say at least a hello-goodbye before setting off to my part of the world again. It was like being completely invisible, like I had been written off or maybe never had existed.)

MM: If I go into a store, folks think I work there. MC, the woman I live with, says it has to do with the fact that I am so absorbed in whatever I am looking at, and that the regular culture does that when they are working, and so it is assumed I am an expert at what I am looking at. Somehow my intensity makes people think I know what I am doing…and there I sit reading the difference between the chemicals that go into my wet vacuum, there are so many different ones to choose from but I am learning the milder smelling ones, and up comes another person asking me where the lamps are, and I point to the lamps, and I have learned that pointing to a section of a store with no words added is easier than saying, I don't work here. Besides, my strange obsession with the store makes it so that eventually I do know where everything is.

Another aspect of NT social life we struggle to grasp, is the essence that binds social groups together. For example:

Coa: I hope that if I share these accounts I've written with my NT companions, maybe they will see another way (mine!) of viewing the things we did together, my subtle difficulties and the consequences. Do you think they would finally get it?

Sola: My guess: not likely. As I read your accounts, I noticed something. You respond to contents, but they don't really care about contents, that's just a hanger to carry the real stuff, an excuse. What the *real stuff* is about, is a little hard for me to describe. (Well, I am AS too!). Probably it's all about being together, and feeling that there's something that binds the group together, and leaves strangers out. Stranger is anyone who does not belong. And I fear that you do not belong.

Jane: That's like what I wrote about the Girl Scout Camp (see "Growing up Genderless", this volume): "there was something there among the other girls from which I was excluded. Something had happened to them, individually and as a group, during the weeks of the camp, that had not happened to me."

Sola: It doesn't matter *what* binds them together, what matters is that they are together. The worst thing that Coa did, was to know better than them. I know too well what a crime that is…and to back me that I am not paranoid, I was relieved to read in Deborah Tannen's books analyses that described just that…that, especially among women, being different, and behaving in ways that might be understood as trying to be better, is like excluding oneself from the group—immediately (even if the outcome might be good for the group). It's not that they are stupid or jealous people, they are just NT…and I don't believe that they will be ready to see themselves in a mirror held in front of them by you.

The following discussion illustrates some of our own views of NT social principles:

Jane: I've been experimenting with applying the concept of *added value* to our social development. As I understand it, added value can be explained like this: A pile of raw material (e.g., gold) has a value. Say a certain quantity of the material has the value 3. After a skilled crafter or artist has worked on the gold, it increases in value, say from 3 to 5, with the increase representing the added value of the artist's time and skill. The American Heritage Dictionary defines *value added tax* as: "a tax on the estimated market value added to a product or material at each stage of its manufacture or distribution, ultimately passed on to the consumer." My idea is to look at the *manufacture* of social persons along the same lines. Each stage in maturation produces a value added product—for an NT child. An eight year-old does not have the total added value of a 35 year-old, and is not expected to. But among other eight year-olds, she is expected to have reached a certain stage in value adding, in acquiring social skills and habits. If she has not, she is devalued by her peers. AS children are oblivious to the elements and processes that impart social value to one's behavior. We are unable to participate in this kind of social self-production. Our raw material remains unrefined.

And this, I think, has special implications for girls growing into women. (Not that it has no implications for boys growing into men, but that the implications are different because we live in a society with gendered expectations.) In many ways, as the social theorists point out, gender is a performance that is enacted. Learning one's gender role (how to enact it) has been the key channel through which girls have become value added social participants. That's what make-up is about, for example.

Daina: I must say that I intensely dislike this value-added way of looking at it. How about just plain *conformity-added*? Simon Baron-Cohen keeps talking about how social people don't live in a world of perceptions, thoughts and feelings, so much as in a world of "meta-representations"—that is, representations of representations of representations. In other words, a fantasy world (albeit perhaps a pleasant one) made of smoke and hooey. It isn't just a question of social skill (I have plenty of that, when I get paid for it), but of believing in the social agreement. What is the social agreement? The agreement is that there is an agreement.

Sola: This is so true. Reminds me of Jim's presentation (Sinclair, 1995) on the communication deficits of NTs. He said that NTs do not care so much about the absolute truth but about what is perceived to be truth by society. When there is controversy about facts, NTs will not go check directly what is true, but will negotiate among themselves to reach an agreement. This sounds incredible, but since I heard that, I've noticed it over and over again. Jim also said that this observation is supported by scientific research on the human memory and the reliability of witnesses in court. Anyway, for us ACs it looks insane! Sometimes it's so simple to go check on facts and for the life of us we can't understand why the others don't just go check; while they probably get mad at us for refusing to participate in the process that seems so obvious to them and instead go off on our own to "prove to them that we are right," i.e., to try to impose our viewpoint rather than be cooperative.

Patty: If working in public affairs I am perfectly presentable. It's the fine line between business/etiquette and moving on over into official friendships that trips me up. I might be able to do it now, but I used to be plagued by impulses to blab everything I was thinking at people who didn't care. I think I could at least control most of the impulses at this point. But what is the point of relating to someone if you have to hold back 98 % of yourself and you know they wouldn't like you if they knew you!?!?!)

Jane: Hmmmmm. This may be one of those areas where we notice differences among us. Unless I'm reading you (two) wrong. You make it sound as if your NT emulation is better than mine. As if the only area where you lack social skills is in intimate (non-business) relationships. That's certainly not true for me.

Morgan: Definitely not true for me either. Makes me sad, because few people will really take me seriously.

Liane: The entire time I pretend to be social, I'm thinking one or more of the following: What? Who in their right mind would act like this on a daily basis? Does anyone know or care what they look/sound/act like?

Jane: Most NTs (apparently) do not realize that they live in a made-up world of "social" unreality where they are judged (and judge others) in this commodified fashion. NTs window shop through life, as far as I can tell. (Although I must add: there are significant and wonderful exceptions.) ACs are considered egocentric at least in part because we focus more on what we perceive as real (and therefore important)—the aspects of our world that are not composed of layer upon layer of value-added socialization. For most of us, the largest available chunk of real reality is our non-value-added selves, hence we are "egocentric."

Gail: Yes, I call this social stuff superficial phoniness. People think they have relationships when they really don't. What they have is other people who do this ritual well which gives the appearance of having a relationship. I saw through that a long time ago. I can't be bothered with it though I can do some of it. It always puzzled me because I could never understand how people could be satisfied with such a phony way of relating.

Sally: Mmm…Ditto big time! Luckily for the most part I don't have to interact with new people much apart from shops and stuff, which is different again but still weird sometimes and a bit disconnected. But I agree about the phoniness of it all. When I was younger I thought people really wanted to know how I was and I'd launch in to a whole catalogue of stuff. As I have got older I have come to realize that it's only them being 'polite', so I just give the monotone "fine," I suppose that has been in last two or three years maybe. So now I can play it, but isn't it just breathtakingly superficial?!

Gail: People who bother to get to know me always comment on how "real" I am.

Sally: Ditto. Or "down to earth," etc.

Gail: They know that what they see is what they get, good or bad. They don't have to wade through lies to get at the truth.

Sally: Yes, true, unfortunately makes us sitting ducks for anyone who tries to do a number on us—I have been victim to that more times that I can count—although at 31 years old I am starting to learn to put up barriers with the help of my partner although I still think he is far too untrusting—but he reckons it's normal to be that way. I just think it's sad.

Gail: A lot of people appreciate this. I really can't stand to talk to people who do this phony baloney stuff well. All this false politeness and good will. I feel like smacking them and saying, "Tell me what you are really thinking!"

Sally: Yes, I know I find it most irritating when it is someone that I know quite well—it's the old, "Is it them hiding or is it me reading it wrong?" dilemma!

Gail: Sometimes I have challenged people. For instance, when someone asks me how I am, I just might say, "Do you really want to know?" Takes people by surprise, and yes, they consider me rude for saying it. I consider them liars for pretending to be someone they're not.

Sally: Yes, and if you don't buy in to all that they think you are standoffish anyway! The thing is, is it just us that can see through all this superficial rubbish? Surely not, I know NT's that find it just as pointless but they play ball…

From our perspective, NT social communication commonly involves mind games that profess to show manners and caring, but may be traumatic for those of us who can't follow them:

Sola: Another thing that I realized is that often NTs don't say what they mean, but still expect us to guess what they really mean and to act accordingly. If we take their words literally, they get mad at us for being inconsiderate…For example the hostess says, "please don't leave yet" and we are supposed to say, "yes I must, I have to get up early tomorrow," and then leave. If we do stay instead, then the hostess will resent us for being inconsiderate by keeping them up late; but if we say, "yes, I'll let you go to bed," then it would be an even worse breach of code, which might result in an argument: "No, I really want you to stay," etc. There are many other examples. This leads to NTs not taking messages for what they are but trying to get into the soul of the other person, evaluate merits and drawbacks of a certain choice for the other person, deciding for them and then trying to convince them that this is what they really wanted. Reflecting on my reaction to such experiences in my own life as an AC, it occurred to me that it's like what happens to a young child exposed to age-inappropriate stuff like sex. It is a feeling of something imposed on us, that on the one hand is incomprehensible and with no context in our system, and on the other hand is so invasive that we can't just wave it off. I find the effect even worse than physical invasion. And it's what NTs call basic manners in simple cases and caring in more complicated cases! I'm not sure whether it's relevant here, but I learnt from reading Deborah Tannen why NTs play these games rather that just tell the truth and take things literally. Because it's fun! She says that communication is so easy, that it would be boring to have social life without those games; it's like when someone has a skill, that it's fun to develop it further by inventing challenges. Now, imagine what that would do to someone who does not have that skill to start with!

Pattern of Behaviors and Interests

Behaviors and interests that seem unusual to the NT observer, may have meaning and value for us, as we discuss:

Jane: I don't know whether this would apply to any/many but me: Do you have ongoing relationships with animals and/or with inanimate aspects of the world that are just as strong/important as (or more so than) your relationships with humans?

Kalen: Do computers count? I *love* my computers. They're not quite just as important as my most important humans (family, close friends), but they are significantly more important than the majority of humans.

Wendy: Jane, I don't think you are the only one who feels that way, when I as growing up, I had a lot of friends who were stuffed animals, but I didn't think of them that way, they were alive to me, and also friends. I wrote stories about them. Also, I had emotional attachments to certain toys, and even now I feel a sort of affection for my car, not that I am materialistic, but that it's beyond being an inanimate object. I get upset when it gets damaged, not for reasons most people would understand, but that I feel sorry for the car. I keep cars until they can no longer run, but still feel sad when I sell/give them away.

Diane: I fixated on cats. But isn't it sad that, so often, our parents and others have tried to take away these very fixations that have made our hearts open? When growing up (and even still now) I was frequently criticized by my family about liking cats so much.

Wendy: I talk to my cats like they are people, because I have this feeling that they can understand me. And if I treat them as friends, they become friends. If this is an AC thing, it's an interesting one.

MM: I, too, related first to animals. There is a large black and white photo of my mother looking beautiful as usual, her friend's child, and my brother and I fighting over the bunny in the box, all of us on the front steps. I am in anguish, crying from the bottom of my soul. My brother has that typical, five year old selfish-ownership look that humans get over things they think they have a right to. But I don't want the bunny. I just want to return it to the realm of animals who understand that life is not a show.

Daina: As a youngster, people meant nothing to me. But the spot on the floor did, and the texture of fur—and many other textures and shapes.

Jane: That's very interesting about texture being the basis for you. I have a thing (both tactile and visual) about certain shapes and was relieved to read in Gunilla Gerland's book that I'm not the only one. I used to get to my office every day by going up the stairs in the western end of the building, but now I use the other stairs because I kept getting hung up (pleasantly but inconveniently) on a particular curve in the wooden banister. I had to caress it with my hand, and then I didn't want to use that hand for anything else because it retained the feel of the curve. It's also interesting how you learned to hide your predilection for shapes—and so early, too. We do that (the hiding) so skillfully, we high functioning autistics. This may be a major distinction between high and low functioning autism. Maybe we internalize our wants, learn to look for satisfaction (for the balance of want and fulfillment of want) on the inside of ourselves because there are always barriers outside. That may be one factor behind our "inwardness" and "selfishness"?

Coa: As a preschooler, I would spend all day enthusiastically studying textbooks while other children played. Then when encouraged to take novels out of the library instead, my way of choosing them (having no feel for characters or plot) was to start systematically at one end of the shelf with the "Aa" authors (an enraging exercise because each time I went back to the library, I would find other "A" books that I had missed out from my sequence because other people had had the nerve to take them out of sequence and disturb my orderly plan!) I gave up long before I got to the "B"s and went back to the textbooks. Only in high school when we were taught how to "study" literature, "understand" characters and motives, etc, did the doors to understanding other people, both real-life and fictional, open: there was a way it could be worked out!

Toni: I too always enjoyed the library. The fiction I enjoyed most was set in an all girls' school and much of the dialogue was the teachers talking in the staff room about the girls. I realize now that this was my attempt to figure out both children and adults. I also really enjoyed my stamp collections. When I look back I am sure I often chose to work on my stamps rather than go play with the other kids.

Sameness and repetition (perseveration) may likewise be important to us for reasons the NT observer might not suspect. For example:

Jane: Something else I've wondered about: Many NTs who get into a rut stop noticing what's around them. If they have to engage in repetitive activities, their senses become dulled and they no longer see/hear/feel as keenly. They may express this as saying that they are bored when things remain the same. As an AS person, I tend to like repetition and sameness. It's true that I sometimes zone out and lose contact with the outside world. But that's different; it's an AS shutdown (or vacation from the NT world), not the NT boredom-reaction to routine. In fact, I often notice that I become more observant with repetition. I walk to work along the same route almost every day. Every day I see the same things, but actually I see particular details. The picture builds up slowly, and it changes over time. I don't get bored, I don't stop seeing, I don't stop developing my picture of what is there along the route.

Coa: Sameness in environment, I like and need too (and react if too much changes too fast): either so I can focus better on the content / purpose / meaning, e.g. on a walk like you mentioned I too might notice different or more enhanced details every time. Or in other cases I like things the same so I don't get into a state looking for things (such as items in a strange supermarket), so I can finish before I get too overloaded. Or all the things I mislay myself if I follow a different routine such as when I sat in a different chair last week: looked and felt exactly the same but was positioned differently in the room, so I lost my lists-of-things-to-be-done by dropping them in places I never would have thought of looking—led to a whole day of searching, and getting none of the list-items done, till I finally remembered what I had done differently to usual.

Diane: I used to be a great fan of talk radio. Listening to it calmed me and made the time pass when I was doing something boring like housework or yard work. I had a schedule I could follow so I could plan to clean the toilets when something good was on the radio. It also helped me get to sleep at night and having a show to look forward to was enough incentive to help me resist my urge to overeat. But now all (yes, all) my favorite shows have gone away. So as a result I am much more anxious at night and having trouble getting to sleep, as well as eating more than I used to. It is interesting realizing how much benefit I used to get from talk radio, and how much it calmed me. As they say, you don't know what you've got till it's gone. I'm even worried now that the anxiety I am now having as a result of not having talk radio shows to listen to may raise my blood pressure. It is as if talk radio were a part of my routine, and a comforting part at that, and now it's gone. Maybe talk radio somehow made up for the lack of interpersonal interactions I get in my daily life, as it was sort of a way to vicariously participate in discussions of issues, even though I never called in.

Jane: I can only enjoy and fully apply myself to those things in which I have an interest. The list of such things does not include idle chitchat, trading personal information with acquaintances, or discussing clothes, hair, weight, relationships, etc. Over the course of my adult life, I have learned how to redefine many topics in order to make them interesting to me. I did this partly by nature (I home in on the little flakes of interesting-to-me material buried within what everyone else considers a different subject altogether) and partly on purpose. There are times when I need to have an interest in what is before me. School/university was a prime example. I needed to be interested in the courses I took or else I would fail them. So I would delve into the material presented until I could dig out the interesting-to-me elements. Either that or I would "re-invent" the material, interpreting it into something I could use to hold my interest.

This process mostly worked well for me, thanks to my ability to impress teachers with my writing. Even if I took their subject off into some unexpected byway, they gave me points for how I presented my ideas. Outside (and occasionally inside) the classroom the process has some drawbacks. People who notice what I am doing, who realize that I am "distorting" everything so that it fits my own interests/needs, see me as self-centered and stubborn. (They mostly don't know the word perseveration). And isn't that another example of how a survival mechanism, a skill an AS person (me, in this case) has learned in order to negotiate her way more successfully through the NT world, becomes a "symptom" of a "disorder"?

Values and Spirituality

As we editors discussed when we met in Boston, it's not this planet as a whole that we feel alienated from (which is why the book-title bears a question mark), just the neurotypcial-social aspect of it. Our interests, as the reader will find from our writing, include such things as spirituality, environment and ethical issues:

Diane: Is it the AS in me that is making me like this? I just can't get away from the awareness of my actions on the environment since I have learned about it.

MM: I don't know. I do know that I have always lived simply and that I don't see any value in collecting material possessions. They feel like pilgrim progress burdens. I need to live as simply as possible because it feels like my head will explode if I have too much to worry over. I have found that I am uncomfortable with people who have large houses and nice cars when they do not fill them. And so when my son says he wants to live in a mansion, then I tend to say, then fill it with people, because most of the world doesn't have adequate shelter. I think I am more sensitive to the needs of the earth because

I seem to be able to feel the trees, the rocks, the water and voices from the past of a land. I also think I don't understand money and why I live in a society that uses money instead of other means of survival. But as far as relatives and childhood chums succeeding, I tend to cringe, but don't feel judgmental. I still love the person even with all their extras. I see past the materialism to the person I want to connect with.

Ava: Many of us here clearly feel a connection with rocks, plants and animals. For me, this is not just an intellectual thing, it is something passionate and living, that I experience deeply in mind, emotions and body all at once (e.g. my response to a familiar tree). Bound with that is a sense of love, respect & responsibility for life, that is most simply and purely experienced in the world of nature, but which also extends to the complexities of human life and the wonders of the wider universe. That's also the basis of my own religious experience, and my understanding of people: thoroughly grounded in what I can experience through my own senses. Definitely not because others have told me what to believe (though I might store what others tell me as a sort of myth or metaphor which may or may not turn out to be useful/true in my own life). This can be a good way to listen to other people (without pre-judgments or the limitations of opinions and belief systems, just listen without assigning them to categories).

My religious beliefs I have come to first via my own senses and my own experience in life. They are neither limited to only the aspects of life that science can prove (e.g. that a tree is a combination of certain material substances), nor arising from wishful thinking (e.g., any wish of mine to be a tree), nor from human opinion/reactions/what is socially trendy to think (a mystery to me!). This is another approach. For me it's more comprehensive and real than orthodox science, religion, or social convention (and I can re-validate it at any time by just leaning against a tree and gazing upward). This spiritual approach to life (which I find best described by anthroposophy) involves seeing through the physical to the spiritual within the natural and human worlds.

MM (*discussing her work as chaplain*): My definition of spirituality is very broad. It is a lifetime of treasure storied in your heart of hearts. It is my job to explain that (e.g. in my Alzheimer's patients) that is not lost just because some of their brain cells are scrambled. And death is a natural process of moving on to the next world. I feel honored to hold the hands of patients. It is a very sacred moment to be asked to be a part of that.

Diane: Does anyone in this group meditate on a regular basis? I'm meeting more and more people who do, especially in the environmental movement, and they say it helps them keep grounded and centered. One of the theses of the book *Spirit Matters* by Michael Lerner (a great book, which also explains human nature in a way I feel could help others with AS as it has me) is that it won't be possible to save the earth unless environmentalists develop movements and organizations based on spirituality. This book together with other reading I've done has really convinced me, and as someone who has always been interested in saving the Earth it makes me want to do my part and develop a spiritual practice, the center of which is meditation. (It also stresses community action but I'm already doing some of that). This viewpoint is that all religions have something to teach us, and the task of mankind is to develop universal ethical practices and get beyond the idea that ethics is relative without promoting just one religion. While spirituality as practiced by many new agers is very self-centered and ignores the problems of the world, to be truly spiritual you face the problems of the world and do what you can to make the world a better place, which goes way beyond just looking inward. But I'm asking about meditation as I did try it a few times when I was younger and found it extremely difficult. My mind always wandered. I am worried that maybe as an autistic, I cannot meditate.

Coa: Hi Diane. Decades ago I practiced Transcendental Meditation until I was thoroughly put off by the way some practitioners were so disconnected from reality, e.g., not noticing when they hurt a friend. Their answer to everything was that if we all did more and more meditation all would be fine...Something similar happened with various religious groups I briefly tried, back in the days when I was still desperately trying to belong somewhere). More recently I practice autogenic training, a westernized form of relaxation, which uses the physiological techniques of eastern yogis but without the religious beliefs. It's good for restoring some physiological harmony. Because it's short, the mind is less likely to wander.

Empathy

Empathy is frequently discussed by us, being an attribute both expected of women in general, and one that folk with AS are popularly regarded as lacking (along with closely related attributes like feelings and theory of mind). How is it then, that we can succeed in mothering, intimate relationships, and the types of work where empathy is considered essential? Our ranks include autistic caregivers, teachers, pastors and therapists who not only manage such seemingly unsuitable jobs, but also are regarded by our clients as being extra-good at empathizing, even though our AS-related difficulties are still disabling in other aspects of our lives. As the following thread explores:

Jean: Ava, you said something about your clients feeling listened to for the first time, then later on, something about your interest in knowing how it is that people like us, in the professions requiring lots of social contact, do it. I'd like to explore that as a thread, especially since so many of us here are in or aspiring to professions that involve people, something that on the surface seems unlikely.

Sue: I too have people who respect and listen to what I have to offer professionally…and I do "help" people. I actually empathize with the children I work with and advocate for them tooth and nail…sort of like fighting for the self that I didn't fight for. Strangely enough, I even get along with the parents and teachers (who can also drive me crazy at times).

Ava: I'd love to help dispel the myth that the only suitable jobs for us are ones with minimal human contact. I think some of our AS traits can even be an asset here. Work is one of the few contexts where others value my oddness. Spatial thinking helps find novel solutions. And my difficulty with words means that there are more silences. Well silences can be therapeutic! For example, enabling the other to suddenly say the most significant thing of all, something they maybe needed time and courage to voice that wouldn't have happened if I had plunged straight into a quick-fix answer. And the client seems to appreciate my putting time and thought into their problem, so has patience, knowing their problem is complex (attempts to solve it elsewhere having failed) and they really do want an accurate answer, unlike in social life. Secondly, even when there aren't silences, I generally get the client talking and say as little as possible myself, which elicits a fuller more accurate story than firing questions does. Work is often the only part of my life where I *can* express myself creatively. Not by talking *about* myself but by talking *from* myself.

Jean: I also went to great, great lengths teaching myself how to teach *out of what I have* rather than what most people have.

Sue: Interesting…I never really thought about it but, ask any of my colleagues and they will tell you that I *definitely* do my job in a way that is unique from the way they do it. I've even lectured others on *my* way of doing my job…but I've never thought about it until now that I was simply doing my job the only way I knew how…using what I had to give to the job…and doing my best. Since I've started looking at myself from an AS perspective, I can see very clear patterns of what has worked for me and what I've done to compensate for what isn't me but needs to happen.

Jean: My students say I'm excellent at conducting discussions on sensitive topics in such a way that they feel free to open up because they're in a safe setting. And I can be diplomatic about a lot of things in settings that aren't threatening. This is a consequence, though, of an awful lot of thinking and deliberate learning campaigns on my part.

Sue: Maybe choosing a people profession was my way of learning how to deal with people…sort of like learning under fire, deliberately taking on what I found most challenging. I have learned a lot about people over the years and my people skills have gotten a lot better as well.

MM: My work with persons with Alzheimer's disease is like coming home. They are people who also have a neurological difference. They are blunt and honest, no longer hiding behind cultural norms. They don't expect greetings, they live in their own world, they are discriminated against as they lose their ability to speak. Where I have a problem is having to report and attempt to explain to NT administrators. It is an uphill climb that frustrates me to no end. I get very tired of the dehumanization of people with dementia. Most people ask them the wrong questions, and treat them like a little child instead of the adult that they are. So they are going to get angry. I am a good chaplain because cultural norms are dropped during this time. NTs fall apart and don't know what to do. It is an area in which instinctively I do well and shine. I approach what I do with an autistic intuition and assurance that I am doing the best possible job.

So we believe we are fully capable of empathy. Perhaps we show this more readily at work than in social settings, because of such things as the slower more flexible style of one-to-one interactions, the clearer roles and scripts, and emphasis on problem solving? Particularly if able to adapt our work environment to reduce overload and suit our idiosyncratic processing needs.

Ava: In the work setting roles, rules and purpose are clear. So it's free of most of the coverings and games that confuse meaning for us in social situations: the client has come because of a problem they want solved so they nearly always describe it as clearly and honestly as they can. And since it's usually about the "core-person" not their coverings, maybe we can reach that more easily than NTs precisely because we're no good at the social coverings so see straight through to the core. Also, meeting on this deeper level, our lack of traditional social skills may be irrelevant, barely noticed. Most of the people who come to me, whether AS or NT, are struggling with difficult life situations, and I think the signs of my own lifelong struggle somehow show and help.

An AS characteristic that may give us an advantage over many NTs, is that precisely because we have difficulty recognizing such things as social categories and norms, we may be all the more likely to really listen to another person as the individual they are. More likely to hear their content without being misled by status, style or popular norms. As we continue:

Jean: I hear from my students that I do it well, and I know that my particular way is much more inclusive than that of some teachers. Because I have no capacity to put people in social categories, I take what students say seriously.

Ava: Jean, you have put that very well! Is that the reverse side of our social difficulties? If we don't have preconceptions or assumptions, everything we meet is a mystery, and responses have to be worked out from first principles, which makes us clumsy and vulnerable socially but open to more possibilities in other situations.

Some of us have become excellent observers and listeners, through having had to painstakingly figure out the social world for ourselves that way. And have learnt another key to empathy: to ask rather than guess or assume (Baker, 2000; Sinclair, 1988 & 1992). Even when we do seem to lack empathy, this may be due to other factors (Baker) such as hyperfocus on something else (so we are unaware of a situation for which we might otherwise have empathy), difficulty showing our feelings or knowing how and what to do about the situation we feel empathy for, or confusion and hesitancy from a lifetime of being pulled up for our errors and shortcomings. We discuss some of these issues:

Ava: I've acquired the art of listening through years of listening listening listening because I couldn't participate in conversations. When one gives up trying to make oneself heard, it's more possible.

April: My neighbor said I couldn't have AS because I seemed to understand better than anyone else how she felt. What she didn't realize however, is that though I had observed her (as I have observed others most of my life) well enough to be able to predict or imitate her, that didn't mean I was emotionally attached to her—far from it.

I have learned to focus on what the other person has to say. And I do take the other seriously, because I know only too well how it feels to be misunderstood.

Gail: I have gotten in trouble all my life due to my social cluelessness. I have gotten accused of deliberately being rude when it was the furthest thing from my mind to be, or doing or saying things to get people mad.

Evelyn: Dear Gail, I know exactly what you mean—got the t-shirts and the bruises to prove it!

Gail: I still am so clueless to my own body language. I have little to no idea how I come across to people. Many, many times my husband has gotten asked why I act so strange or rude. Most of these times I am doing (or not doing) something that people are offended by, I have no idea! I don't enjoy hurting people, either intentionally or unintentionally. It hurts me more than anyone can know. So to have people so totally misunderstand me without questioning why I might have acted a certain way is really discouraging. Because of this I personally try to give people the benefit of the doubt and clarify what they mean before I get offended at them for anything they say or do. I just wish people would do the same for me.

Evelyn: I think because we AS people *have* to try so much harder to be understanding, be good listeners, develop social skills, I think as a result of that we become people who are firstly never totally acceptable socially, never really safe in those situations, yet, secondly, able to do social things nearly as well as NTs most of the time, and thirdly, able to do some things far better than NTs: like, I've been told so many times I'm a good listener, because I can focus in on the other person and their problems and not be sidetracked by my own issues, when I have decided to *be* a good listener to that person.

A perhaps startling suggestion, is that we may even have learnt empathy and other moral attributes, through our early relationships with the nonhuman world, despite a common NT assumption that fascination with the nonhuman risks making us more robotic. For example:

MM: We are always sewing souls into the things we create.

Jane: Yes. I think soul (essence of being) is created through creation of a relationship. I call it a moral relationship (which I know sounds prissy or sanctimonious to some), by which I mean a relationship where there is acceptance/acknowledgement of agency and responsibility. When I relate to an object (whether it is another human or a bear I have created out of cloth), with my moral (aware) consciousness, when I acknowledge my power to affect (recognize, hurt, heal, shine like the sun or nourish like rain—even to destroy like lightning), I also give power to the other (the object) to affect me. So that other is as alive as I am (in this sense). We are in a moral relationship that gives life meaning. That is why I know the bears who are my most intimate and daily family do help me be/have whatever is good in who I am and what I do. It is the relationship that makes us who we are (that makes me who I am). And I say that even though I have a strong tendency to want to say/feel, I am I, alone. That fraction of truth lives inside the larger truth of relationships.

MM: Most of humanity is ignorant for not hearing and seeing what is around them. I hear the rocks and trees. Wish me well and tell me I am one of them, one of the silent ones who has now been given a voice, and that I must come out of hiding to protect others without voices: in my case I tend to give voice to persons with Alzheimer's disease. My washer and dryer speak to me, and so I painted a face on them and gave them names and make sure I don't over work them. When I worked in a copy shop I could produce more copies than any other employee. Yes, I could understand the physics of the machines and their limitations from overheating etc. But for me the machines were talking to me and I talked back regularly.

I was raised by our Siamese cat I could understand her language better than the human language, and so I spoke Siamese way before I spoke English, and I thought the cat was my real mother because I could understand her more than I could understand humans. I speak to children, babies, machines, rocks and trees as if they can hear me and they know what I am talking about. That is why my success with Alzheimer's patients is so high: I treat them with such great respect and assume they know what I am saying. And I wonder why the rest of the world is so ignorant as to treat others as stupid and dumb and things and animals so terribly because they are somehow less than us? Well I think that is a very arrogant stance to think we are better or more alive then these others who very much have a soul.

Imagination and Creativity

These too are controversial attributes we debate about. Though Hans Asperger wrote (1944, p70) "Autistic children are able to produce original ideas. Indeed, they can only be original", the dominating professional view has been that "lack of imagination" (one of the three components of the "triad of impairments") is a key feature of autism, and only very recently are some professionals challenging this (e.g. Jordan, 2002).

Those who do show imagination, are likely to have the possibility of an AS diagnosis dismissed. While those with AS who appear to lack imagination, may be engrossed in imaginary play of a different kind or stage, may have no interest in expressing this in a social context, or may have difficulty translating it into a language (such as words or drawing) to share with others (Baker, 2000). Or there may be creative blocks, as we explain:

Daina: I've noticed that it runs in circles. I get enthusiastic for a while, then depressed and wonder why on earth I ever bothered, and then I get excited and creative again. I wonder, however, if during the blah times some sort of mental process might not be going on. Not subconscious in a Freudian sense (I have no subconscious that way) but sort of mental activity that isn't coming into awareness yet, but is brewing something. I believe that the creative times are rooted in the blah times.

Diane: I am creative and imaginative. However I find it hard to be creative when told to be or told what to create. It has to be something coming from within or something that captures my interest before I can be creative. At work, I have never been praised for my creativity, because there I'm told what to do and am not self-directed.

Since social recognition is rarely our motivator, and may even be an inhibitor, we may not reveal our talents at all, or we may develop them in atypical directions, as per the following discussion:

Daina: I had a "world premiere" of my film today! Some people thought that my images were very disturbing and one woman even got angry and upset.

Yet when I showed my images to Jean, MM, Judy and Ava in Boston, no one got upset. Each preferred some images, but it was either "I like this one" or "I am indifferent to that one," but never "This one is creepy, disturbing, yucky, etc. Could there be something in us more accepting of images?

Jean: I'm not sure. I think maybe we don't find images loaded with dread/joy/nihilism, whatever, as often or in the same way. Our associations aren't codified as much. We regard things more as phenomena than as rational, cogent entities and events...so along comes a, a, a, um, a giant floating puffball or a string of fish vertebrae in a meadow and it just is. And we also have the kind of imagination (speculation, here) that allows us to consider puffballs of enormous size with blissful freedom and consider the symmetry of the fish bones. Sort of free association. As I think of this I'm free-associating now, remembering my daughter's in utero ultrasound to assure she didn't have spina bifida. And seeing that absolutely perfect spinal column on the screen and either thinking or hearing someone say, "Just like a string of pearls." So now I'm speculating about replacing the fish vertebrae with pearls that have perfectly symmetrical bones arching out from the sides, like, like, like, um, finely crafted flying buttresses, which now puts a gothic cathedral into the mix with the string of pearls and the bones. Mmm, wonder how to make a crea-tion or a crea-ture out of that? I really don't think NT's think this way. (Now who are the unimaginative ones?) Some things do give me the creeps but it's often not on predictable lines. I also had no trouble getting the idea that animals, plants, and mechanical things were interchangeable—maybe connected to our thing about relating to non-humans and even non-beings.

Daina: My pictures are almost like an NT vs. AS screening test. NTs like my pictures but seem kind of lost, like they've fallen down Alice's rabbit hole. They seem to clutch desperately at things they know, like images of people, but don't like the images that are more like textures. There seems to be a female-AS aesthetic. Perhaps this is some sort of evolutionary mechanism for repetitive activities like sewing fishing nets, planting row upon row of seeds, collecting berries one after another after another; a desire and tendency to do such things might give some sort of survival advantage. Maybe there are two survival methods: collecting food for oneself (AS) vs. depending on others, specifically men (social).

Ability

Our lives on the autism spectrum may seem a paradox, a puzzling (to NT observers) and frustrating (to us) mix of ability and disability, success and failure, insight and naivete. Very likely in autism spectrum conditions, as has been shown in other forms of neurodiversity, such contradictions are inextricably linked, two sides of the same coin (Grandin, 1999; Happe, 1999; West, 1997), and may have a survival value for the human race: persons with different ways of thinking may be needed for the crises the world faces (West). With understanding and support, we can develop and use our unique capabilities rather than be dismissed as disabled or made marginally functional by trying to fit neurotypical models.

Wendy: I've written about being gifted in some areas, (such as art and creative writing) while struggling with doing the everyday things in life, yet because people saw my gifts, they thought I should be quite capable in other areas of my life, and couldn't understand why I wasn't.

Diane: I've been going through a list of AS strengths and weaknesses. What this seems to confirm for me is that maybe AS isn't really a defect. We have traits that may be actually needed in society, and if only society would start listening to us instead of marginalizing us, maybe solutions could be found for the world's serious problems that currently seem to be unsolvable.

Neurodiversity, as we hope you will discover from our accounts, can be a source of richness to all, a source of mutual understanding, learning—and celebration!

References

Asperger, H. (1944). 'Autistic psychopathy' in childhood. Translation by Uta Frith, 1992. In U. Frith (Ed.), *Autism and Asperger syndrome.* Cambridge: Cambridge University Press.

Baggs, A.M. (1999). *Being a spatial thinker (one kind of autistic thought).* http://www.autistics.org./library.

Baker, A. (2000). Life and community on the spectrum: insiders' insights. In *Proceedings of "Next Step" Conference, October 2000.* Autism NZ, PO Box 7305, Christchurch, New Zealand.

Baker, A. (2002). The invisible end of the spectrum. In *Unity through diversity: Proceedings of Inaugural World Autism Congress,* November 2002. Or www.autismcongress.com.

Baron-Cohen, S., Wheelwright, S., Skinner, R., Martin, J., & Clubley, E. (2001). The autism-spectrum quotient (AQ): Evidence from Asperger Syndrome/High-functioning autism, males and females, scientists and mathematicians. *J. of Autism and developmental disorders,* 31 (1), 5-17.

Blackburn, J., Gottschewski, K., George, E., & Niki, L. (2000). A discussion about theory of mind: From an autistic perspective. *Proceedings of Autism Europe 6th International Congress, Glasgow 19-21 May 2000.* Also on http://www.autistics.org./library/

Garfinkel, H. (1967). Studies of the routine grounds of everyday life. In H. Garfinkel *Studies in Ethnomethodology,* 35-75. Englewood Cliffs, NJ: Prentice-Hall.

Gilberg. C. (1999). *Seminar* presented under auspices of Autism NZ, July 1999, in Christchurch, New Zealand.

Grandin, T. (1996). *Thinking in pictures and other reports from my life with autism.* New York: Vintage Books.

Grandin, T. (1995). How people with autism think. In E. Schopler & G.B. Mesibov (Eds.), *Learning and cognition in autism,* pp. 137-156. New York: Plenum.

Grandin, T. (1999). Genius may be an abnormality: Educating students with Asperger's Syndrome or high functioning autism". *Autism 99 Web Conference: Papers: In our Own Words,* at www.autism99.org/text.

Happe, F. (1999). Why success is more interesting than failure. *The Psychologist,* 12 (11), 140-146.

Hermelin, B. (2001). *Bright splinters of the mind: A personal story of research with autistic savants.* London: Jessica Kingsley.

Jordan, R. (2002). Education and autistic spectrum disorders: Advances and prospects. In *Unity through diversity: Proceedings of Inaugural World Autism Congress,* November 2002. Or www.autismcongress.com.

Richer, John (2001). The insufficient integration of self and other in autism: Evolutionary and developmental perspectives. In J. Richer & S. Coates (Eds.), *Autism: The search for coherence* (pp. 36-53). London: Jessica Kingsley.

Sinclair, J. (1988). *Thoughts about Empathy.* The MAAP Services Inc. Also available at www.jimsinclair.org.

Sinclair, J. (1992). Bridging the gaps: An inside-out view of autism (or, Do you know what I don't know?) In E. Schopler & G. Mesibov (Eds.), *High-Functioning Individuals with Autism.* New York: Plenum Press. Also available at www.jimsinclair.org.

Sinclair, J. (1995). *Cognitive, communication, and interpersonal deficits of non-autistic people.* MAAPing the Future, September 15-16 1995, Indianapolis, Indiana, USA. The MAAP Services Inc.

West, T. G. (1997). *In the mind's eye: Visual thinkers, gifted people with dyslexia and other learning difficulties, computer images and the ironies of creativity.* New York: Prometheus Books.

Williams, D. (1996). *Autism—An inside-out approach: An innovative look at the mechanics of 'autism' and its developmental 'cousins'.* London: Jessica Kingsley.

Williams, D. (1998). *Autism and sensing: The unlost instinct.* London: Jessica Kingsley.

Who Is That Woman in the Mirror?

Different on the Inside

Susan Golubock

To look at us
You and I appear very much the same.
Yet I have learned that we experience life,
And therefore view our experiences,
very differently.
I have learned that I just don't think like you,
no matter how hard I try,
and believe me I have.

My nervous system seems to be
configured differently.
I've learned to do what you do,
at least the mechanics of it,
but I don't understand
why you do it.
I've memorized the words you use
and can repeat them fluently.
Figuring out what you mean
and why you say them
is the hard part.

I process words literally, concretely and naively,
which often leaves me baffled and confused.
I thought that by pretending to be you,
I would someday understand you.
But I don't.
Anymore than you understand me.

There are times when I join in
and truly enjoy interacting with you
but I rarely feel that I belong.
I can focus on you
or I can focus on me
but understanding the complexity of relationships
is very much beyond me.
There are times when I can connect
with my feelings, or yours

but never both at the same time.
And some emotions not at all.
There are times when I really think
I understand you
then you change, and I don't.

Even though I have stopped trying to
be like you
I haven't stopped trying to understand you.
It would mean a lot to me
if you would try,
just for a little while,
to understand what it must be like to be me.

Remember those awkward social moments
as an adolescent or pre-adolescent
when you were trying to fit in,
but didn't really know what was *in*
or what was expected?
You stood there in conspicuous silence,
rehearsing everything you wanted to say,
waiting for a chance to speak,
then blurting out some untimely statement.
Or more than you really intended
not knowing when or how to stop?
Imagine having those moments occur regularly
with family, friends, and strangers alike.
Your best defense is to
memorize the required smalltalk,
keep your mouth shut,
and let others talk about themselves.
Meanwhile you struggle to filter out
the background noise they so easily seem to ignore,
processing maybe 50% of what they say.
Then there is the feeling of panic
when the dreaded unexpected question appears
requiring you suddenly to shift from processing to production
without the time you need to do it.
It makes you wonder,
with interactions so difficult,
why so many people consider socializing
to be so much fun.

Remember the time when you were startled
by a car horn? Or fire alarm?
Or a touch on the shoulder that you didn't expect?
Think about what it felt like.
Your heart raced.
Your senses were being assaulted.
Your mind was suddenly jolted out of focus
for a millisecond
until you realized what had happened
and could calm back down again.

Imagine instead the panic escalating as you
struggle desperately to register what happened,
causing you to feel violated, angry, and disorientated.
Then imagine being asked to function in this state
for the next number of minutes or even hour
that it takes for your system to pull itself back together again.

Imagine what it is like to be startled
by everyday experiences,
like the sound of a cup touching a saucer.
Or someone suddenly making a gesture with their hand
in your direction.
Think what it is like to have your nervous system put on edge
by the sound of someone chewing
or the thought that someone just might come close enough
to brush up against you in a crowded room.
Your environment becomes a minefield.
The bathroom, car, and bedroom are your foxholes.

Remember those occasions
when you couldn't retrieve the names
of people or places or things
you know that you should know?
Imagine that happening three, four, five times a day.
Not being able to make those connections,
or any connections,
without setting memory triggers
and practicing words that you want to say in advance.
All this just to remember what you need to do or say
with people you work with every day.

Have you ever reached for something

that you expected to be there,
and it wasn't,
just when you needed it most?
Do you remember that moment of panic
and how you froze with indecision
as to what to do next?
Living life spontaneously
would be for me
a continuous series
of panics and indecision.

Despite my many years of experience,
my brain still yearns for consistency,
yet finds none.
New responses require a lot more time
than the milliseconds it requires for you
to review all the possibilities.
So my brain either freezes
or falls back on old responses.
Either way I'm stuck.
Later I can think it through
and pre-plan for the next time.
Only next time it is likely to be new again.

Among the words
I most dread to hear,
yet hear so often,
are "Lighten up!"
"Don't be so intense."
"Don't take life so seriously."
In essence you are telling me
to stop functioning

Remember how hard you worked
to learn a sport? Or play an instrument?
Or drive a car?
Remember how the task initially seemed so overwhelming?
You might have thought you would
never reach the ease that comes with mastery.
Imagine succeeding
but never being free of the need
to think your way through each task.
Not being able to listen or talk

and put a pot of water on to boil at the same time
because each requires your exclusive mental focus to perform,
each and every time.

Remember those times when you had more to deal with
than you thought that you could handle
and you were ready to blow up in frustration
or collapse in utter fatigue?
Perhaps you closed yourself off from others,
vegged out in front of the TV,
re-organized your closet,
or found some sensory pleasure in which to engage.
People seem to understand this need
in themselves and others,
on occasion.
For me this need occurs throughout the day,
every day.
When I appear zoned out
in a world of my own
or obsessively organizing,
I'm just trying to conserve energy
or forage through the thicket of input
that overwhelms me.
I can't wait to get home to collapse,
and I can't proceed without planning.

To calm my overstressed nervous system
I have had to learn alternative strategies
such as leaning, propping,
rubbing, squeezing or stretching.
Whatever I can get away with
that gives me the body movement
and deep pressure input
I need so desperately throughout the day.
(I leave the rocking and stimming,
more natural ways of coping,
for when I am alone.)
I have learned that *my* way is unacceptable.
Thus, even my coping behaviors have become
just one more thing for me to hide.

Most people hold on during a crisis and
relax when it is over.

I hold on and hold on
unable to let go.
Instead, when the crisis is over
I collapse
because modulation is something
my nervous system has never learned to do.
It must be hard to understand.
I appear, because I hide things so well,
like someone who can handle so much.
Yet, inside I experience a roller coaster
that is either up or down,
rarely if ever experiencing solid ground.

If you stop to think about it
you do know what it feels like to be me,
briefly, in a less exaggerated way,
just as I experience
briefly, on my more integrated days
what I imagine it must be like to be you.

As you grow
practiced tasks get easier,
allowing you to add complexity and variety to your life.
My practiced tasks only get memorized,
not generalized.
Each situation must be struggled through
as if it were new.
Complexity only overwhelms.
There is no energy left for variety,
yet what is expected of you and me
remains the same.

Think back to a time
when you were experiencing an event or period
that was particularly difficult
and someone said to you,
"Oh yeah, I've had that happen to me," or
"That happens to everyone at some time or another."
I've been told that the intent of these comments
is to encourage you
to do what you had to do to get past it,
to avoid making a big deal out of it.
To me those words are particularly painful.

The way my nervous system operates
is an event that happens every day.
Not a situation or feeling that will pass with time.
It is what I have to deal with.
I accept myself for who I am
and I do what I have to do.
yet sometimes,
being me does feel like a big deal
and some encouragement would be nice.
When I talk about what is particularly
hard or frustrating for me
I'm not pitying myself nor the life I've been given to live.
I'm not suggesting that your difficulties are any
more or less than mine.
I'm not looking to blame someone
or be excused from what I know are my responsibilities.
It would mean a lot to me though
if someone would recognize
just how much effort I put into
meeting the expectations in life
that you and I share
with unequal resources.

I am not looking for recognition for what I have accomplished,
because I am not driven by accomplishments.
Most of the time it only serves to remind me of
what I have had to compromise within myself
to achieve these things.
I want recognition for myself as a person.
Recognition for how hard I work,
because of and despite my differences,
to function in a world
that does not readily accept those differences.
That would make me feel good
about how far I have come
and encourage me to keep on trying.

Is being me a tragedy?
Far from it!
In fact, if given the freedom to live and do
the best I know how,
at the pace and in the way I know works for me,
I would quite enjoy myself and my life.

Alone time is something I very much cherish.
It's people time that challenges my nervous system
and if I let it,
my self-esteem.
In some ways
my differences have enabled me
To develop talents
I might not have without them.
By using intellect rather than emotions
I have earned the respect of co-workers
as a mediator during stressful events.
My ability to hyperfocus
once I start on a task
means that others can always count on
a job done well
down to the littlest detail.
Processing new
and especially abstract information
is often tedious for me.
I need to see and experience things
before I really comprehend them.
But once I do
I am able to use what I have learned
in highly creative
and holistic ways.
I enjoy having and using these talents
just as you do yours.

I am fortunate that I have found a profession
in which my talents are appreciated
and my differentness accepted.
I know others who are less fortunate.
They are never given the chance to show their talents
because their differentness is considered a disability.
It seems odd that we value so much
the beauty of diversity in nature
yet seem afraid to share and appreciate
the differences among and between ourselves.

I'm not asking that life's expectations
be changed for me.
I seek only acceptance for the ways I choose to meet them.
Remember what gives joy to you

is often very uncomfortable for me.
The way you would do something
is often not the way that would
enable me to best succeed.
Or more importantly
find pleasure or self-satisfaction
in what I might accomplish.
I don't experience loneliness
or have the same needs and wants that you do,
so don't pity me for not having what I don't miss or want.
I recognize that your life,
with all its complexities,
has its own set of difficulties.
Your definition of accomplishments
and what you find encouraging
go beyond the simplicity
which defines me.
I'm only asking for the same rights
and freedoms you seek for yourself:
To be accepted for who you are,
To be the best *you* that you can be.
Don't assume that I want or think or experience
the way that you do.
As nice as you may think it is to be you,
I only want to be me.

© Susan Golubock

Social Skills or Being Oneself?

Susan Golubock

I overheard a teacher in the lunchroom one day tell another teacher that she likes to observe her students in their physical education class because it tells her so much about how successful they will be in life. She explained that in PE it is easy to see the children's social skills and how well they work within a group. "Without social skills," she proclaimed, "they'll never make it in life." I'm not sure I can say why that hurt, but it did. Perhaps because for the first time I was becoming aware of how widely held that belief was and the very real implications it has for so many. Perhaps it simply reminded me of the price I personally paid to meet this definition of success.

It took me a lot longer than most, but by age 55 I think I have acquired the social and group skills this teacher was talking about. Well, the mechanics of them anyway. Several years ago, a co-worker who overheard my conversation with someone about a work-related matter told me later how wonderful my phone skills were. I found that perplexing at the time because I thought I was just doing what I had been taught one ought to do. If you are taught to do it that way, what other way would you do it? Of course, my socially correct phone skills only apply to work-related calls. I still don't do social calls comfortably, so I rarely initiate them. I am a well-respected member of the team where I work, but eating in a lunchroom with others continues to be awkward. I am married and have traveled and lived all over the world, but still prefer my *own* world when it comes to leisure time or I'm pressured into shut down. I have learned to make smalltalk and even tell a white lie (which I struggled with and resisted repeatedly before finally getting it), but I still fail to see the purpose to either one. Ironically, I pushed myself to learn social skills simply because I didn't know I had the choice to be anything other than like everyone else. We didn't share feelings much in my family and, growing up, I never found anyone who understood what it was like to be me. I simply assumed that someday, if I tried hard enough, I'd understand other people, which I felt was the key to *being* like other people. I often wonder if the more passive/compliant role expectations of being female allowed me to hide better the fact that I could only mimic the social skills I learned, without truly grasping their meaning.

I was diagnosed as being on the autism spectrum at age 54, after several very difficult years of self-discovery. I had always sensed that I was different. I just never understood how or why. I honestly thought that, once I had succeeded in learning the mechanics of socializing, I *would be* socializing. People would share information about themselves with me, yet I didn't know what I was supposed to do with it. People would call themselves my friends, but I couldn't figure out what I was supposed to *do* with a friend. Without this sharing of thoughts and feelings between myself and others, I had no clue just how much I thought or felt differently from others. It was quite a shock when I finally did discover how much of my self I had hidden even from myself all those years.

At age 48, I was working with a pre-school class when the teacher commented that she was having one of her young students evaluated because she suspected she might be a high-functioning autistic. I had been observing this child with particular interest as I worked with the class, because she was the first child I had seen who seemed to be a carbon copy of myself as a child. The frustrated and perplexed look on her face when others said or did something out of the ordinary, the following other children around mimicking their actions with no purposeful interaction of her own, even sensory sensitivities and swallowing difficulties, were all me as a child. I had never heard of high-functioning autism, but that came as no surprise to me. I was forever mystified by how little I knew that seemed common knowledge to others. At first I was excited that I might possibly have found something that would explain me to me. I read all I could, and the more I read, the more I saw me. My readings took me in many different directions, but nothing explained me so completely and so well as what was written by those on the autism spectrum. At last, people who perceived the world the way I did. I so desperately wanted someone to talk with. Someone who might help me understand what I was discovering. Someone to validate what I felt to be true.

I found a co-worker who worked with the autistic population. I am forever grateful for her presence in my life at that time. She listened and never judged. She gave me honest, open, feedback on what she saw. She wasn't quick to accept completely everything I was revealing to her, but over time she agreed that I did indeed appear to be on the spectrum. I had another therapist friend at that time who was also non-judgmental and willing to listen to the inner me talk. I started to reveal the inner me more and more to my husband as well. I was actually beginning to gain some confidence in the acceptability of the self I had hidden for so long. Then, my friends moved on. Not out of my life, just busy going in other directions. I didn't understand. I felt abandoned. I blamed myself. Surely I did something to cause them to disappear from my life. I didn't understand that this was a natural thing people did, moving on, shifting directions. I didn't understand that it didn't mean they weren't my friends anymore. Not knowing what I had done wrong, I stopped sharing myself with my husband as well. Just when I thought things were starting to make sense, confusion and frustration took over once again.

I sought out the director of the local Autism Resource Center. Her response to all I told her was that she didn't see how she could help me since I "seemed to be succeeding already in everything that could be expected for someone with Asperger's." I felt crushed with that response but couldn't articulate why. I just knew she missed the point. I had proudly told her how I had recently learned to do lunch in a restaurant with a group of friends from work (which until then had only overwhelmed me). She asked me, "What did you learn about your friends from having lunch with them?" I was taken aback. I had no clue that was why people "did lunch" together! I had succeeded, but at what? I could feel no pride in having worked so hard to succeed at something that others understood but I did not, something that over time did become more automatic but never easy, something that made me look like everyone else but was not really me.

I sought out a psychiatrist who claimed to work with adults with Asperger's. I found it odd, when I went to his office, that someone who says they work with AS adults would have so many white walls and fluorescent lights. I already knew I had a limited tolerance for these conditions before reaching overload, so I started off anxious. He told me, after listening to me talk, that he thought I appeared quite calm and collected (when actually I was extremely anxious) and then at the end (when I collapsed in frustration and disdain as I listened to his analysis) he said I appeared very anxious to him. How could anyone help me if they misread me so badly? He also told me that since I used the word "vow," a word I often heard growing up in a Catholic home, my "anxiety" must be related to my religious upbringing. I was totally dumbfounded. I pulled inside even tighter. Yet, I still desperately yearned to come out. The world kept telling me I needed to "lighten up," to "be myself," yet no one would tell me what that meant or how to do it. Seeking help only confirmed my conviction that talking to people made things worse. I did what I always did. I turned to books. I turned to the internet. I would find out the information I needed by myself.

I read voraciously. I learned the language to explain myself to myself. I discovered a friend on the encephalitis support group who taught me that some friends don't go away. That reaching out to talk with people can be other than painful. It can actually be helpful. By understanding her own challenges, she helped me to see and understand mine (and surprisingly to me, I helped her too). I was beginning finally to understand what being and having a friend meant. I was learning to trust. She patiently listened to the questions I had stored up over all these years, and just as patiently explained what I needed to know about the social world around me. I began opening up again to my husband. I sought membership in Autism Network International. I found another friend who helped me see and value the self I had abandoned so many years ago. Trusting didn't come easily though. I had so many fears, so much anger, so much confusion. What was wonderful, though, about developing friends through this internet support group was that it was in writing! I could see and re-read their words. I could respond or not respond as I was ready. Things didn't move at the rapid pace that overwhelmed me in real-time. Most importantly, these people understood me. They experienced life in much the same way I did. I was valued for the inner me that I shared with them. I didn't need to play the social games the world seemed to expect of me. I went to visit my new friends. I began the process of un-learning the self-defeating strategies I had learned in order to survive in a world I failed to understand.

The problem came in trying to generalize what I had learned about friends and self in these support groups to the world in which I lived. It didn't help that I was going through hormonal changes at the time. I suspect these changes contributed to the intensity of my reactions to what was happening. The walls I had built to protect myself from my own emotions so that I could function were crumbling. Every emotion was intense. I developed tics and a sleep disorder, which my neurologist finally determined were related to my having had encephalitis. I feared going to doctors because they wouldn't listen when I talked about my sensitivity to medications. I lost many a work day to sleep because I was overmedicated before I was able to convince my neurologist that baby doses worked much better. Meanwhile, my lifetime of mental ruminations was becoming so obsessive that even I was becoming weary of them. Finally, I sank into a deep pit of depression. What surprised me was that no one, not even my husband, could see it. I had memorized facial expressions as a child but had no experience in how to communicate emotions. I knew that I didn't do moderation well. I never sought out other people when I was upset. I couldn't deal with my emotions and their concerns at the same time. I needed to be alone. Over the years of our marriage, my husband thought of me as extremely emotionally stable and calm. He had witnessed an occasional blow up (the few that I couldn't hide), and he had let me know that it was not a pretty thing to see. I was afraid now of what would happen if I tried to express my emotions to other people. What would happen to my job if this self was unleashed on the world? Of course, the opposite was a problem too. There were many times, even when later I wanted to feel, that I simply couldn't connect to any emotions. I felt nothing. How was anyone to understand that? My husband, who has worked hard to understand and has stuck by me throughout all of these changes, finally encouraged me to try again to seek professional help. This time, I called a parent group for information on where I could find a psychiatrist whom they trusted to understand their children on the spectrum. Two years later, with proper support and help from medication to assist me in meeting the challenges of my brain's erratic chemistry, I have been able to accept the self that I am and bring that self into the world.

Does that mean that I am now like everyone else? Far from it. I'm not so unaware that I don't recognize just how weird my sudden string of verbal tics is when I am releasing tension, or how my rocking when anxious, or hand clapping when excited, appears to others. When my husband teases me about being an "alien from Zyrcon" (a planet we invented between us), I giggle. I know he is pleased with the person I am now and wouldn't want me any other way. And that is a wonderful feeling. I know now and accept that I think and experience life differently from others, and my actions are going to reflect that difference. My selves and characters are coming together. I no longer spend energy on hiding. Just because I don't work so hard at being me any more doesn't mean that being me is easy. I estimate that I make anywhere between one and five or more social mishaps a day, depending on how many people I come into contact with and whether the day progresses as planned.

The most common social mishaps are misinterpreting, or not being able to interpret, what people are saying, and not remembering who they are. Names are a continual embarrassment for me. I'm well aware that everyone forgets names now and then. I struggle to remember names most times on most days. Not just their names but who they are and why I know them. These are people I work with every day! I have yet been able to retrieve someone's name fast enough to return the "Hi, [name]" as I pass them in the halls. I'm often mumbling it under my breath minutes, hours or days later as I finally make the connection. Unfortunately, I fail to retrieve it again the next time. I still haven't figured out how people know what they know, and why I don't. I really do try hard to read the paper and newsmagazines. I go down to the lunchroom thinking it is where people exchange information. I just recently discovered the school bulletin boards are where a great deal of information is posted. What I don't do is spend time chitchatting with other people. I suspect this is the hidden information source.

I'd learned over the years that if I just let people talk long enough, I would often get the answers I was seeking without having to ask. Ironically, I have earned the reputation of being a good listener as a result. Of course, I miss 50% of what they are saying and generally don't know what to do with the other 50%, but I've always tried to listen carefully because I assumed there was a purpose and a reason for people telling me things. It was quite a shock when my husband told me, in his patient efforts to explain to me what I did not understand, that people often have no purpose or reason behind what they say! They are just making conversation. They just like connecting with other people. It really doesn't matter what is said.

All those years of trying to decipher what people were saying, only to find out that it all meant nothing! I now know that I had been focusing on the wrong information. Now, since realizing that I can only process one thing at a time, I focus on the intent that I sense behind a conversation rather than the words. I can now better appreciate conversations for what they are, an attempt by one person to connect to another. That doesn't make them easier to do, just easier to understand why people do them. It still is uncomfortable for me when people reach out to touch me, even though I recognize their intent in doing so. My interests are still pretty focused and limited, so I still don't have a great deal to share with others. I am still pretty much ignored when I go down to the cafeteria because my timing in initiating or joining in a conversation is pretty bad, but I don't dread or fear these people any more. I know that if they overwhelm me with their chatter, or shatter my nervous system with a sudden burst of laughter, they did not intend to hurt me. Knowing that doesn't make it any less painful. I just like not being so afraid of people.

I've learned that my objectivity, my lack of emotional connection, is seen by others as valuable because I can listen and use logic to redirect team meetings that are being de-railed by others' emotions. I may be unable to connect to others enough to sympathize with their particular concerns or emotions, but I am quite good at empathizing with the pain emotions can cause people. I am learning where I share common experiences with others and where we diverge. When it comes to the students with whom I work, both parents and teachers have thanked me for helping them understand what they could not see or comprehend in their child's way of experiencing events that diverge from the way in which they experience events themselves. I may not be able to read or comprehend the minds of those who do not experience life as I do, but I have little trouble interpreting or anticipating what someone who thinks like I do will say or do or feel. I don't think that anyone can know what others are thinking who do not think or experience or interpret events in a way that is similar to their own. I hear teachers and parents talk about how baffling a child's behavior or response is, yet it is no mystery to me. It is those who do not experience life as I do who I find a mystery.

What I have learned by the age of 55 is that one need not make a choice between learning to live in a social world one doesn't understand and living life in a way that makes sense and gives pleasure to the person that you are. What I don't recommend is the road I took to get where I am. Unfortunately, I've seen no small number of my students heading that way due to the pressures put on them to memorize and repeat rather than acquire through understanding the social skills that others feel are essential to their success in life. That saddens me. Social stories are a wonderful tool to aid in understanding. I have seen dramatic changes in self-esteem and social skills in the older and more verbal child on the spectrum through use of a social skills group where their questions are encouraged and honestly answered.

My desire for social interaction may not be the same as others, but I have many wants and needs that are. I want to be accepted. I want to be liked. I don't want to be packaged with a convenient label and thus pegged in other people's minds as to who I am and what I can do or can't do. Yet people do it to other people all the time. An autistic friend of mine wrote to me, "It is dangerous to measure myself or anyone else by 'what I can do' instead of 'what I am'."[1] I have that quote framed where I can see it every day. Succeeding in life need not be an either/or choice between being oneself and learning social skills, in my opinion, if the first is respected when acquiring the other.

---

[1] *Amanda Baggs, email correspondence, summer 2001*

I Wish

Sola Shelly

I am tired and sick of playing it strong
Say I'm all right when so much goes wrong
Put a neat costume on a bag of hash—
Well, sooner or later I will probably crack.

I must keep running, or else I will freeze
I shouldn't give up on the struggle to breathe.
My feet might carry me to the end of this dash
But at the finish line I am going to crack.

Am I a winner for what I achieved?
Depends on how success is perceived.
Everything that I got, I paid for in cache,
And now, all I want is to drop out and crack.

Do not cheer me up, "you are doing just great."
Nice, empty words only make me irate.
Being around people is a never-ending clash.
I wish you just left me alone to crack.

The Perils of Diagnosis
(Or How I Became Bipolar?)

Patricia Clark

In 1982 I lived on Guam, where I had been taken by my U.S. Navy spouse. He then filed for divorce. I had a job there, even though I was practically unemployable. With two children, 3 and 6 years old, it was up to me to raise them and provide for them. I was 38 years old, with an income of $8,000 per year and an $80,000 mortgage on the house my husband left us with. I had to maintain babysitters in order to work (they were notorious for quitting with no notice), and pay them. He would pay the mortgage for up to three years while I tried to get rid of the house or increase my income.

About a year into this I started having extreme problems coping. I drove both children to a sitter halfway across the island in the morning, where one caught a bus to gifted and talented preschool. I then drove the other child back to our neighborhood and dropped her at school, then went to work for eight hours. This was a demanding photojournalist job where I drove all over the place, took photos, did information setups like Armed Forces Day exhibits, and interviewed people (pure hell for a person who was autistic and didn't know it). Then I would go pick up the older child at her sitter's after work, drive halfway across the island to pick up the smaller child, return home, cook dinner, do laundry and dishes, do all the regular stuff, and sleep if there was any time left. In the meantime I was playing the organ at church, since no one else knew how, and doing some other things because, for my sanity, I needed to do something I was interested in as well as what I had to do.

One day I was vacuuming. On Guam, the house was always hot and I have never tolerated heat very well. The little wheels of the vacuum were seizing up in the tropical humidity, and as it was an expensive and very good vacuum cleaner, I knew I could never afford another like it without a husband. I gave it a yank and it fell over instead of coming to me and that was it. I just went nuts. I screamed and threw my glasses against the wall. They didn't break, so I threw them again. I threw the vacuum cleaner's body out the door into the driveway, crying and shouting, unable to stop. I really wanted to trash the entire house and run screaming out into the jungle and never come back.

Things had always been really hard for me, and I had no clue in my autistic fog that I was under extreme stress, raising my kids without any family backup, 9,000 miles from where I grew up, with no time off to look forward to. I felt that I was either a failure as a person for not controlling myself better, or else insane. So I went to the health care place assigned to me under my workplace

81

health insurance and told them the circumstances. I said I had lost it while vacuuming, felt that this was not normal, and was turning myself in. They interviewed me a couple of times and announced that I was bipolar and had to take medicine for the rest of my life. So I took it for 13 years, terrified that I would end up institutionalized for insanity, having no idea what was going on, or that my behavior was actually normal for a person in my circumstances.

Amazingly, I had always considered myself normal, yet had no realization of normal people suffering in ways that I felt I suffered. They seemed calm, so how could I justify being upset by the requirements of my own life, which actually had no comparison in amount of difficulty. I only measured myself against the *outward appearances* of others, always felt lacking, and my only effort to help myself was to tell myself I did not measure up and I had better try harder and complain less.

So, that's how I *became* bipolar. Eventually getting stuck in the California mental health system for many years, I learned that I had *no* problems in common with the other people around me in the system, so I began looking for another explanation for my anger/depression/inability to cope.

© Patricia Clark

If You Prick Us?

The Hearts & Minds of AS Women

Coming Alive in a World of Texture

Daina Krumins

One of my earliest memories, a very strong and meaningful memory, is of the texture of sheep. I remember a yellow-beige texture that communicated an infinite softness to me and was very, very important. I also remember that this love of this texture somehow caused people to be angry with me, and to punish me. Their anger did not make me love the texture any less, but it did teach me, early on, that what I perceive and love and what other people perceive and love, are two different and incompatible things. I learned to be a quiet, private child.

As an adult, I asked my father, who was an Aspie of a different type, what this memory of sheep could have been all about. He told me that in the refugee camp in Germany, when I was about two years old, I had been playing outside in the yard with another little girl and when my mom had looked out the window we were both gone. My father told me that the little girl and I had been found walking down some railroad tracks in the direction of the sheep meadow.

What is it about textures? Why is it that textures have such a strong effect on how I see the world. Most people who see my work as an artist/filmmaker notice the textures, but they assume, or I assume that they assume, that I am like them with this added fixation on textures. It is not that way. My world is organized around textures. I have been playing around with sounds and when I sent a cassette of my computer sound compositions to a friend, he said that they were very "textural." This way of seeing things replaces the neurotypical way of seeing things. All emotions, perceptions, my whole world and how it has been created in my mind have been heavily influenced by textures.

A Pelican Flying over the Ocean: Aspie-cognition

All my life there has been a feeling of isolation, and a kind of sadness that goes with it. What's more, I was always blamed for this. People would say, "If you could just enjoy the same things that other little girls enjoy, you would be much happier." This was another thing that convinced me that people were crazy; I knew it was possible to do things you don't want to do, but how do you make yourself perceive what you don't perceive or feel what you don't feel? And yet people seemed to believe that this would be possible for me, like turning on a light switch.

There is a Bach cantata I find particularly hilarious called *Tritt Auf den Glaubensbahn,* which means, loosely translated, "Step up on the Wagon of

Faith." It is a serious cantata, not a joke, but it seems so cuckoo to me. It is like saying, "Sprout wings and fly to the moon." Yeah, sure! And yet, most people find this cantata serious and meaningful. There must be something in their minds, some mechanism that allows them to put aside all reality and logic and simply believe what they think they should believe. How is that possible? There is nothing in my mind that corresponds to this; it is as alien as the thoughts of a pelican flying over the ocean.

As I grew, my texture-driven way of understanding and loving the world became more complex and sophisticated. I had collections of rocks, sea shells, feathers, stamps, coins, slices of tree-trunks, and even snakes, which my father helped me preserve in formaldehyde. He also had a relationship with visual things and was an excellent photographer. When we first came to the United States from a refugee camp in Germany, he had to take whatever jobs he could in the beginning, and one job was in a machine shop. He was fascinated by the shapes of the metal chips formed by the various metal-shaping machines, and very often he would bring his favorite chip-of-the-day home to show me. I was not allowed to touch them because they were sharp, but I joined my father in admiring the various shapes and textures.

As a child, I had my own world, my private agenda, although even now I cannot explain verbally what it was and still is. It is not intellectual, but something within my mind where visual images combine with emotions. From the time I first set out down the tracks after the sheep, I was searching for something and finding some of it here and there.

One place where I found it when I was about seven or eight was in the second-hand lumberyard (actually more like a dump) across the ditch behind the house where I lived. There were stacks of wood from demolished houses, some up to 15 or 20 feet. One day I saw a cat crawl under one side of one of these lumber piles and crawl out the other so I decided to do the same. I got maybe seven or eight feet into the pile and was quite happy there; lots of rusty nails and spider webs. I couldn't get any further so I crawled back. If I had gotten stuck in there, I doubt anyone would have thought to look for me under the woodpile, at least not right away.

My parents and I would spend the summers in a cabin in Sussex County, New Jersey and I was fascinated by the pipe through which an ice-cold stream flowed under the road. Naturally, I had to crawl through it without any concern for the frogs, snakes and crayfish that lived in the stream, to say nothing of sharp rocks. I was aware of the physical world in ways that most people are not. (Even as an adult, I can still tell if a snake is moving through tall grass by the sound of its skin scraping against the blades of grass.) It's not that I could hear better, although I could hear much higher pitches than most people, but I was aware of what I was hearing. Most people attend to voices above all else. I attend to everything the same way with no discrimination, so that the caw of the crow in the tree is as clear and important as the voice of the person I'm walking with.

Gypsy Soup: Not like NTs

When a bird flies between two cherry trees, one with thousands of cherries and the other with just a few, does the bird know to go to the one with lots of cherries? How about a ladybug walking down a branch and coming to a fork, one side with lots of aphids in view and one with just one aphid? Does it know which way to go?

I don't know the answer, but it seems there must be some mechanism that tells the bird to go where there are more cherries. How does the mechanism work? Does the bird know how to count? Certainly not! There is not enough room in that little cranium for numbers. Perhaps, to the bird, it just feels better. Perhaps it makes the bird happy in some way.

Is that it? Is that what is going on in my mind? Has this love of seeing *more* of something determined my whole life? I think it has. A few years ago I wrote to Mark Tilden, the guy who makes little robots, that he should teach his little robots the concept of *more*. A little robot vacuum cleaner that scurries around the house would be a lot more efficient if it could seek out the spots with *more* dust, leaving the spots with less dust for later. A little robot that is taught to pull up dandelions could scan the yard and start in the place where there are *more* yellow spots.

I know that seeing the essence of myself in such simple terms might seem flaky. I am a fully complex adult human, with zillions of brain cells doing who-knows-what. It's just that I notice a similarity in the pattern. Just as a small fractal pattern repeats itself and repeats itself until it gets larger and larger, so a pattern that started millions of years ago on a small scale in a primitive mind repeats itself in my mind.

Imagine a small amount of iron filings on a piece of paper, in a small area along with a small magnet. Bring the magnet close enough, and a pattern will form. Now imagine a huge piece of paper, like a football field, with a huge magnet. Again, a pattern forms, but the pattern will not be the same as the small one, although the patterns will be related. Perhaps, if the field of iron filings grows big enough, the central magnet will no longer be able to affect it and the psychologists will start talking about "defective central coherence."

In the same way, a pattern started to form in my mind-wiring when I was a baby. Certain things were important, some were less important, and other things were not important at all. The most important things—visual things, textures particularly, but also shapes, colors, movement—were the things to which my heart opened. Secondary things, like people's faces, were not that important and I can hardly remember a face from my childhood. I just remember a person's temperament and personality and something about them like red hair, height, or freckles. Faces escape me, and as an adult I can never recognize anyone I knew as a child.

As a child I was constantly aware that my perceptions were different from everyone else's around me. Most normal or NT children's way of organizing sensory information is either inherently similar to their parents or, perhaps by watching and perceiving their parent's reactions to things, their mind wiring comes into line with that of their parents. This did not happen with me, and I knew that my world was not the same, *literally not the same,* as anyone else's. This was, and is, the absolute, constant truth that underlies every moment of my life.

When I was a kid my mom used to make something called "gypsy soup," which was not made with cooked gypsies, but with lamb and cabbage. The fat would come out of the meat and come to the surface, where it would slither around with the slimy slivers of cabbage. Just the sight of it would nauseate me, and the feel of it sliming around in my mouth…blech! And yet, everyone else at the table would be eating happily and praising the stuff. This convinced me that the other members of my family (and most Latvians) were just plain crazy. Either (a) they didn't perceive the food as slimy and disgusting or (b) they liked slimy and disgusting food. I truly felt as though I had arrived on a very strange planet where the senses of the inhabitants were different from mine.

Dolphins and Stiff Corpses of Small People: The Meaning of *Alive*

When I was a little girl, I was afraid of dolls. I knew that live animals are warm and malleable, but dolls were cold and stiff, like dead frogs that had been run over by a car and had dried out in the sun. To me dolls seemed like the stiff corpses of small people.

I could not *ever* imagine what pleasure little girls could have in playing with them. And yet, people would persist in giving me dolls for my birthday. They even expected me to play with them. My mom actually went so far as to make dresses for one of my (?) dolls and insist that I dress and undress it. I would comply: dress on, dress off, dress on, dress off. "Mom. I took the dress off and put it on five times. Is that enough? Can I go outside and play in the woods now?"

The *Toy Story* movies give me the creeps. The nice thing about toys and other objects is that they sit still and *shut up.* How would it be if you went to make breakfast in the morning and your coffee pot said "I don't like you today—comb your hair differently," and your toaster said, "Don't toast raisin bread today, I want to toast whole wheat!"? I'm sure you would throw these appliances in the trash immediately!

At that time *everything*, even these inanimate things were somewhat alive to me. Perhaps the face-processing ability most people have enables them early on to distinguish what is alive and what isn't, what is human and what isn't. The things that are *human* become very meaningful, non-human things that are *alive* are less meaningful, and the things that are inanimate are least meaningful. My mind did not, when I was a child, make this distinction. There was very little difference in meaning between the children next to the lake that I was playing with and the turtle sitting on the log. Of course I knew the tendencies and capabilities of each, but neither was more important than the other. My feelings were drawn more by the turtle than by the children.

It seems that when most people think of something being *alive* they really mean, *kind of human*. Almost as if the thing could express human thoughts if it could. This is a mistake the scientists seem to be making when studying dolphins. They show the dolphin an object—a box, for example—and the dolphin makes a certain sound, so they assume that that sound means *box*. But maybe not. Maybe it means the way the water swirls around the box, or how the box changes the color of the light, or…anything. We really don't have a clue what's going on there. And even if we can train the dolphin to do what we want, it is never doing what *we* think it is. Whatever it is doing, it is doing it on its own terms, which are not our terms.

So what is alive and what isn't? What makes the atoms in the lake different from the atoms that make a human being? Perhaps we are just snobs and assume that our atoms are of better quality? Or perhaps we are bigots and think the lake atoms are not sentient.

A Raccoon on a Football Field: Aspie-spirituality

Almost my entire life I have had a desire to make things, and when I was a child one of the things I decided to make was jewelry. My father was a dental technician and he had a small laboratory in the basement where he made false teeth and gold crowns and bridges for his friends. He used the lost-wax process. The first step was to make a mold and casting of the person's teeth. Then he would shape the crown or false teeth out of wax, embedding the factory-made teeth in the wax. This would be embedded in plaster to make a mold, which would be boiled in water to remove the wax. Finally it would be cast, either in gold for a crown or bridge, or in pinkish acrylic for false teeth.

Naturally I was not allowed to cast things out of gold, which I didn't want to do anyway. However, the pink false-teeth plastic was cheap, and my father had a lot of extra unusable teeth hanging around. I made a bracelet out of pink wax, stuck a whole bunch of these teeth in it, and, with my father's help, did the whole lost-wax procedure until I had a bracelet of pinkish plastic with lots of teeth sticking out of it. My father helped me polish the bracelet with the spinning brushes on the motor.

Then I wore it to school to show to the other girls and the teacher. Need I say more?

I've always had a taste for surrealistic, odd, visual things. When my parents sent me to Sunday school, they didn't realize they were falling into a trap. I was considered odd, eccentric, and creative as a child in most circumstances. However, in Sunday school and in all religious settings, the stakes had been raised much higher. The Bible is filled with surrealistic visual images: water turning into wine, thin ears of corn eating fat ones, thin cows eating fat cows, resurrections, food multiplying magically, Christ walking on water, etc. I was fascinated by these things and totally uninterested in any conventional meaning they were supposed to have; I made them part of my world, my fantasy world. I would watch a glass of water in the kitchen and expect it to turn into wine. When my mother found out I believed all of these things—in reality, right now—she told me that I wasn't really supposed to believe them literally, just symbolically.

Well, how do you believe something not-literally? To my concrete-thinking mind, something is either so or it isn't so. And if it isn't so, then why had everyone been telling me that it is so? I decided that adults were totally crazy. First they would tell children a lot of lies, and then get angry at the children for believing them. I got my revenge by asking the Sunday school teachers logical questions like, "If the thin cows ate the fat cows, what happened to all the extra meat? It obviously won't fit into the thin cows. Did they make poop real fast?" You can imagine how that went over in the class, and how popular it made me with the parents of the other children, who now had to deal with similar questions that I had put into the minds of their kids.

Religion often requires that you *believe* in a certain way, and if you don't, you are made to feel terrible: bad, evil, damned. But what happens if your brain structure just doesn't allow you to believe something that everyone else's brain structure enables them to believe?

In Sunday school, I felt that, according to the ideas of the people around me, I was forever damned and lost because I could not produce, within myself, the effect of *belief* that was required. No matter how hard I tried, it was impossible. The *real* world, the world as my purely intellectual mind constructed it from my senses, would always intrude, and there was nothing I could do about it. I remember someone saying to me, "Now why can't you believe? Wouldn't life be much easier if you could?"

Of course it would be much easier, but that didn't enable me to do it. Apparently, believing what is socially and conventionally required is like turning on a light switch for some people, and they cannot understand how another person simply cannot do it. This could present a real danger to the self-esteem of AS kids who are sent to Sunday school.

To me, as a kid, it seemed that I was expected to put my intellect aside and believe in fanciful things, which I did, with terrible results. On the other hand, if I didn't put my intellect aside, how could I deal with spirituality, God, and all that? Certainly not in the way it is presented in most religions.

If a raccoon wanders onto a football field, do you think you will be able to explain the game to him?

© Daina Krumins

Nothing but a Flower

Sola Shelly

In the spring two years ago I was still on automatic pilot. It was not the first time that I was functioning like this. For the past few years, I had been cycling, beginning with a period of superficially adequate functioning (on automatic pilot), while cut off of my inner being. Then this façade would break down, and I would enter a period of greater connection to self, but depressed, and functioning minimally, day to day, or even hour to hour. But this time, my superficially adequate, cut off state had been a few months long, and I knew sooner or later, I would have to take a break. I knew that the longer I stayed on automatic pilot, the worse the breakdown was going to be.

The change was unexpected. I received a note in the mail that a package was waiting for me at the post office. I went for it in the morning, on my way to work. The package was from my friend overseas and I don't remember much of its contents, just this thin envelope. Taking out the card that was in it, I squealed at the picture of a cute squirrel. My friend knew my thing for squirrels, and would send me cards or pictures from newspapers when he would come across them. Then I opened the card, and found a sparkling earring attached to it. I knew what it meant. My friend once had told me about his way of sharing: to buy a pair of earrings, keep one of them, and give the other to his friend. Now, I was the one to receive the other earring.

On the way from the parking lot to my office, I was walking on air. I looked around, and felt as if I saw the garden and path for the first time in my life. All felt shiny, and somewhat unreal—as if it were remote scenery, at the background of the immediate reality—my inner being, and the card, and my friend. Yet I was extremely aware of things—the vibration of a leaf in the wind, the sparkle from a window glass.

I entered the building, and ran my employee card through the attendance clock, then took the elevator to the sixth floor. At the office, I turned on the computer, and sat there, not even looking at the monitor, but just staring into space. I knew that I had to start working, but just the thought of it was extremely painful. Continuing to connect to the inside, and to feel this closeness with my friend was even more painful. It was both forbidden (as interfering with my ability to do my duties), and also too intense to experience in this insecure environment, where a colleague might knock on the door at any minute. I froze, unable to concentrate. The space between my ears was filled with a constant scream whose meaning I could not grasp. I don't know how long I stayed like this. Luckily, there was no one to consult with me that morning. I wrote the following poem—in an impulse of just a few minutes:

The Scream

I hear the scream again.
It's calling on me to return
to a place, where I should not be.
I feel the scream blow,
but there's nowhere I can go,
for it's shrieking inside me.
The rooms are cold and hollow.
Even if I choose to follow,
I've already thrown the map to my heart.
I want to cry,
but my eyes are dry.
No one's going to watch me fall apart.

I emailed the poem to my friend. After sitting some more, aimlessly, I went out for a walk. On the other side of the building, a flowerbed was all shining in purple. Coming closer, I ran my fingertips on the finger-like, furry lobes of the leaves. I stayed there a little longer, taking in the purple perfume of the bunch of butterfly-like flowers, touching furry leaves and stalks. On the days to follow, whenever I felt that I could not stand that bloody scream, I would take a walk, and visit this flowerbed. Meanwhile, the plants started to carry seeds, and I would touch also the thick, furry pods. When the seeds began to dry, I picked a few pods, and took them home, in case I might want to plant them in the small yard in front of my apartment.

Weeks passed. The scream, together with the acute awareness faded, and I was back on automatic pilot. The squirrel card rested at home, in a drawer in my night chest. I didn't take it out. The awareness of its existence remained, and from time to time I would retrieve its image in my mind. But it belonged to another life that now seemed remote and unreal. So was my friend. We continued to exchange email, and we were still involved with what was going on for each other. I could maintain this connection, because it was confined to cyberspace, and to the late night or early dawn hours, when I was alone at the computer. Outside of these boundaries, it had no presence in my everyday life. Now that I was back out *there*, I no longer could let this connection touch things in me that had no context in everyday reality. I had to stay away from what might resonate with my core.

Messages from the electronic support group that I had been on for a few years continued to accumulate in my mailbox, but usually I was careful not to read them. Doing so might expose me to contact: a highly vivid awareness of other minds, of the presence of other beings—even though I have never met these people in real life. I could read descriptions and recognize the difficulties

I faced. People were inspired by the same things that let me breathe and gain space. It felt good to be in a place where language did not need continuous translation, where people's expressions and reactions made sense, where the issues of mutual interest meant so much to me. This closeness was overwhelming, and drew me to absorb more and more, and to become more and more absorbed in it. The urge to join and share was so deep, that if I surrendered, it might not leave any resources to cope outside, in real life: to pay attention to so-called social relationships; to watch myself closely so that I didn't violate normal expectations; to defend myself from exposure to contamination or to a toxic atmosphere. Switching from the intense but safe space of the support group back to real life would be painful and dangerous. It would take too long to wait till I was desensitized, till I re-established the protective shell that I needed to survive. I was never sure that I would have the chance to undergo this transition reasonably well, so I preferred not to risk contact. The people and the discussions still meant a lot to me, but they had to remain unreal. It was more important to preserve my ability to function.

Avoiding contact indeed enabled me to function reasonably—as a mother, an employee and a decent citizen—for a long time. But that period came to an end last autumn with enormous fatigue that did not seem to have any apparent cause and was not reduced by increasingly many sleep hours. This period was followed by weeks of numbness: I would indifferently see myself not feeling anything, even when reasoning told me that a similar situation in the past used to raise rage or sorrow or joy. I was probably depressed by then, but deeper depression came a few weeks later, when I would wake up at dawn, all soaked with sweat, and barely manage to drag myself through the day. Moving was so hard, as if my limbs were all covered with sticky grease. Trivial tasks, like doing laundry, required deliberate effort, and made me want to cry. Interaction with people, even a very short, technical discussion at work, left me totally drained, and required a long time to recover enough to be able to proceed with work. The scream blew more and more frequently and loudly in my head. The hardest of all was, to keep a facade of normalcy, at least to pretend that I was still functioning.

I knew that I had to do something, because sooner or later I was going to collapse. Finally I started to go to counseling. The therapist did not help me much with the problem of mode switches. I could not get her to see why there had at all to be two distinct modes of being. One suggestion, however, was helpful: To make a habit of daily walking. The only time I could find for this was lunch break at work. It was already winter by then, but I would not skip this walk even on cold or rainy days. While walking, I often felt an urge to stretch-out my arms or twist my wrists. I used the opportunity when no one was around to do that. Moving, stretching and just breathing fresh air gave me a short break from that relentless scream.

Spring was nearing, and during the daily walk, I started to notice changes in the garden. One day, new, small leaves caught my attention. I came closer, and recognized the furry, finger-like leaves of the same plants that were to grow tall and have the butterfly-like, purple flowers. This was, then, the right time to plant them! I recalled the seeds that I had collected, and as I returned home, I found them and planted a few of them in the small area near my front door. By spring, there were already furry plants with finger-like leaves in my front yard, and tiny purple buds indicated that soon there would be flowers too.

Then one morning, when I was trying to fight off the scream so that I could get some work done, I gave in to a sudden urge and downloaded private email. One discussion that was going on in the support group dealt with getting help, with recovering from years of automatic pilot functioning and regaining the long suppressed self. The experiences described, and the language used were so on target that I was shocked. My first instinct was, to close the email folder, and to shut down anything that related to that matter. After sitting for a while, still shocked, I posted a short message: "It's that pain again, and feeling unreal. The recent discussion is too much for me to handle, but from previous experience I know that going *nomail* is only going to make things worse. Talking about recovery and healing, can anyone give a clue about how to make the first step?" Then I went out for my daily walk.

The response from the group was overwhelming. I was encouraged to hang on and not shut down again. People shared their own experiences with connectedness, and overload, and coming to terms with who they were. Although I didn't say much, they understood exactly what I was talking about. There was *contact* again, with its incapacitating intensity. But this time I had nothing to lose, because I was not functioning anyway. The next morning, after the kids went to school, I sat at the computer and read more responses. Some things resonated so strongly with my core that I had to get up and walk around in the house for a while, till I could sit down again and continue to read. That morning I was two hours late for work. But still, it was an achievement to make it to work at all.

The responses also suggested coping ways that made a lot of sense to me, although I was not sure if I had any idea how to go about implementing them. One response that described relationships with nature in terms of friendship puzzled me. The way I took in sight, sound and texture, and absorbed them never translated to personal or even emotional relationships. Their impact was mainly sensory.

Then, on one of my daily walks, I came around a corner where a small flowerbed separated the building from the sidewalk. And there they were: tall, furry plants, carrying purple bunches of flowers, closely crowded in a small area. "Hello, old friends," my thoughts said silently. I smiled, and stopped by to smell the flowers and to touch the leaves. The following days, I made a point to go this way, to visit my friends. When they started to carry seeds, I picked a few pods. They were still green, so the seeds were not ready to plant. In fact, I didn't need more seeds, because I still had some at home. I took the pods to my office, and whenever the scream was too strong to deal with, I would reach out and touch a furry pod with my fingertips. There was some comfort in this sensation, and I let myself feel it.

It is summer now. The gardener uprooted all the dry plants, so there is no sign of them in the garden. I still have one pod in a drawer in my desk at work. It is all dry and brown now, but it still keeps its furry texture, and it did not break open. Occasionally when I look for something in my desk, I come across this pod, and I smile, and let the furry texture touch me once more. I still hear the scream sometimes, and I still don't know how to handle contact without losing my ability to function. But I do know that I will no longer shut out my inner reality, nor will I try to stay away from my people. It is going to be a long learning course, and probably not an easy one. But I am ready to start now.

© Sola Shelly

AS Paradox
Rational Anger

Jane Meyerding

I was a sunny, cheerful child, for the most part, with few sensory problems that I remember. There were certain foods I couldn't swallow without gagging, and I had severe motion sickness. But the most painful area of my life was hair. Hair hurt. Having my hair combed was torture, and it was the beginning of a series that lasted through my childhood and youth: occasions when my descriptions of my world and my experiences were disregarded or denied by everyone around me. I wasn't accused of lying (I was a transparently honest girl); either I was exaggerating wildly, I was told, or else my self-reports went unheard because they were too far off the norm to make sense to parents, siblings, other adults, and age peers. It was common for people to tell me how I felt about things ("Oh, you must feel very _____ about that"), and perhaps that is a normal thing for adults to do with children. In my case, it was confusing because so often my feelings did not agree with those ascribed to me. I worried about these discrepancies, and by the time I was about 12 or 13, I was looking actively for an explanation of why I was flawed in my emotional reactions.

I used to think I never got angry. In situations where people expected me to react with anger, I didn't. For example, when somebody assaulted me verbally or (less frequently) physically, I remained emotionally detached and intellectually interested. "How lucky," I told myself, "that you stay calm instead of having your responses dictated, as happens to so many others, by anger."

The first kind of anger I recognized in myself is the kind that wells up when I find myself in a situation where someone is being what I consider illogical, especially if that person has the power to impose his/her version of reality on me. In essence, this kind of anger is extreme frustration, and my response to it is to cry. It is horribly frustrating to cry when overwhelmed by anger, because so often people misinterpret the crying as something other than anger. For example, when my co-defendants and I were being sentenced to prison for an anti-war action, I was furious about the irrational nature of the criminal justice system and its role in society. This irrationality was taking over my life (and my friends' lives) in a very literal way, setting off a volcano of anger in me that had no place to go, considering how angry I already was about the war itself, and there was nothing I could do about it. I had done the best I could, and at that moment it seemed as if our efforts were being nullified (because our statements of conscience had been declared to be crimes and dealt with as if they had no more moral content than a case of idle mischief). My anger was intense, and all the more so because I realized that my crying would be interpreted by many in the courtroom as fear.

Eventually, my anger about the criminal justice system became chronic and ended my life as an activist. I got to the point where I was angry not only with the system and its bureaucrats/employees but also with other activists who didn't share my anger. This made it very hard for me to work with most of the people engaged (as I had been for years) in nonviolent activism. Plus, my anger was so ever-present (with respect to the criminal justice system) that it prevented me from speaking coherently in any of the various kinds of contact with the criminal justice system into which nonviolent activism inevitably brings one. My anger idled me. It forced me to become passive—and this was after 20 years of intense concentration on this *special interest*.

That was the kind of anger that was fairly easy to recognize in myself, as can be seen in the fact that it took only about a decade for me to figure out what was going on inside and how that internal situation affected my interaction with the world.

The much harder kind of anger to recognize (in myself) was the kind that scared my mother. Maybe scared is too strong a word. What I realized very gradually (finally achieving some amazed clarity about it around the age of 35 to 40) is that my mother was very careful, always, to steer away from situations that might anger me. I think it was my eventual ability to notice her reactions to me that enabled me to figure out what was going on. Once the idea entered my mind, I began to be able to look back through my life and identify many occasions when I had flown instantly into rage—all too often at her expense. I guess the reason I didn't recognize my anger as anger is that I thought I was reacting reasonably. *Reason* and *anger* did not go together in my way of thinking, so as long as I was being reasonable (and I had no idea I ever was anything but) I couldn't see that I also was angry.

My fits of sudden rage were invisible to me because I wasn't able to recognize emotional content as distinct from what I saw as the substance of the situation—"the facts of the matter." It amazes me, in retrospect, how patiently my mother put up with my recurring anger/rage and how much effort she put into trying to avoid setting me off.

My mother wasn't the only one who noticed my anger. No doubt I was unaware of how it affected many people, but every once in a while someone would react to me in a way I recognized as a reaction to anger. This always took me by surprise, and often I was able to discount such reactions because people so often misinterpret my behavior and words, ascribing incorrect emotions to them. Only occasionally (and only as I reached middle age) did someone get through to me with what I realized was a true perception of me as angry.

One event that helped me "get in touch with my anger" (as the relationship gurus say) was the three-year period between the time my first novel was accepted by a small publisher and the time the book actually appeared. I was angry for so much of that time that I pretty much had to notice it. My anger became so debilitating, in fact, that I was forced to recognize a basic problem I always had with all kinds of anger, which is: I didn't know how to get out of it. Once something flipped the switch, I was stuck in anger mode. I didn't know how to change gears and move out of or past the anger. Being angry in such a sustained way during the book publishing years was unbearable, physically as much as mentally, and I had to look for a way to de-anger myself. The search for this technique helped me recognize as anger the smaller (but nevertheless intense) rages I'd been having all along, and to realize with increasing regret and disquiet how unjust it was for me to inflict this anger on my mother. I felt especially bad when I began to perceive the whole process (sudden rage followed by varying—but always too long—period when I didn't want to be angry any more but didn't know how to stop). Apparently anger makes me obsess, and I had to find a method that would enable me to cut off each obsession as soon as possible after it occurred. I'm getting better at it, I think, as I go along.

There's another thing that happens to me occasionally that I know looks like anger. I'm not sure what it is, though. It happens when I am totally overloaded, overwhelmed with interpersonal contact. When I feel trapped, stuck, enmeshed, smothered in a relationship that has become so constantly present in its influence on my life that I cannot find an instant of time in which to decompress and be my self again. I haven't let myself get to that point very often, and it gets easier to avoid as I get older and have less and less identity as a potential friend/lover. The result when I have been in this state is that I burst. I tantrum wildly, and twice I have gone to the extent of performing my own version of self-mutilation: breaking the lenses of my glasses. Since I am virtually blind without my glasses, and since their lenses are made of sturdy, shatter-resistant plastic, breaking my glasses both requires a tremendous lot of work and represents the most extreme rejection (short of suicide) of the world around me. I know it looks like anger, but it feels like despair.

© Jane Meyerding

Fantasy Realm

April Masilamani

One thing as problematic in its own way as having personas is my fantasy world, the imaginative realm I invented to inhabit, that helps shut out the outside world. It is on a par with reading and fulfils a similar role of keeping me mentally safe and happy while having to exist as a real person. I am reluctant to elaborate on the details of what I inhabit, as I would hate to risk losing it by having to describe this world. (I would probably go mad without it—what then would stop the flood of outside data?) Reading is extremely efficient as a block, but can be too efficient. It is a concrete wall that doesn't allow me to drive or perform physical tasks, whereas my imagination is fluid and allows me to slide round and navigate my way through the real world. I can remain protected but also nearly conscious at the same time. This fantasy realm cannot engage, as far as I can tell, with other humans; the personas do that. I probably spend 60% to 70% of my time, engaged in this world, maybe more. It's especially useful when in crowded situations, or with strangers, or in bed at night, as I cannot go to sleep quickly.

This might account for the gaps I experience in memory. It is a wonderful world completely under my control and fantastic things happen there. I can become the things I have no ability to ever be. For a start I'm extremely brilliant, a mathematical genius and a concert violinist. In relation to the real me I could say that this person often seems more real than I am and I know more about her than I do about myself. This sounds quite stupid, almost on par with those women who read *mills and boon* books so talking about it reminds me how pathetic I am. But then again, if the object to everything is to try and function and get things done, then I could hardly function or manage without my different levels of retreat, or withdrawal.

I wonder if this helps create problems with self-awareness for Aspies, though. In the struggle to understand and comprehend the outside world, or conversely shut it out, we end up with no energy left to see ourselves. Also, as we so seldom have ourselves, or our inclinations, or ways of being reflected back at us, we then have limited access to data concerning *us* that we can make sense of. I have recently joined an Aspergic group, and although connections are slow going (like cranking up a rusty machine), I feel I am seeing a miracle in action as we discover in others' words and descriptions (sometimes just chance comments) insights that illuminate vast vistas of comprehension that have remained so long in darkness for so many of us. A worldwide effort to support these connections could be vital to enable ACs to make the most of their sometimes extraordinary abilities that are so often stifled under a blanket of NT misunderstandings.

© April Masilamani

Jewels and Tools

Sola Shelly

I wear a squirrel pin
to remind me of who I am
and of all the things that bring me joy.

The other day, I wore a turtle pin
to keep me aware of the armor
that stays with me to protect me,
and to show me the blessings of slowness.

I also have a butterfly pin
which reminds me
of how fragile I am,
and brings back memories
of my dear friend overseas
and our visit to the butterfly conservatory,

And a snail-shaped pin
with little blue stones
to remind me that I am,
that inside my rigid shell
my core is vibrant
and my mind is free to fly
and meet kindred souls.

I don't wear jewelry much
the touch of necklaces and bracelets
irritates me
but small pins, attached to the shirt
are like treasures I carry.

I love to wear velvet
and look how the rich texture
plays with the light.
When I need to
I can rub the tips of my fingers
or the back of my palms
and let the smoothness soothe me.

But I should be careful
not to let people
think that I pet myself.

When I have to go out there
to impress the world
and make people appreciate me
for things I am not,
I paint my face with war-colors
and blacken my eye-lashes.
Behind that mask, I am safe.
But mostly, I don't use makeup.
I wear my special symbols
and let their secret
be my shield.

© Sola Shelly

Walking the Labyrinth

Jean Kearns Miller

I think a lot about a recent experience with a spiritual exercise that goes back to the Middle Ages, walking the labyrinth. At a daylong session on spirituality and nature, participants went out onto the campus of Siena Heights College and the Dominican Sisters' motherhouse, where retreats and such are conducted. There are some wonderful blessed yet pagan (one and the same?) installations on the grounds, like a fire pit and poles with flags resembling Tibetan prayer flags and loud, clanging wind chimes. (It was very windy.) After walking down from the house a ways across the prairie, we came to the labyrinth, a replica of the one set in tile in the floor of Chartres Cathedral. The Adrian Dominicans' is set in paving stones with paths about 15 inches across. Paths winding one way are only inches from paths going another. You can't get lost or stuck and you'll eventually get to the center, but you'll wind close in and back out a number of times before getting there. And though you do it in silence and meditation, others wind silently around you all the way. I wasn't sure about it as a spiritual big deal but I knew that getting into it, for me, was going to mean going barefoot and taking off my jacket so the cold wind could circulate freely inside my clothes. The cold was everywhere. The cold was nowhere. And I thought immediately of a poem I wrote, my first legitimate poem. It's called "Albert Shea" and it's about a little boy (me!) who's out exploring and everyone is yelling at him and ridiculing him for not wearing his coat and shoes. I ended the poem with "Albert knows…that sensetouch must be tested, teased, then put aside." This by me in 1966 at 17. This field in Adrian was not the backstreet cobblestones, where I was as a kid in England, but on paving stones, and not making my way through the cave like buildings of my soot-covered hometown but on a prairie—still exploring! And I couldn't make my mind go blank. Instead it started making art and poetry and observations furiously. And I moved very slowly and with my eyes looking down and doing ballet steps and arm stretches, even though there were others around. I felt they were like fellow animals whose shapes and movements and tempo and animal heat were what distinguished them as my kind. Everyone was silent and proceeding on their own. Every sensation was heightened. There was nothing else but being. It wasn't delight I felt, but ecstasy. I was the last to weave my way out. I don't know how this fits in but I've been bursting to tell it!

Albert Shea

Jean Kearns

Walking
along the black cobbles
between the backyard gates
and the black houserows
of Everystreet and Bishopstreet
a small boy age about six
with tattered vest and
shabby greywool shortpants
and no-shoes, urchin
red of hair, blue of eye,
fair of cheek and freckledy,
skinnylegs and very much
akin to the name Albert
though maybe not
runs his toe along the
grates peering into the sewer
for lost threepenny bit, brooch,
tennisball or dabloon, if lucky,
to the sound of omniscience:
look't Albert the little dafty doesn't
he know it's chilly if he were my boy
I'd box his earholes and
the crazy little blighter going out
on a day like this without his
pullover and shoes he'll catch his
death. But Albert-thoughts we on da—
bloons, and Gene Autry, and them yellow
paper hats they was giving out at
Pickup's shop for a penny-hapenny's
worth of kalai-and-spanish,
nd the chill and lone and grittycobbles
only made Albert-thoughts sharper,
deliciouser,
for Albert knows, as thinkers know,
that sensetouch must be
tested, teased, then put aside,
a matter of nervends says them
that ought know better.

But Albert knows and canst but
spit at Pammy Green's dolly when
she: Albert Shea's naughty boy
his mum's going to leather him good
for that why doesn't he wear his
coat and shoes and play in his
yard like me and t'other children?
But disbelief-hately he screws up his
nose in a frightenful way
and goes on,
Pammy Green doesn't know.

December 1966

Author's note: There's a bit of Lancachire dialect and other funny sound stuff. It's the remembrance of my own disconnection from the common sense world of warm coats (and why), and in reaction to someone commenting on my wandering slowly around campus coatless in December of my first college year. I wrote this about 3o years before hearing about AS. And the only thing that doesn't ring true is the spitting. (We Aspies will do anything *to avoid an unpredictable social encounter!) Thanks to Martha Kate Downey for sending Albert back to me after his visit to her CD,* Tap Dancing in the Night.

The Personas

April Masilamani

This was the most stressful thing to write. Everything else seemed a bit boring on rereading, as it is just based on my memories and I have not lived a very exciting life. But I put it all in, as it was hard to work out what might have been useful, and what wasn't. This, however, is more to do with who or *what* I might be, and it is something I have not analyzed before. So I was not sure where it would take me, especially as, when I try to get to the essence of things, there is a strong pull to go there and never come back, which could be regarded as a form of madness, I suppose, and dangerous, given my present level of responsibility.

My personas developed over the years, usually forced into creation, mostly as the result of shock, not something I deliberately set out to do. Shock is my way of describing what happens when the NT world or interactions with it forces itself into my fantasy—or real (depending on how you look at it) world. They are usually based on nothing one could call a personality, but on a mimicked personality developed by careful observation of what was required by the NTs. However, there is a common theme running through all of them that may be my link to who I really am. (I have trouble with the word *who*—*what* could be a better one.) This theme is slightly manic, humorous, a bit larger than life or larger than what is required, and, even when I'm aware of having to watch my Ps and Qs, it is still inappropriate. Humor plays a big part, as everything seems slightly odd and things are often funny, even when tragic, although I'm not sure that they mean to be. In looking at my personas, it's a bit like looking in the wardrobe for a specific outfit that I've just remembered I've got, instead of putting on the usual blue or gray outfit.

Using my new AS perspective, I've almost convinced myself that I'm not AS, because, if the common theme is a funny, social, nutty person, then that's not very Aspergic. However, most of the time, without the personas, I'm actually nervous, neurotic, worried, grumpy, and stressed. So which part is real? I then thought that maybe when I'm drunk, that would be the real me as there is diminished control, and I'm very aware of always being in control. However, once again, I'm a happy drunk, although extremely inappropriate, according to those who will still speak to me the next day. But, as I don't consider myself happy, then once again I come back to the question, "What is real?" Because the neurotic *me* is like a computer, always analyzing and sifting through the data input, always studying and thinking about the object in front of it (usually human, as they represent the most challenging data-processing), trying to make sense of everything that comes in. And once this is processed, an appropriate

111

persona is activated and goes out to deal with the situation. However this persona is only a front forced into being by the world trying to get in. Behind all this is nothing in particular that I can work out, and I'm really trying. It's more of a trance state, a state of nothingness, that would be perfect if everyone would go away and leave it alone. I am wondering if this is the normal core center for everyone. Perhaps it is. I should ask people. In fact I will. It might be useful for this book. (Attempts to do so, so far, have not proved very enlightening. The NTs asked were hostile. Most felt that they had a strong sense of self, and didn't feel comfortable with me trying to question whether there was a basis for their feeling, or asking for proof—it was apparently supposed to be self evident. Also I did make it clear that I was not talking about a soul concept, as that was even more debatable.) If everyone has this core center of nothingness, then maybe I'm not AS, or is this one of the things that makes ACs different? I can enter this state if left alone playing with water or looking at clouds. Obsessions come close to it as well, as they are so consuming that they become almost all that you are, although I don't allow myself any, as they are like a drug and I cannot deal with the real world or engage personas, and feel I could kill if anyone tries to interfere with them, so I leave them alone, especially while bringing up children. I cannot seem to get a connection between this core, and its interests that keep it contented, and what I would call a personality, or a *me*, if you like, or an interactive connection with the outside world.

Every other engagement that I'm forced to make, then, involves the various levels of other state. My anger is another issue of existence that is not connected to other bits of me, in a way that I can link anyway. If people are not particularly nice, I don't mind too much any more although I can't be pushed around and use an aggressive persona to deal with the problem, usually in the nicest possible way. However if I overload or am pushed into a corner, then I have no control. In fact, I often lose my vision or am not aware of processing it, and just howl like an animal or bang my head on walls and smash things. (This does not happen often now—nobody would push me there twice.) The physical pain that is sometimes created by hitting myself seems to match the confusion and mental pain I am experiencing.

Maybe my overload anger represents the real me, as it represents very little control at all. It is my easiest emotional state because it requires very meager thought processes or decisions to engage. It just seems to happen. Although it is the least deliberate or controlled of any of my actions, it is the most exhausting, and I'm trying to move away from it.

People often say, when coming in contact with my personas, that they have never met anyone who understands them as well as I do. They say things like, "You think or feel exactly like me," and seemed quite pleased. I would always feel like a fraud and feel a bit guilty as I wasn't aware of a connection between us at all, although obviously some people are more engaging or interesting for me and this is usually when it happens. (It's as though the challenge of quickly creating a new persona to deal with them is very interesting to me: Can I do it or not.?) I could now say to them that actually, far from being understood, they have never been imitated so well. Sometimes the imitation becomes almost a parody, which makes people feel uncomfortable instead. I very rarely meet an NT that I have trouble understanding if I study them long enough. By understanding I mean predicting or anticipating their most likely response, though why they do what they do is often still a mystery.

In some ways if men's behavior is far easier to predict than women's, then NTs are far less complex than ACs. One of the things I enjoy about AS contacts is that they follow their own agendas a lot, if obsessively. I find it more relaxing as they are not looking for a lot of reflection of themselves in the person they are with (although we are of course looking for similarities in order to relax and reveal more of our idiosyncrasies without being in fear of being judged odd). Connecting with fellow ACs makes a lot less work for me and I find I can be myself and not have to adopt personas.

People often say I should make time for my self or do I have any interests or do I have mental health days and give myself little hugs (*yuuuaarrrggg!*) as they do. I have always found this a strange concept. Again this elusive sense of self. I mean I guess it would work and there is some logical sense in not stressing out, but it is a hard concept to grasp when you don't seem to be able to define or even create an awareness of a sense of self in the first place. To tell the truth it's only since I've had this Asperger concept to deal with that I've started thinking that I might have a sense of self, which is a bit tiring especially as I now feel obliged to work out where it is or what it is.

I feel like I used to exist a long time ago, possibly when I was born, and I was a little transparent egg filled with liquid of some sort (mercury perhaps, my most favorite) and then somehow the outside world tried and kept on trying to get in, forcing the egg to be aware of its own existence and the existence of the world around it. This forced invasion was very painful and the egg had to build up layers to withstand the onslaught, layers of different shapes to cope with this outside attack and then all these layers covered up the egg with so much stuff that it ceased to exist, or forgot its existence. I am now trying to remember or get back to being the egg or core center and yet am obliged to also remain as something that could be called human.

To remember and experience the egg state and exist as human may not be possible. Maybe it comes down to a choice between the two, maybe I've already made the choice and exiled myself, maybe the two can never co-exist and can never meet, or maybe that's what death is. I was always comforted as a child with the thought of lying in a grave, ceasing to be, joining nothingness again. Rebirth or heaven sounded scary, this contact with people would never end. So maybe that's what it is, in my half remembered concept of my beginning is also a concept of my end.

While I observe that I exist and am aware that this constitutes existence the same as for everyone else, the comfort and certainty this seems to afford most people (I imagine) isn't there for me. This existence is just imposed on me or was at the beginning. It is partially created by myself based on choices I have made. And I am forced to acknowledge this (and in many ways very grateful for it) but it's not what I had or have as an expectation for existing, which lies for me, more in a state of nonexistence as a core truth for being.

© April Masilamani

Wandering Has Its Advantages

Kim Motola

You can't stay too long
you can't combine
you can't go wrong.
But when they ask you to stay
you know it's the beginnings
of getting hooked.
And forced to leave again
takes you back
to the warm rustles of the wind.

From whence come the fears, the sighs,
of the pain of love?
From within,
beneath the gloom
of unsatisfactory wisdom.

across the alley, the day is done.
But within these halls of tinseled stress,
there toils one man.
He knows not where to begin
the search.
But he continues, nevertheless.
And when this dawn is dimmed,
for him…

Three Poems

C.J.

1

Poetry is said to be a release to say
Words that do not come easily any other way.
Sounds a thing in which to try to do
To explain what our life's like to you.
Words are so hard to tell
Sometimes I wish they would just yell
But on paper they flow with an ease
So we'll start if you'll be patient please.
No people around within sight
No reason to get uptight
The body can relax, the hand can flow
The words come out fact, no reason to go slow
What comes next may be asked
For there must be structure within this task.
It is unknown where to begin to explain
How most days feel like we are insane
Those things others have with ease
Are not available in every way to me.
Even if we do not appear to be there
Every word that's said we can hear.
We learn to cope from what we see on TV
The actors explain so much to me
For if there was a script to life, a role to play
Life would be easier every day.

2

Asperger's, what does it mean?
Not a lot on its own it seems
To me it explains why my life
Seems to get me in so much strife
Feelings are the most confusing
All those words people keep on using
Like happy, nervous, angry, sad
Connections to these I have never had.

116

Noises can be a painful thing
Some voices can sound like a constant ring
I often hear only half what is said
It's much easier if the information is read
So if you were to write me a letter
You would find we'd communicate much better
For then when I loose the plot
I can go back and start at top.
Lots of people are too much
That it's hard to ignore as such
The easiest thing is solitude
But that's when people think I'm rude.
There is something in this poem
If you like a kind of omen
As I have got a little older
I have also become a little bolder.
Knowing what I now know
What people have showed me how
That this is really not so bad
All those strange habits I thought I had
Are really just being me
And that's the way I need to be.
I'd like to thank those people who
Have taught me how to struggle through
Who have nurtured me along the way
Have sat with me when I've nothing to say.
I'm not ashamed that I am me
But to explain to everyone you see
Would be like over-wiring a computer chip
It makes me want to jump ship
But since I learnt to write it down
It's like being on top of town
I can express what I want to say
In my own unique way
That it is different we may be
It makes us no worse that he or she.

3

You have a gift that you can use
To help your friend be less confused
It is so simple when it is explained
It is not so difficult and will cause no pain

117

The truth is that we need to learn
The knowledge that we so often yearn
The things that you can take for granted
Within our minds need to be planted
The things we have no knowledge of yet
Until in our minds they are set
Names for feelings that are unknown
Until you have explained and shown
It is ok to feel these things
Even though they have a confusing ring
The point is not to give up after once
But use each opportunity as it comes
To point out what each thing means
Even if to you it seems
That you often repeat yourself to no effect
Because it seems we have not got it yet
The truth is that it will take some time
But if you persist you may find
The benefits are worth the wait
If with patience and time you take
The opportunity to show and share
That we may surprise you unaware
That we learn to accept and often tolerate
The things for granted that you take.

I Don't Remember Signing up for

This Planet

Mary Margaret Britton Yearwood

I don't remember signing up for this planet. I suppose when the assignments were handed out I was given somebody else's. I wonder if she feels as lost on the other side of the galaxy as I do on Earth. None of the angels caught the error and so I was birthed in 1961 by a 5'2" human who calls herself Mama. The Mama already had a boy child three years my senior.

The boy would become My Boy in my mind because he assigned himself to me to explain the complicated terrain that caused me so many problems. There was another human that came and went to a place called New York City the first two years of my life. He worked on something called computers, was 6'2," and My Boy called him Daddy. The Daddy man left the rest of us in Miami while he flew to New York City each week. The Mama woman was an elementary school teacher.

It helped her feel good about herself. I was not like My Boy. My Boy was cuddly and used something called words. I could not be cuddly because I did not fit in my thin human skin. When The Mama tried to pick me up it burned and pinched even though she wasn't burning and pinching from her side of things. I would scream and scream and it hurt the Mama in her heart. The Mama did not know what to do. How could this be her child? When she left me alone I was happy to explore this world by myself all alone in my crib. The Mama described my behavior to doctors and they told her I was something called spoiled. They told The Mama and The Daddy to make me use words instead of letting me grab and grunt at things I needed.

I do not remember these things. The Mama and The Daddy told them to other people and I would leave my world of one sometimes to listen to what was being said about me. It was like they were trying to figure out a complex riddle. How could their child be so odd, so different? But The Mama and The Daddy had places to be and things to do and life went on. I slowly resigned myself to being assigned to the wrong part of the galaxy. I was not leaving anytime soon.

My Boy is classic Asperger's. He knows everything about everything. He has always read the encyclopedia in every free moment because he thinks it is fun. The words on the page hurt my sensitive eyes, and words are a mystery that I must translate back to my land of pictures that live in my brain. Therefore My Boy is my informer about many written things. My Boy says that his readings have shown him that Earth is a remote planet on the far side of the galaxy. We who live here have agreed to a lonely existence far removed from the greater activity of the universe. We are a planet of explorers on a remote, isolated island. Only I did not volunteer for this mission. I was drafted accidentally. I feel the remoteness of our position deep in my soul. I am an island on an island. There are others like me scattered about the face of this planet. We know each other when we look into each other's eyes. We see the intense loneliness of wearing the wrong skin.

We are inmates of our skin prisons.

© Mary Margaret Britton Yearwood

How I Feel Tonight

Mary Margaret Britton Yearwood

there is a loneliness
a hole so deep
from not being held by my mama and daddy
because of this autistic skin
that can never be repaired

no matter
the amount of therapy
no matter
the people who love me

but the pain it brings cannot
break me to the point
of removing me from this world
because
though it grows worse
when i have to take care of others
namely my children
it
is for my children's sake
that i remain on this earth

i refuse to
make their lives worse than my own
by taking my own life
i refuse to
make them live with a premature death of their mother

chris, my loving therapist, reminds me
regularly that my children
will never know
the pain i know
because i held them
and continue to do so

and then that leaves me

what do i do with me

how do i walk through this pain
that
both stifles and propels me
in new creative directions

today i have been working on a simple love story
of my own making
i enjoy writing something fun every once in awhile
it is a tiny break
in the middle of everything else
in my life

i will make it through this dry time in my life

i will both feel the pain of loneliness
that i wish on no other person
but i see in the eyes of other autistics
and
i will demand of me to try to use my energy
to push through the pain to
the love
that can be felt
if i only let others touch me

to live
is the most difficult
thing for me

to others it comes naturally like breathing
but
for me
i must fight an uphill battle
just to exist
without falling in on myself

© Mary Margaret Britton Yearwood

The Savant

Wendy Peabody

Words are labels for thoughts that we wish to convey to others, and hopefully others will understand those thoughts enough to be empathetic towards the initial thinker. It could be that people who are labeled *savant* have an unusual ability to perform certain tasks, well above the average performance level of what is generally known as a neurotypical person. There are many different kinds of savants in the autistic world, and at many different levels. Some are not very noticeable to others, because the savants may keep it largely to themselves, likely due to a communication glitch with the outside world. Some are quite apparent to observers, even casual ones, and that is where the attention is directed.

On a personal level, as someone in the realm of Asperger Syndrome, I am self-centered. It is difficult for me to relate to and empathize with other people, and I tend to make observations based on intuition, which is in itself an inexact science, so I will decline to speak for anyone else. But I hope that someone who is dealing with these same things will understand and relate, and hopefully will be encouraged by this writing.

Since I was able to hold a pencil, I have been drawing. I am a visual thinker, which is, of course, not unusual for those on the autistic spectrum. I tend to record images and store them somewhere in the recesses of my brain's memory banks, to be later drawn in great detail. Since my drawings were easily understood by the grownups, they made a lot of fuss over them. They saw a lot of things that caused them to react in astonishment. They called me unusually talented, and even a kind of prodigy. At the same time, I also enjoyed reading, creating worlds in my inner mind, and writing stories about them.

What happened was that, later, as my schooling progressed, I was told that I should make a living with these talents. Kindly, well meaning people enthusiastically told me that I had great potential, and filled my mind with all sorts of notions regarding my success in the material world, if I went to art school and applied my talents to something marketable. Not that there's anything wrong with this, in itself. But I found that I was unable to do this as well as they expected. I found, that while doing assignments for art school, I struggled as much as anyone else, and my talent didn't count for anything. I found this burdensome and depressing. I was constantly told, "You have so much potential. Why was this so difficult for you?" I couldn't say. I can only search for the most likely explanation in words.

What I didn't know, and neither did anyone else, was that I had a great deal of trouble with perceptions of what people said and implied, and there were times when the meanings of words changed and created a different reality. And it was when that reality didn't coincide with my internal sense of reality that the confusion came. Everyday tasks, such as getting to places on time, organizing my work, communicating with the right people, were very difficult, more difficult than for the average person. I did not finish art school, which left me with an accumulated financial shortage that caused me to abort my professional education. Not that I wanted to quit art school, but, while I did enjoy many aspects of it, things were not happening the way they should for my success.

I have found quite recently that it was when my lifestyle was lined up the way I wanted it to be, and I was in a comfortable situation, that is, there were no distractions, no sudden changes, no irritating people, and no conflicting ideas, that I could tap into what some called *flashes of brilliance.*

This savant ability to draw and write fiction from an internal world led people to believe that I could perform at a high level in many other areas of my life, and I wondered sometimes if this talent only served as a double edged sword. Then again, one will not know what she can or cannot do, until she experiments and makes attempts to find her boundaries and limitations.

It was far easier to keep my accomplishments to myself, and only show them to a select few. People in general didn't seem to get what I was doing, but they didn't really look. I began to realize, that I was not like everyone else, in that they didn't see things with as much detail, or think about things as much as I did. Yet, there are people who *can* do this, and those are the people that I gravitated to. The only thing that was a problem was our mutual inability to socialize consistently enough to keep up friendships.

People drift in and out of my life. Some incidents are soon forgotten, and others replay in my mind as though they were on a film loop. People will react how they will, and my ability to understand them is not at any further point of enlightenment than it was when I was 6. I continue to draw creatures, taking what is *seen* on an internal projector, and then putting it down in great detail. And then I build what J. R. R. Tolkien called a Secondary World, to put down in a tangible medium what exists only in my mind, up to that point.

The only way I can see to my personal success, is, having paid my dues in school, I can now throw away most of what I have learned, keep some other things that I deem valuable, and go back to my Secondary World. It's entirely possible that when this Secondary World has been completed, translated onto paper, in both words and pictures, it might be publishable. In the meantime, I struggle with average and below average abilities in dealing with every day life. Knowing it is a necessary evil to do these things, I wade through the swamps of the outside world, knowing I can come home to the sanctuary of my Secondary World and continue in its bliss.

© Wendy Peabody

Our Family Album:
AS Girlhood

Cartwheels and Silent Tantrums

Susan Golubock

I was born a "good baby." At least that is what my mother always told me. I never cried for attention or food. She would hear me babbling to myself, or later, rocking and banging my head on the head of the crib. It was the only way she knew that I was awake. She never found that to be odd, only "good."

I've always been slow to acquire most skills, but once I have them, I don't lose them. When I was two, my mother would bribe me with cookies to say single words. When I did start to speak, I spoke in whole sentences. Receptively, I heard what people said; I just didn't understand what they meant. My family delights in telling the story of how, after my first few days in first grade, I came home quite bewildered. Everyday, I told my family, my teacher called out the names of the children in the class and they were to respond by raising their hand. Everyday I listened for my name, but she never called it. I also observed that she called out the name of another child who was never there. I commented that this other child had the same first name. My family asked what her last name was, and I told them. It hadn't occurred to me that there was any connection between these two observations until my parents explained to me that my teacher was simply mispronouncing my last name. I was the missing child! The next day I raised my hand. As I grew older my family stopped providing explanations. My queries and observations were met by laughter or silence. I wouldn't have minded the laughter if they would have answered, but they didn't...or couldn't. I realize now, that I was supposed to know the answers by then, or be able to figure them out on my own. But I didn't and couldn't. I just knew that their silence hurt, so I stopped asking.

I was definitely not a promising candidate for success—if indeed it is based on group and social skills—when I was a child. My sisters tell me that I never initiated play with them, nor with my many cousins who came to visit. Maybe 50% of the time, if invited, I would consent to play with them. When I did agree to play it was more out of curiosity about what they were doing. Since I didn't understand what they were doing, I would simply wait until someone told me what to do. Later, I learned to ask for certain roles. I realized that if I asked to be the *servant* or *child* in pretend play, that someone would always direct me. That way I didn't need to figure out what the game was all about. It was the first of many ways I learned to hide my social confusion. I never did catch on, but I was learning to be like them.

The other 50% of the time when I was invited to play, I chose instead to play alone with my two clothespins. I remember those clothespins. My sister said I spent hours with them at a time. One day they disappeared. That was

OK. I simply substituted play using my fingers as *people*. When I was a little older, my aunt bought me a doll to which I formed an attachment. I liked to look at it because it had dark hair like mine and wore a red dress, and I liked anything red. But, I never played with it. When I played *hands* I mostly remember playing with sounds, intonations, actions and emotions…not actual situations. Later, I created moving pictures in my head, and would walk down the street talking to myself as I played them over and over in my mind. I played out very elaborate scenes in my head. I don't feel that my form of play lacked imagination. What I recognize now that I lacked was input from outside of myself. Playing with other people only overwhelmed me and made things more confusing. I turned inward where things made more sense. My mind became my playground. I was safe there. Today, I am well respected for my creative solutions to problems within my profession. I visualize in my head what others appear unable to see. I never understood what harm there was in this form of play. I just knew that I was increasingly being pressured to spend more time with others and given less time or opportunities to be alone. My uncle recently showed my husband and me a home video of my sisters and cousin dancing. My guess is that I was at least seven. I was serious and entirely focused on performing the dance. I have no doubt that I thought that dancing was the sole purpose of what we were doing. How was I to know that we were playing, and this was supposed to be fun? By the time I reached 50, I still had no concept of what *fun* was. I never experienced a natural laugh until my late 40s, when homeopathy allowed me to experience what it meant to come down from the *flight, fight, fright* state I had lived in all those years.

I remember experiencing panic often when expectations were made of me and I didn't know how to respond. One day, my father was taking a group picture of my sisters and me and he called out, "Smile." I froze. It suddenly occurred to me that I didn't know how to do that! My family has told me that when I was younger I simply opened my mouth when told to smile. I was older now. I needed to learn this. I remember spending hours in front of a mirror practicing facial expressions (that I learned from watching Shirley Temple movies). I watched TV a lot growing up and Shirley Temple fascinated me with her expressions, but it was the logic of Mr. Spock on Star Trek to which I related best. I also read a lot. Both were acceptable ways of retreating into *my* world. Today, my husband would say my escape is my computer, and he's probably right. Even now, I think that I learn more about people by watching their interactions on TV, reading about them in books, or in Ann Landers' column, than I do through direct interactions. I started a comic strip collection several years ago in an attempt to understand how people perceive humor. I collect the ones that I can relate to as a way of knowing what perceptions I share with others. It's a small collection, but growing. Humor is not something that I get very quickly in real-time interactions. In comics, at least, the words stay there so that I can take the time I need to make sense of them.

In addition to books and TV, I learned to play board games and card games. Those were safe ways of playing with others. You didn't have to interact too much. There were few surprises. I also took dance lessons, and learned to play a guitar, and twirl a baton. These seemed to be things that my parents decided that my sisters and I should learn. I never questioned why. I suspect now if they were somehow connected to things that young girls were supposed to learn in those days. My favorite activity was the stunts and tumbling lessons. I practiced cartwheels and backbends for hours on end. If these were supposed to be social activities, I think that I again missed that point. They were simply activities that I could do with others without having to actually interact with them. They were structured and I could spend time practicing on my own. I learned to practice many things in my mind that I needed to know to avoid that panic feeling. Life began to fall into predictable routines. I was content.

When I was 10, we moved to a new home and a new school in a new area of town. I lost my good child status right about then. The change was too much. I went beyond panicking; I became angry and irritable. This change in me was not at all understood by my parents, and definitely not considered to be acceptable behavior. I could not verbalize what I did not understand myself, and I had no outlet for expressing it. The pressure inside of me built. Whenever my parents would leave my sisters and me alone in the house, I would immediately throw myself down on the floor and have a full blown temper tantrum. My sisters, not knowing what to do, did nothing. When I exhausted myself, I would stop. Over time I learned to hide my pent-up frustrations.

My youngest sister has told me that she remembers finding me sitting and rocking on the corner of my bed, in an area that was not visible from the open doorway. (I had learned that to close the door invited someone to check so it was safer to leave it open.) She said that she would quietly sit and rock with me. Eventually I would stop and sometimes talk with her. At the time I didn't realize how special her attempt was to reach out to me. I do now. I had language skills, but it didn't do me much good. People didn't understand what I was trying to tell them. It didn't get me what I wanted, nor did it answer my questions. It was better to remain silent. As long as I was being *good*, people left me alone. I learned that life was easier for me that way.

I was fortunate in that I was never teased as child. Someone once suggested that was because I was pretty, and smart, but shy (which, more accurately, meant passive and trying to avoid interactions). Being pretty and smart was socially valued. My parents praised me in front of other people all the time for that. Apparently, since I didn't draw attention to these facts myself (by being "shy"), I wasn't teased for being stuck up. I never have seen the value in these traits. How is it to my credit if I was born that way? It made me angry anytime someone would compliment me for being pretty or smart. I didn't want praise for something that I could see no value in. It wasn't something that I made happen. What I did desperately want though was for someone, anyone, to notice the *inner* me…the me that I felt I had to hide because it was not acceptable. I wanted someone to recognize how hard I struggled. If I couldn't have that, I wanted to at least be left alone. When I was left alone in my own world, I enjoyed being me. Unfortunately, I didn't seem to have the ability to communicate what I wanted. What I wanted and what other people wanted for or from me didn't seem to be the same. It never occurred to me that I had any choices. What I finally learned was that if I wanted something, and couldn't get it myself, it was best to give up that want. Eventually, I stopped wanting altogether. I just did what other people wanted. It was less painful.

I remember quite vividly the night that I finally shut down emotions completely. I was lying in bed having my now-nightly silent tantrum that I couldn't explain so had to hide. I was tired of feeling confused, angry and frustrated, with no way to express it without getting into trouble. Play and fun were non-existent concepts to me. If I zoned out from overload, someone would get in my face wanting something from me I was in no shape to give. Something had to go. It took too much energy to deal with emotions, mine as well as others. (I didn't realize then that I was hypersensitive to others' emotions and felt them just as intensely as I felt my own.). I needed all the energy I had to figure out how to function in a world that I did not/could not understand, and no one seemed able or willing to explain. I realize now how big a role emotions play in understanding the *why*s of social interactions, and in understanding and building relationships. As a child, though, social skills did not come naturally or easily. I was overwhelmed with trying to figure it all out on a cognitive level. Instinctively, I did what I thought I had to do. I went robotic. I allowed others to direct and control me. I still experienced emotions, but only when I was in *my* world, not when in *the* world. I built a wall between the two and it made life simpler for me.

© Susan Golubock

I'll Never Make Eraser Balls

Kimberly Tucker

"What's with the sweater?" Jason asked.

I stared at the oversized clock on the wall, which had roman numerals. I could cheat a little because I could count to where the number should be and write down the correct answer. However, when the assignment called for a number over 12, I was clueless. This is what Jason was supposedly helping me with. It was fifth grade. I was the "calm in the eye." The classroom was the storm.

"You wear that sweater every day. Don't you have any other clothes?"

I nodded. Of course I had other clothes.

"Why don't you talk for cripe's sake? This is great. Just 'cause I'm smart I got to waste my time on a dummy who can't talk or do math and wears sweaters every day in this weather. Its almost summer for cripe's sake!"

I loved my white sweater; so very soft to the touch, like a rabbit. I needed comforting things in this particular classroom. It was the first time I'd ever had a male teacher. He was witty, always making jokes. The kids were understanding his jokes, laughing as if on cue, as if they had scripts. They seemed not only to laugh at his playful kidding, but to enjoy it.

I wished I had canned laughter that I could operate when the others laughed. Or maybe one of those flashing signs overhead—"Laugh!"—that cues the audience on TV: Then at least I'd be prepared. To me, his words were riddles I couldn't solve. Although I sensed he was loved by all the kids, perhaps more than any teacher I'd had thus far, I could not relate. I wanted the teacher I had the year before, the lady with the bun on her head.

In this classroom, I did not understand why suddenly we were to replace ordinary numbers with roman numerals, which were lines, and not symbols at all. I was not Roman. I resisted learning the new replacements and for the first time ever I struggled in school and was given an impatient "tutor" to help teach me math during class.

I liked Jason. He was quiet and serious and produced artwork with a sure placement of lines. He seemed to enjoy drawing and drew well. But no matter how many times he explained roman numerals to me, I did not get it. He became angry with me and belittled my appearance instead.

"She wears that every day for cripe's sake!"

It became necessary to skip school on gym days. The teacher told my mother I must have Mondayitis. Now that the classroom was as stressful as gym class, I had to cut back somewhere to preserve energy. Gym class had to go. Every Monday my mother came to expect a war getting me to go to school.

My teacher knew that we had gym class on Mondays. Why did he not say, "Let's get her out of that awful stressor!"? Instead he made the Mondayitis joke.

It was a playful atmosphere in his classroom that set me more on edge than I normally was at school. I didn't respond to innuendo. Or to learning games...played after moving desks out of their routine arrangement and sitting on the floor in an informal grouping. How did one sit upon a floor, accidentally touching other kids' limbs with feet and with no desk to put one's elbows on?

I probably wore my sweater all year, every day. Tiny buttons and feathery to the touch. He could not take that away from me the way he took my erasers, could he? I needed routine and structure, not informality and spontaneity. The sameness of the sweater kept me from disappearing completely.

I knew he liked a neat classroom so I kept my desk exceptionally in order. If it was crammed with papers and books with torn book covers, I knew it would draw his attention on me. I wanted to blend in as much as I could, to prove I was as normal as anyone else. So as we stood in the lunch line at the side of the room, I could look into the mouths of the desks, and I knew mine was the neatest. Then he made a joke at me.

"Kim, do you really think you're going to make that many mistakes?"

He was pulling his red beard and he had that amused grin. Other kids apparently got the joke because several were already laughing—*oh dear oh dear oh dear oh dear oh dear*—I cocked my head to the side. Should I laugh and pretend I *got* the joke? Or does the joke have meaning and require an answer from me? Does the joke call for some action from me? I just didn't know.

"I think you should take all but one of the erasers home. I'm confident you won't make that many mistakes in my class."

Most of the class was laughing. Did he say *erasers*? So that was it! They were clearly visible from his vantage point, lined up uniformly in the front of my desk: I stacked them three-high and four-high. There was my six-inch eraser I'd gotten from a souvenir shop with "Niagara Falls" painted on the front in black ink. Stacked on the big one were my small rectangular pink ones and one white ink eraser. Propped beside those were my multicolored ones shaped like spacecraft and aliens that I'd gotten from cereal boxes. There were red and green and blue ones too with holes in them so you could top a pencil with them.

More kids laughed. I scooped the alien erasers up and started stuffing them in the pockets of my pants (the ones my mother insisted on calling khakis). I stood there cramming in eraser after eraser. (I'd always liked the movie where Jerry Lewis doesn't speak through the entire picture. He reminded me of myself that day.) I tried to force the six-inch eraser, my favorite, into my bulging pocket but it was not fitting. Fresh laughter from my peers as I shoved and rearranged my pocket and tried to force that big eraser in.

"I think you can put that colossal one in your desk until the end of the day. Just don't forget to bring it home with you today, okay?"

I nodded. I put the big one in the front of the desk and one little pink one directly in the center of it. Frowning, I returned to the line thinking, could he next demand I not wear my sweater?

Pink and so soft, my erasers smelled perfect when I sneaked them to my nose during classroom discussions. They came in so many shapes and sizes. Various colors too, but I liked pink best. Why, I'd just started my collection! I'd have to find a special place at home for them now; perhaps next to the pencil shaving collection…but then I'd not be able to appreciate them in class, which was where I really needed them. Could I one day rub the sides of them smooth until they formed perfectly round and soft pink balls of many sizes? Would they then bounce? Would it be easiest to rub the corners against paper until a sphere took shape? Or rub the corners away on the inside of the desk itself? Would some balls be easier to shape, depending on the brand of eraser? Oh, how I'd planned on cherishing my eraser balls and filling little boxes with them to keep. Forever.

It had always been my plan to rub each of them into tiny balls by smoothing the corners. I'd planned to work on that project with my hands hidden in my desk. Now I'd never get the chance.

How I Acquired the Name

Cry-Over-an-Apple

Coa

I was about 10 when I acquired this name and I have worn it ever since. Before that age I had been a confident if rather odd little girl, totally oblivious to how I was perceived by my peers. Happy and busy with my own projects, on my own or coercing others into them. For example, holidays at the beach would be a strange succession of lots of swims (the exact number and timing each day recorded in my diaries) and teaching myself French from the French books I took with me everywhere. At school, when I wasn't busy standing on my head, or gathering four leaf clovers, I did appear to do social things, but usually this involved organizing other children to take part in my projects. For instance, I wrote a series of plays depicting life in other cultures. I was the writer, the producer, the star actress, the costume-maker, and I was the person who went boldly up to each of the teachers in the school and told them we were coming to perform the play in their classroom. Not exactly a shy or anxious child, I simply but politely told other children (and the teachers) what they would be doing.

My ideas and behavior were generally the sort pleasing to adults. At home, I pestered my mother with the question, when would I be allowed to make my own bed? Once she had answered, "When you're seven." That was fine. I just excitedly marked off the days till my seventh birthday. At school, perhaps because I had decided I was going to be a teacher, I set about doing everything in the classroom as correctly as possible. A model child, the adults would say. (I have since been told that some concern was expressed by teachers about my social skills, but that this was fiercely contested by my mother who was sure that her quaint little darling would grow up just fine).

Then it happened. Rather like for Adam and Eve, the taking of an apple expelled me too from paradise. It was something that must have seemed so trivial to others. I only dimly remember the actual incident itself; it was what followed that overwhelmed me. The group-chant "Cry over an Apple. Cry over an Apple. Cry over an Apple." I can still hear the exact taunting, sneering, jeering, lilting intonation. I can still feel the spot of the big asphalt playground where I sat. I don't know how many children were involved or how long it went on for, but the way I heard and still hear it, is as though it was every child in the school, all the rest of my schooldays. Someone had stolen my apple from my lunchbox and it was when I tried to find it and get it back that things got really

135

confusing. I discovered there was not a single child who would help me or tell me the truth, or understand why I then got so upset about it. How could this be? I'd always been such a good girl. I'd never stolen anything of theirs. I'd always told them the truth. What had I done wrong? Why were they suddenly treating me like an enemy?

And that's when I began to notice I was different. Being good wasn't enough, and having wonderful ideas and projects only caused more problems. There seemed to be other things that went on among children that I just didn't get. And I've been trying very hard to get it ever since.

Back in schooldays, I learnt there were things I would have to hide: my interests, my passions, my ideas, my embarrassing successes. I still remember the spot in the library where I hid, holding my breath, from classmates in case they asked me what I got in my Latin exam and I would have to admit 100% and that would mean more taunting. But it became clear hiding wasn't enough. There seemed to be something else one was supposed to do beyond just hiding things. For instance it seemed strange that another girl who was about as bright as me was one of the most popular girls in the class, and she didn't even have to hide things. So it wasn't brightness that was the problem then. It must be either selfishness, or not trying hard enough, or both. My diaries of my late teens, which I recently rediscovered, record some of these dilemma, together with repeated resolutions to begin life anew, to try even harder to get on with other people, and be less selfish.

To quote my diary (age 17):

19 November: Have just been to choir. Afterwards both ____ and ____ asked me to Coffee Club. I refused and I feel so miserable now. It would have been my chance to come out of myself and I feel I was rude to refuse. Why can't I think clearly at the time? I think I shall become a psychologist—the way to become unselfish is in the suffering of others. Life is passing through my hands, I am getting older and older, and I do nothing to grasp it. From now on I must live every second to the full in love of others and not myself.

then

13 December: The world is such a bustle that everyone is only interested in themselves and to me it is so hard and painful to realize that a little thing like me cannot possibly mean anything to anyone else. What can I do? The only people who notice are those needing help, e.g., mental patients, and the only way one can endure the age is through books or music—this would also help others in my predicament, as say TS Eliot's poetry and Tschaikowsky's Pathetique *console me. I think I will write books and be a humanitarian. How I have wasted these 17 years in the attempt to impress others who couldn't care less. I somehow imagine myself in 60 years' time, an old lady surrounded by fragments of a wasted lifetime. There are, no doubt, other people like this and perhaps I could help them. I do not think I can believe in God—I cannot tell—but I can certainly be glad at being alive to love my neighbor as myself.*

Looking back, I wonder how many of my socially successful peers, swept along by their natural social abilities, did such battle with selfishness? It was shortly after finding and reading these diaries that I attended an international autism conference where a prominent speaker explained that a key feature in distinguishing persons with Asperger Syndrome is their selfishness!

I have made it through another 32 years since I wrote those diary entries. And I am indeed surrounded by fragments of many things, but I think, nothing quite as disastrous as fragments of a wasted lifetime. I still hide things, but I don't hide everything. I have discovered I have wyrd sisters hidden away in obscure parts of this universe, and that it's safe to show some of the hidden treasures to one another and have them actually recognized as the treasures they are. I have also discovered that hidden treasures can be used and drawn on, in solving one's own problems and helping others solve theirs, without having to reveal what one is drawing on. Not that I'm ashamed or embarrassed any more by the things I now know to be treasures, just wary, because I still find most people can't really comprehend the full reality of lives such as ours. I still cry most days, usually when attempts to participate or express myself fail or only result in more misunderstanding. To please a boyfriend, I once tried to use my willpower to force myself to go longer and longer times without crying. But I never made it to a week, and even then I found I had to revert to other ways of relieving the pain instead, such as biting my hand or scraping it on concrete till it bled. So Cry-over-an-Apple I am still, and probably will be till the day I die.

I still don't fit socially, I still have enormous difficulty expressing myself in conversations other than one-to-one, but I don't give myself such a hard time over it as I used to. As my children will testify, I am often to be found of an evening, pacing up and down the corridor, muttering, "How embarrassing," or, "How stupid," over and over again, as I go over my social fumblings of the day. But once that's out of my system I'm ready to get busy again with new ideas for the next day.

I've also discovered some of the advantages of silence. In particular, when I gave up trying to find a way to slip my words into conversations, I found it was easier to listen well, easier to hear the whole, and to hear it from the other person's viewpoint. And this has grown into an art that proves very useful in my work. I've even found, to my surprise, people saying things like, "This is the first time I've felt really understood."

So I guess there is room for optimism after all.

© Coa Jonassen

Scenes from a Perverse Girlhood

Jean Kearns Miller

I tell everyone to call me Runt.
Runt of the litter.
Can anyone be so timid,
so angry
at the same time?
Just watch me.
What curse is this to be
unable to
disobey?
I'm a teenagergoddamit!
I cannot act up.
I cannot act out.
I cannot act.
I say to myself,
"Runt, you are a
political prisoner,
conscientious objector,
under house arrest.
They lock people up for that."
Runt answers,
"I'm locked up
already."
Mult'ille et terris jactatus et alto.
Tossed about much on land and sea.
Aeneas in school uniform.
No one understands
my anger.
"What's the matter with you?!"
(my sister)
"You're the most
uncharming person
I know!"
I know.
But it's the injustice that
rubs me raw.
I don't suffer fools.
I don't suffer fools.

I keep telling them
But no.
But no.
Brutal injury to me
deeper than flesh
Because no one *thinks*!
Is it so hard?
Would it kill you?
Musa, mihi causas memora…
Muse, recall for me the reasons.
I drop my cafeteria tray and scald
my arm.
School nurse bandages.
and the schoolgirls say,
"What happened?"
"To your arm?"
I say,
"I tried to commit suicide
but they caught me
just in time."
I think they are staring
at me
but I haven't mastered eye contact yet.
I do know
there is no laughter.
No one ever
gets my jokes.

© Jean Kearns Miller

How I Came to Understand
The Neurotypical World

Daina Krumins

As a child, until I was perhaps 13 or 14, I simply accepted that I was different from most people in some way and didn't worry too much about it. My inner world of textures and imagination was fascinating and satisfying and my father was a willing assistant in developing this world, partly because his own inner world was similar. My mother was frustrated that she couldn't get me to play with dolls or be interested in makeup, but she enjoyed my creativity and was proud of it. I was always doing something original and fun and this charmed adults and interested other children, who would play with me as long as what I was doing was fun.

When I was about 13 or 14 things changed, rapidly and traumatically.

My grandmother, a tough-minded Russian woman who had had a horrible childhood in Moscow as a child laborer in a candy factory, came to stay with my family for a while in the woods in the summer. She had never liked my father and she had a dirty mind. She had noticed that every other day or so, my father and I would go walking in the woods and she started imagining things. She told my father that going away with his 13 year-old daughter, who was becoming a woman, was not appropriate. What would other people say? What would they think?

Of course, being a man, my father had perhaps noticed that my body was becoming womanly and felt a little uneasy about this, as fathers do. However, he knew how important the forest was to me and he also knew that neither he nor I would ever, ever, ever do anything improper, so at first he shrugged my grandma's ideas off. Soon, however, because of what my grandma had said to him, he became more and more self-conscious about the situation, and stopped going for walks with me. Suddenly, my helper and assistant was gone.

My grandma had assumed, as many people might, that I should be going around with my own friends, start wearing makeup, and start thinking about boys. What she didn't know was that these things were denied to me because my mind simply didn't produce the effects that are necessary to make these things meaningful. She also didn't know (how could she?) that the main point to going into the forest with my father was the *forest*, not my father.

Now, I had to go to the forest alone, and I did, for miles and miles. I knew that if I told my parents or anyone what I was doing, they would watch me more closely (for a time, anyway), so I lied. I always had some other explanation of where I was, being careful to make it plausible: "I was trying to catch turtles at the lake, but they kept coming up in different places from where I thought and I finally gave up after three hours." Actually, I could catch a turtle in ten minutes if I wished, since I knew their behavior, but my parents didn't know that.

Was I frightened going into the woods alone? Yes, but where else could I go? Where could I feel at ease, and loved? I knew that people loved me, but when I was alone in the woods, I could *feel* that. The tension of being with people, of having to figure out the right thing to say and do, would obliterate that feeling.

This is how I began to understand the neurotypical world.

One summer, maybe when I was 13, I was sent to a Latvian summer camp in the Catskills. The other girls hated me, except for the two that enjoyed having rowboat races with me when no one else was watching. All of the activities there, the sports were useless to me. On the other hand, there was a forest all around. I would go hunting for bracket fungus, the kind you can draw pictures on, and I finally had a whole collection drying behind one of the cabins. I would have liked to play chess with the older boys but that was not permitted because I could beat most of them. Out of boredom I decided to try to study some insects, so I borrowed a jar from the kitchen and went hunting for them in the woods.

Every morning at seven o'clock we had to go to a religious service around a Latvian flag before going to breakfast. I decided to bring my insect collecting jar with me and while the religious and nationalistic blah-blah was going on while we were standing at attention, I put the jar down on the ground by my feet. Nothing happened at that time but after my parents brought me home from the camp my mother told me in private that the pastor had had a long talk with her and had told her that I was an inherently bad person. I asked my mom why he had said that, and she said it was because of the jar on the ground during the morning ritual around the flag. Looking back, it was probably the bored expression on my face as well, but I didn't know that then.

Just recently I saw a program on PBS about a pride of lions and there was one lion who was not accepted into the group. The narrator said that no one knew why the one lion was not accepted and said that perhaps it was a cub killer. But he was missing the point. The lions sensed that this one lion was neurologically different and if it had been neurologically the same, they would have accepted it, even if it were a cub killer. The narrator thought that the rejection was logical and moral but I'm sure that it was not.

As my teenage years unfolded, I was increasingly isolated and depressed. I also knew that most people would be against me because it was their nature to be against me, so I decided that I had to become smart and sophisticated to compensate, just to survive. I embarked on a massive reading project; adult books, as sophisticated as possible. I read my way through Steinbeck, Dostoevsky, Dos Passos, Dreiser, Jean Genet (a favorite), Proust, Becket,

Virginia Woolf, as well as Mary McCarthy and anything else sexual I could lay my hands on.

Looking back, I wonder what effect this literary self-education had on my work at school. My comments in English and history class must have been quite different from the other students, although I don't remember anything specific.

I also realized that I would have to be very, very perfect in my manners and behavior. Normal people have an inherent desire to abuse people who are different, and any imperfection that I revealed would give them a stick to hit me with. This is a heavy burden for a teenager. To make it easier on myself, I stayed away from social occasions as much as possible.

One summer my parents and some of their Latvian friends had gathered near our cabin in the woods to celebrate *Jani*, the summer solstice. However, it was raining and I had cramps and was sitting under the gazebo reading Jean Genet. One of my uncle's friends, an artist, came up to me, very angry, and said I was not behaving properly for Jani. He said I should be laughing and gathering flowers and making wreaths and drinking wine like a real Latvian young woman. I'm sure I must have looked at him with a blank expression and said something like, "In the rain?"

As a child I had enjoyed wearing jewelry but as a teenager I stopped because I saw that jewelry was actually a costume for the social play. If I wore it, it would make me feel that I should now be part of that play and since that could never work, it made me sad. I stopped wearing it.

Two events stand out from high school. I enjoyed chemistry class because I had, and still have, a relationship with the physical world. I enjoy the way my senses present *the* world, or *a* world, to me. I enjoy bubbles, explosions, textures, shapes, colors, and all of their permutations. During the theoretical part of chemistry class I was a normal student, but when we did experiments, I would be happy and I would laugh in delight sometimes when the bubbles would fizz through the liquid. One day I was called to the chemistry teacher's class after school and she told me that I was immature and I should not behave that way in class.

This baffled me. If I was immature (whatever that meant), what could I do about it? It was like saying, "You are bad because you have big feet." On the other hand, I realized that my enjoyment of the physical world, my private relationship with it, was considered evil by many people, the chemistry teacher included. I learned not to laugh, not to have any expression at all. Perhaps this is one reason why autistics are thought to have no emotions: they have had bad experiences when they have revealed their emotions and have learned not to.

The other event at high school was something that enhanced my understanding of the social world. Being an artist, I was invited to help paint the prom decorations and I enjoyed this very much. Some kids were supposed to tell me that there was a planning meeting one morning and that if I didn't go, I wouldn't be allowed to help put up the decorations. They didn't. I accepted that as normal behavior. (I expected no less.) But the teacher should have known that the other kids could not be trusted to tell me this, but maybe she just didn't. Anyway, I was not permitted to take the day off to help put up the decorations. OK, I guess. But after school that day, I wanted just to peek a little to see what they looked like, but the other kids wouldn't let me into the gym, saying, "You can see them at the prom." Of course, I wasn't going to the prom, so I never saw the decorations properly displayed, which was all I really wanted.

Despite what the chemistry teacher said, in some ways I was actually an adult by the time I was 15, because by then I had removed myself from emotional dependence on other people, parents included. I had learned some hard lessons about society and I knew that I would have to find my own way, from scratch.

© Daina Krumins

Adolescence:

The Beginning of the End

April Masilamani

I can remember the day childhood died for me, I still don't know why it happened and can only assume that it was a normal part of the development process that I didn't see coming. I came home from school one day and prepared for my usual frenzy of play, and it didn't work. Nothing felt right, and I rushed from one thing to another, toys, hobbyhorse, hut, and then the boys I played with, to organize one of my games, but that was it. The magic was gone. I had somehow been abandoned, left behind, as though childhood had continued without me and left me waiting at the station. I was shut out of this realm forever. This was devastating for me. I wanted to die, and felt very scared because these games helped me shut out everything else and I felt very threatened by the now very present, outside world. I almost feel I would have tried to kill myself if I had had any concept of suicide. However I soon resigned myself to living in this gray, without magic and with very little purpose. I still played my games and acted normal (my normal), as I had no idea what else to do. This was in form one, between the ages of 11 and 12. I still played cowboys and Indians with the boys, and painted the usual war paint on myself. I even painted circles of paint round my budding breasts. This drew me to the attention of the neighbors and I got in to trouble with my parents when they were told (God knows why they didn't notice themselves) I was apparently embarrassing everyone. I felt quite ashamed and angry at this trouble. It's as if others' dirty thoughts can sully you.

My physical development was also a shock. Although I had been given a talk by my mother, it was an explanation from a medical text book and I could talk knowledgeably about progesterone and such, but had made no connection between that information and what was happening to my body. And while I felt scared when I went to the toilet, it was a case of out of sight out of mind and I just stuffed my pants under my bed, and forgot about it. The hunt for the missing undies resulted in my discovery, and my mother was most surprised I hadn't told her and that I seemed to not understand what was happening. I remember sitting in a tree hating all men and boys because they didn't have to have this horribly invasive experience. I remember calculating how many periods I would have to endure for no reason, as most women have so few children for the number of years of menstruation they endure.

I cursed God a lot to. We had very Christian neighbors who often tried to civilize us and they had told me that God was responsible for everything, so it was his bloody fault. I was also always afraid of "his all-seeing eye" they had told me about. You can imagine what that sort of imagery does to an Aspergic child. I could imagine this enormous eye wrapped round the world and I never felt comfortable picking my nose in the toilet because he would be watching. I would often poke my tongue out at him in defiance, but later rationalized that he couldn't possibly watch me all the time as I was so boring. We were taken to church by these neighbors for a while. I would get up and dress my sister exactly like me (which she hated and I loved), but when I drew the Red Sea red and got told off for being silly (too literal) and then got into more trouble for arguing that the teacher was stupid for calling it the Red Sea if it wasn't (which really shocked the other children), I then felt angry with the whole institution and I never went back.

One thing I found puzzling about children was that when I had finally upset a teacher so much that she walked out of class, the children as a group would often turn on me and be very angry with how mean I had been. And yet although I had no real affinity with most children, I thought it was at least clear that the adults were another controlling subgroup that we as children wouldn't support, or protect. I cannot recall at all what I did to upset the teachers so much, but if my son's behavior is anything to go by then I feel sorry for them now.

I enjoyed intermediate school more. It was small and we were given more respect by the adults, more autonomy. But my anxiety levels and neurotic thoughts started in earnest then. I was very worried, to the point of being sick, by almost everything, but most of all by having to engage in conversation with anyone and I always felt I was being watched or looked at. Also my headaches became worse: they were migraines and affected my vision and lasted for two days in which I could only lie in a darkened room. They have abated in ferocity over the last ten years (better pain killers), although I still get them and I often get common headaches. I was still always reading to shut people out. I became very self-conscious, which was a shame as I had always just lived in a body that I gave no thought to, that just did what I wanted, and I enjoyed that very much. But body image was something that was on everyone else's minds, apparently, and boys started making comments about our breasts or faces. The biggest shock I got was when a group of girls in the library period started talking about who was the prettiest girl. It was a surprise for me to hear that, and to try to figure out how any one could notice what any one really looked like, let alone then judge a degree of looking. I remember trying to analyze this alarming new information, when one of the girls said, "Well I think April's one of the pretty ones." This was an even greater shock; it felt like a physical blow, as I had no idea that people could see me, which sounds really stupid but I guess I just didn't process people well and thought that I was also invisible, or of no consequence.

This, then, led to speculation (by me) as to how I really looked and I couldn't wait to bike home and check. When I looked in the bathroom mirror I was shocked that I was a blond girl, and not the dark-haired boy of my own real world. I was also not generally very impressed with what I saw and it was the beginning of a lot of anxiety I developed when people looked at me, which I can still only stand if I don't think about it.

I find it hard to recognize myself in a mirror if I'm not expecting to see myself, and will often think, "what's she staring at?" If I really look at myself and it's not just a grooming exercise, I end up pressed up against the mirror staring into my own eyes trying to see who is in there—nobody, I think. Anyway, I got myself a duffel coat (which, along with corduroy trousers, has to be part of the Aspergic uniform), and wore that all the time both summer and winter. In summer I would just wear my undies and sandals underneath to cope with the heat of it but it made me feel very safe and hidden.

Coming of Age

Susan Golubock

My parents decided it was time for me to become more independent. That meant going away to college. This was traumatic to put it mildly. On the drive to the campus I had an out of body experience, I was that terrified. I had no choice but to learn to live in the world on my own. I dove into college life as if it were a course unto itself, a course I desperately needed to learn. I resumed my delusion that if I just did what everyone else did, I'd figure out the mysteries behind why they did it. So, I joined: clubs, committees, even a sorority. I had to know how people thought, why they thought the way they did. That was especially true about women. After all, I was one, but had no idea what that meant in terms of what was expected of me. I earned several honors by the time I finished college for all the joining I did, and my social skills and independence definitely improved, but I was still clueless as to why I was doing all of this. It was what was expected and what everyone else did, so I did it too.

Socially, I learned to attend dances and to sing and work within a group. I even was convinced by my roommates to date. These dates were mostly disasters and were rarely repeated. I remember once, though, accepting a number of dates from a young man I liked because he was nice and would make me laugh. Then he invited me home to meet his parents. I thought nothing of it and accepted. It didn't occur to me that this had some significance. When he started talking about the idea of marriage, it suddenly dawned on me the direction I had let this dating take. That was the end of that relationship.

Academically, I did well. But it wasn't easy. I took a remedial reading class in my freshman year, which turned out to be a speed-reading class. I was processing words one at a time when I read and still had difficulties understanding the meaning behind them. Speed-reading helped me scan text to get the big picture of what I was reading. Then I could commence deciphering the individual abstract words whose meaning eluded me. My most challenging classes were the physical education classes. My body awareness, and thus control over my movements, left something to be desired. I chose social dancing, gymnastics, and bowling. Gymnastics was the best, and hardest, class I took. I worked exceedingly hard at it. I never did succeed in doing a headstand, but I finally achieved the wondrous feeling of leaving gravity behind as I did a no-hands flip. I felt for the first time what it was to have control over my own body. I liked that feeling.

I crashed regularly throughout college. Reaching a state of overload, which resulted in an intense emotional meltdown, followed by extreme fatigue, was a pattern that repeated itself often. During my earlier encephalitis, I received regular injections of B12 and other B vitamins. I continued to receive them "as needed" for years afterwards. "As needed" turned out to be pretty much once a month. They are what kept me going throughout college. Even after I eventually stopped the injections, the crashes continued. I didn't understand them. I just accepted their presence in my life. My attempt to control everything by responding robotically wasn't working so well any more.

Cracks were starting to develop in the walls I had built.

In between the crashes, I was at least learning what I had set out to learn (or so I thought). I had learned as a child that asking others for answers to what I did not understand was futile. I now realize that not asking meant I was not getting the feedback I needed in order to learn. I knew that people thought things about me, because I would hear them talk about what they thought about others. It was not polite, however, for them to say what they thought about you *to you*. I hated politeness. It meant denying me the honest answers I needed to learn about myself. I had one professor, though, who, I think out of frustration, dared to break this social rule. I don't recall what we were discussing, but after who knows how long (my poor sense of time), he suddenly blurted out at me, "Why don't you ever look at people when you are talking to them?!" I was taken aback. It never occurred to me to do so, nor did I realize that I wasn't. I accepted this honest feedback, however, and set out to learn to give eye contact. I didn't realize how hard that would be.

When I looked at a person's face, the light reflecting off it made it painful. Gradually I learned to train my eyes to focus on a select spot on the face, initially the mouth (since it sometimes helped me interpret what they were saying) and later the right eye. To look at their face as a whole made me dizzy. The body and facial movements were too much for me to process. Better to pick one spot and focus only on that. The problem was, to do that required effort on my part. The extra effort plus the added visual input were distracting, so my understanding of what they were saying dropped even more. My husband will testify to the fact that I do not multi-task. I can listen or look, talk or do, but not both at the same time. To compensate for my decreased auditory processing as I visually focused on people's faces, I learned to nod, smile or frown to make it appear I was listening. Sometimes, I would become aware that my response was the wrong one. But for the most part, people didn't seem to notice. It just kept them talking. Later, I learned from watching a friend how asking questions kept conversations going. I would catch a few key words and form it into a question. I was learning the give and take in a conversation, or so I thought. I often wondered, though, why no one ever asked me to talk. Didn't matter. It was too hard to shift gears from listening to talking anyway. Years later I tried teaching myself to lip-read in a desperate attempt to follow people's conversations in noisy environments. When the stress became too much, I would excuse myself to use the bathroom. I learned early that the bathroom is the one place where I get to be alone and need not be afraid of my space being invaded. The car has become the other respite place in my life. For all my social skills learning, I still had no clue why it was so important that I learn all of this. I simply knew that I had to in order to survive in a world that expected it of me.

During my junior year, I decided that I needed to know more about the world outside of the college campus. I saw a sign advertising a two-month humanities seminar to India and Japan that summer. I marched into the office sponsoring the seminar and announced that I wanted to go. I was learning very well how to get others to teach me what I needed to know, by joining and letting them tell me what to do. It was during that trip I met my husband.

There was something special about him that attracted my attention. He had a quiet sensitivity that I felt, in some way, matched my own. We've discovered over our 33 years together that we balance each other in many ways. Our strengths and limitations are quite opposite, but we both have a strong desire to respect and understand and learn from each other. I decided it was time to put a drawbridge in the wall to my emotions in order to work on this relationship. I had just come back from experiencing the world. Now I was taking on a relationship. The crash that followed this time put me in the hospital. Change was not easy for me.

I had decided on my course of study before going to college. In high school, we had a future teachers and a future nurses club. For women those were the choices. My instincts told me there was no way that I could handle a room full of children in order to teach. I also knew that handling bodily fluids went far beyond what my sensitivities would allow. A neighbor who was a nurse brought over pamphlets on physical and occupational therapy for me to consider. A physical therapist meant touching people, so that was out. Ah, but occupational therapy appealed to me. I could teach, but on a 1:1 basis, without a lot of physical contact. Plus, I would be in a non-messy medical field where I could learn more about the brain, which fascinated me.

For a long time, I got past the social aspects of work by keeping my mouth shut and a low profile. I focused on my work. I developed competency. I stayed one step ahead of everyone else. I earned respect for what I could do. Socially, I was considered "sweet" and "nice," period. Those were the only descriptions anyone ever had for me. I had so succeeded in hiding the person I was in *my own* world and performing the role expected of me in *the* world, that I guess this was all there was to observe about me. It never bothered me until I overheard someone say that I had no personality. I decided I wanted a personality. I looked around and decided that people who had a personality often spoke out. They said what was on their mind. So I started saying what was on my mind. I let a little of that inner self out. The Christmas of my second year of working, I received a mug from my "Secret Santa" that said: "Bitch, Bitch, Bitch." I went back to being nice. The inner self went back to hiding.

I think my *character* started in college, at least the social one. The professional one developed over the years of working. I suppose they both were an outgrowth of the robotic character I used in my younger days to survive. Only, these were more specific. The professional character knew all I needed to know to do my job. The social character learned the skills needed to meet the social expectations of, well, being a couple and having friends. My characters did not develop consciously. It was simply a matter of survival. To compensate for what did not come easily or automatically for me (understanding words and social situations), I had to figure things out on a thinking level. There is only so much one can think about at a time without becoming overwhelmed! It's amazing what the brain will do when stressed enough. I now had inner *selves* that no one wanted to see and outer *characters* to play the roles the world seemed to value. My walls were becoming much more complex. My sense of self was becoming much more remote. The drawbridge to my inner emotions was less creaky as I opened it more often within the safety of my relationship with my husband, but it still sprang shut very quickly and tightly when needed. The world had not become any less confusing.

In hindsight, it is not surprising that I followed the career path I did. I quickly gravitated toward work with children, and ended up working in a school system where I continue to learn what I missed years ago. I also developed a fascination with the theories of sensory integration that helped me to understand and explain the way in which a differently wired brain like my own processes information. Over the years I have tried vitamins, gluten-and milk-free diets, Feingold and yeast-free diets, auditory training, visual training, light therapy, homeopathy, Feldenkrais, and various forms of alternative medicine, all of which helped in their own way to make life for me a little easier. I never stopped looking. I wasn't really looking for *self* anymore. I had pretty much given up on trying to understand others. I was just tired of working so hard.

I realize now that I was instinctively seeking relief from the internal as well as external stresses of trying to overcompensate for a nervous system I did not understand any better than the world in which I needed it to function.

Work took all of my energies. Before falling asleep at night I would picture all that I expected to happen the next day. I would practice words that I would need to say to people to do my job. I would create plans A, B, and C for how I would react if things didn't go the way I expected they would so that I wouldn't panic and fall apart. I had no other interests or focus. I worked hard to develop the language skills I have now. I was fortunate to be married to someone with excellent language and social skills. I had to be careful, though, to not be too obvious in mimicking him. He wanted me to be my own person, only I didn't know how.

© Susan Golubock

Turning Thirty

C. J.

Turning thirty I did this year
For some you say "What's to cheer?"
For you it appears a hard thing
To hear the celebrations ring
To be no longer classed as twenty
For me the advantages are plenty
People always said it would be bad
For me it was as if I had
Been asleep all this past time
To finally awaken and find
That I am just as important as me
That I am valued as I be
That I have knowledge I can share
This is not a burden to bear
This is a path I chose to accept
A road on which I have taken the first step
It will not be a secret to be locked away
I am proud to be and say
I am me and I am glad
There is no need for pity or sad
I know the road may still be long
There will be times when I am not so strong
But that is OK because what I know
Is as I travel I learn as I go
Each day will bring something new
Some piece of knowledge I never knew
So what this life has yet to bring
Seems no longer such a scary thing.

© C. J. Smith

Close Encounters

Growing up Genderless

Jane Meyerding

Autistics often describe themselves (or their experience of life) as feeling alien, not of the same species as the humans around them. For me, part of that reality has been an inability to identify with other women. I can (and often do) feel solidarity with women in relation to political, social, and economic institutions and the sexist bias they impart to women's lives. My intellect makes me a feminist. But my gut, my feelings, my self-awareness remain stubbornly and radically un-gendered—at least in the terms of the culture that surrounds me.

When I say I don't feel like a woman, people are likely to assume that I mean I feel like a man. I don't. Never have. Nor do I feel alienated by my body, its female shape, its female cycles. When I began to explore feminism, and then lesbian feminism, in the early 1970s, I thought that I had found the answer to my then unspoken questions. It was the female role, the political-cultural Woman stereotype, against which I continually felt myself alien. Among lesbian-feminists I would feel at home, I assumed, because part of the lesbian-feminist project was to reject that stereotype in favor of a liberated and self-determined identity. Other lesbian feminists would escape from the confining shell of culturally prescribed femininity, and we would all be individuals together. These newly free lesbian women would not necessarily be like me, but they would be as different as I was (in their own ways) from the species called Woman.

Surprise, surprise: it didn't work out that way. I spent 20 years on the project of being an ordinary lesbian, of seeing myself as part of a group in which my ways of apprehending and interacting with the world were within spitting distance of the norm, and then I gave up. No doubt my effort was doomed to failure because it was based on a category mistake. The difference between me and Woman was not caused by either of the factors that drew many women into lesbian-feminism in the 1970s: sexual orientation and political analysis (or philosophical beliefs stated in political terms). Although feminist analysis did a fine job in helping me understand women's place in the world, and although lesbian-feminism enabled me (and many other women) to imagine many changes in how women might envision and work towards changes in society, none of it had any reference to me as-me. None of it explained why I felt as distant (and different) from my *sisters* as I had been before the sisterhood began.

This distance was not on the plane of intellect. Nor was it the *human condition* kind of angst. I have that, too, at times, the *essential loneliness* kind of thing. The "nobody understands or appreciates me" days. The "nobody has ever felt this before" despairs and euphorias.

That's not it. What I'm talking about is more like language. It is very, very daily.

Little girls—and bigger girls—are supposed to chatter and giggle and gossip and share secrets and have *best* friends and so on. Much of what they do together is preparation for later, when they reach the age for dating, school dances, and romance. The way they play together is partially a rehearsal for their teen years and beyond, just as other young mammals from social species (e.g., lions) play together in ways that help them develop the skills they will rely upon as adults. Little girls at play are practicing the social skills they pick up automatically from the children and adults around them, skills they will rely upon to form alliances, gain favor, avoid censure (and rejection), keep informed of important news within their social group, attract friends (and a mate), and present themselves to the various facets of the social world in the best possible light. They have fun, and they learn how to negotiate with sensitivity the relationships they establish or that are imposed upon them by circumstance—by school, by family, by community, and, eventually, by the workplace.

I didn't do that. My wiring (the neurological configuration of crucial parts of my brain) didn't let me.

For example, I was enrolled in a Girl Scout Camp one summer when I was about eight. I was a cheerful child from a loving home, and I generally expected the best from everyone. Going to camp every day in a nearby county park was fine with me, and I looked forward eagerly to the one night at the end of the term when, instead of going home at the end of the day, we would be camping out in tents overnight. (My family camped in a tent on vacations, so the idea was not new to me.) Every day I participated in whatever activities the staff had programmed. I learned (with greater difficulty than most) to braid a four-strand lanyard. I helped write a little song for my group (Bluebirds) to sing. I went where I was told, did what I was told to do, never objected or fussed. As far as I remember, it was only on the final night, inside the tent with the other Bluebirds, that I became aware of something odd.

The other girls had become friends with one another. Alone there, with no adult present to direct us, they chatted and whispered and laughed and interacted with seamless ease. How did they know what to say? They weren't talking about anything, and yet they talked constantly. My conversation was limited to specific subjects, not including anything as nebulous as girltalk or smalltalk. Moreover, they seemed to know each other in a way they didn't know me—and I certainly didn't know them. I had been with them as much during the summer as they had been with each other. I had done everything they had done (as far as I could tell). And yet I was a stranger there. The only stranger in the tent. I realize now that one or more of the other little girls in that tent may not have been happy and socially successful. But all of them knew how to put on the act. They may have felt lonely. They may have felt inadequate. But they knew—even at eight years old—how to behave in a social situation. They could, and did, interact successfully, no matter what uncertainties may have lurked within. They knew how to be little girls together, whereas I had no idea what to do at all. I was frozen and silent not because I was shy or scared but because I literally had no idea what words to say, no idea how to move or when to move. It was as if everyone else had studied a script and learned their parts beforehand. In fact, of course, they were improvising brilliantly, thanks to the social code capacity programmed into their brains and to the natural ease with which they acquired their gender identity from the culture around them.

Now (post-diagnosis, post-self-education about autism) I can explain my childhood predicament this way: Normal people live in a social world full of doors and windows. When they meet a person, they immediately perceive ways to reach and be reached. They recognize the psychological door, automatically opened by the stranger, through which they can enter into a conversation. When they look at the other person's face, they are looking through a window that shows them a wealth of information (conveyed through expression, gesture, manner of speaking) they can use as a basis on which to build a connection. They can send signals through their own windows, they can open their own doors, and invite the stranger to engage in the type of relationship they prefer: acquaintance, friend, colleague, rival, superior, inferior, comrade or enemy. Non-autistic men and women share this basic operating system, but women and girls are expected to be *better* at it, to live with doors and windows wider open (i.e., with greater sensitivity) to the breeze of social interaction.

Those doors and windows do not exist in the world of an autistic child. Only with enormous effort are some of us able as adults to train ourselves (like "anthropologists on Mars," to use Temple Grandin's term) to read some portion of the enormous spectrum of non-verbal language normal people take for granted. Some AS women, under the pressure of social gender expectations, begin to learn some of this hidden language even before they are adults. But I didn't.

That is one reason why, like many AS children, I preferred to relate primarily to adults. With adults—if they were willing to treat me with respect— I could keep conversations substantive. Children are not expected to read adults to the same extent as is expected between children (or between adults), so I was not constantly sabotaged by my inability to respond to signals I could not see. This was not true, of course, if I was forced to interact with immature adults who, without realizing it, were trying to fulfill their own emotional needs in relationships with children. I had some very unpleasant experiences with teachers who couldn't accept my assumption of intellectual (and moral) parity with them because their self-esteem depended on having children act out a subservient role. With mentally and emotionally healthy adults, however, I got along just fine.

My classmates in third grade played a game I didn't understand. It involved the girls running away from the boys. I could see that, but I didn't understand why, nor could I figure out the rules. When I tried to join in by imitating, it didn't work. I didn't know how to shriek properly, nor did I want to (it hurt my ears), but I considered myself pretty good at running. The trouble was that nobody chased me. It was a relief when I fell down a hill and cut my legs all up. That accident, and the subsequent discovery that I was allergic to the antiseptic the nurse applied, gave me an excuse to give up that game. I often thought back to it in later years, however, whenever all the girls and boys around me became engaged in some mysterious interaction I couldn't understand. The consistent element (besides my lack of comprehension) that reminded me of my third grade failure was that nobody ever chased me. Whatever the chancing analogue might be at any given time, I was exempted from it by a silently arrived at but universal consensus among my age peers. They tended to detour around me as if I were a tree or a boulder in their midst. Apparently I was as alien to them as they were to me, probably because I was a dead zone in terms of social signals. I neither responded to the non-verbal signals they were sending out nor initiated any of my own.

Life proceeded more or less placidly for me until seventh grade. I had two older sisters who took turns playing with me. They created games and gave me explicit instructions about the role I was to play. When they were otherwise occupied, I enjoyed myself alone. There were occasional opportunities for me to play with some other child several years younger than I was, and I usually enjoyed it. Once, I remember, I strained a neighbor child's manners to the breaking point by insisting that we imitate the ducks in a children's book. I knew the book by heart and wanted to recite it as we repeated—again and again and again—the motions I considered the nearest possible equivalent of the way the ducks tipped their front ends down into the water to feed. My friend was patient for a while, but I am sure she thought such behavior (sticking our bottoms up into the breeze on the parking strip at the intersection of two streets) was beneath the dignity of a 10 year old.

In fifth grade I had a friend who lived across the street. She invited me over occasionally when there was nobody else around for her to play with. I responded with my usual malleability (and lack of initiative) and was happy to spend time under her direction—until I discovered one day that she was cheating at Monopoly. This was incomprehensible to me. I was shocked and alarmed. Confused. And I didn't want to be with her anymore.

Fifth grade also provided my first memory of being adopted, a pattern that would recur occasionally throughout my life. I suspect this is something that is more likely to occur for AS girls than AS boys, but I'm not sure. Generally, I had one *friend* in each class throughout my school years. Whichever other girl in the class was not accepted by the others would end up sitting with me during lunch. She usually had some obvious factor (e.g., she was fat) that made her unacceptable, and it never occurred to me to wonder what it was about me (who seemed to lack all the usual attributes so vigorously rejected by my age peers) that *lowered* me to my accidental friend's level. I was cute as a child; all the adults told me so, and photographs from that period confirm their assessment. Whatever was *wrong* with me, it wasn't physical in any ordinary sense.

The fifth grade class into which I was injected by family circumstance turned out to be divided by a factor new to my educational experience. Half the kids in the class were white and half were black. The two halves sat in the same classrooms but they separated immediately and decisively at recess. Although there could be no doubt about which half I belonged to by ethnicity or ancestry, my white classmates shunned me as unanimously as I had come to expect from all my age peers. The amazing difference was that the black girls took me under their collective wing. "Come on, Jane," one would say to me as the group dispersed for recess. "We don't want to play with those white girls." They didn't even seem to hold it against me that I was lousy at kickball.

There have been times, just now and then, during my life when this scenario has recurred in one form or another. Here's my theory: It's always possible to hope for kindness from people who know what it's like to be treated very badly. It would be unwise to expect this kindness. But experience has taught me to hope.

Seventh grade was the point at which I realized the other children in my class were making fun of me. I had stopped trying to participate in my age peers' games by that time. Nor had I ever found anyone my own age who wanted to share my interests with me. I was preoccupied then by the nuclear arms race and had developed expertise in patterns of fallout, and associated rates of death to be expected from the explosion of nuclear devices of various sizes at various heights over thickly or sparsely populated areas. My other main interest was World War I, to be followed in later years by intense interest in the Russian Revolution, World War II, the Chinese Revolution, and the war in Indochina. (Korea got left out somehow.) At home, I spent hours with a big book full of color plates tracing the history of art from early religious paintings to Robert Wood Grant and also enjoyed reading Shakespeare. I was profoundly concerned about the fact that the United States had dropped nuclear bombs on Hiroshima and Nagasaki, and I had read extensively about the horrors endured by the survivors. And yet I remained a happy child, secure in the love of my family and liking nothing better than going off by myself to the nearest dump to dig through the filthy refuse in search of treasure. My mother was very patient about the finds I lugged home.

In seventh grade, the divide between my precocious intellectual age and my retarded social age finally got too much for my peers to suffer in silence. Either

161

that or I finally became able to read my peers enough to recognize abuse that, for all I know, may have been going on for some time. Class was the part of school I liked: orderly, dependable, usually a *real* subject, therefore adult-oriented. There had been a few problems over the years when a particular teacher's teaching style conflicted with my learning style or turned my slight (undiagnosed) learning disability into a stumbling block. But generally speaking I had gotten along fine academically. It all went to hell in seventh grade, a combination of too many teachers (some of them unequal to the challenge of my difference) and my peers' determination to let me know their opinion of a goody two-shoes like me. It must have been especially provoking for them to encounter a stuck up know-it-all (I thought I was *supposed* to know it all, to respond fully to the teacher at every opportunity) who was socially so far behind. And the incident that finally caused them to turn on me decisively enough to break through my general lack of contact with them was—no surprise—my failure to react appropriately to gender cues.

I'd never interacted with my classmates much. Unless someone took me under her wing and led me around, I watched from the sidelines. It had never bothered me (probably because it never occurred to me) that I didn't get to know my peers well enough to tell them apart to any marked degree. (*Prosopagnosia*, "faceblindness," is common among autistics, but, although I am prosopagnostic, I never heard of it until I was in my late 40s.) Then one day a teacher had us play a game in class. The game involved two teams and I was assigned to one of them. The other students seemed enthusiastic about the game, but I was totally lost. Later, I realized that we must have been playing a version of a game they had seen on television. My own television viewing was limited (compared to theirs), and I had no clue about what was going on. Suddenly I was paired with a boy on my team, and I was supposed to guess a word based on a one-word clue from him. His clue was *neat*. I repeated it: "Neat?" "Not the way *you* say it," he shot back with disgust.

The word I was supposed to guess on the basis of his clue was *fun*. At that point in my life, and for several years afterwards, I had no slang at all. *Neat* was a synonym for *tidy*, period. My brain had zero capacity for picking up the kid slang around me, and I often had no idea what my peers were saying to one another. In my speech, I fit the AS *little professor* stereotype.

Several girls in my class took it upon themselves to explain to me exactly what I had done. That boy I was paired with had *liked* me, they said. Apparently his being my partner in the game had not been random or teacher-controlled. He had been doing the seventh grade equivalent of flirting (do seventh graders flirt?), and I had snubbed and embarrassed him by responding with such incredible and snooty stupidity. This description of the incident surprised me greatly, and I examined the boy with interest next time I saw him. He had never drawn my attention before, and I had not differentiated him from any of the others. From that day on, he never spoke to me. I don't remember after all this time whether he joined with the others in teasing me for my continuing lack of comprehension and my unfeminine aloofness. (I didn't actually hear that word *aloof* applied to myself until a year later. After that, it came up frequently and always to my surprise. I never felt aloof; in fact, I always knew myself to be a friendly sort of person. But nobody else ever saw me as I felt myself to be.) I didn't have time or energy to worry much about my classmates. In any case. I was much too busy feeling mauled and confused by my teachers. At the end of my seventh grade year, I told my mother I wasn't going to go to school anymore.

I spent the rest of my secondary education at a small private school for girls. It was a modest establishment "under the care of" the Friends' (Quaker) Meeting my family attended. At no time were there more than 25 girls in my grade, and being with them for five years made it possible for me to get to know them better than I ever had known any classmates before. I could tell them apart, I knew their names, and I even accumulated information about many of them. I knew that one of them played golf, that another was considered "fast," that X was the "smart one" and Y had trouble taking standardized tests. Over the five years I spent there, two of them became my friends. It was a good, safe environment. And I emerged from it convinced that girls were really, really dumb.

Not including me, of course. I wasn't like a girl. I didn't understand how they could be interested in clothes, make-up, dances, dates, and boys. Boys were people and therefore potentially interesting, but that's not how my classmates related to them. Whenever boys were around, the girls turned idiotic. Totally useless. Silly. Incomprehensible.

At the end of eighth grade, we were instructed to elect a class president for the following year. Nobody was interested, so my classmates elected a patsy: me. I obviously didn't know any better, I talked (boringly) about politics, and the teachers/administrators made it clear that I was "special." Whatever I did or said, the response was, "Oh, that's just Janey." Not only was I bright, I came from a disadvantaged Quaker family: my father had died suddenly in the recent past, leaving the rest of us to struggle along on my mother's salary as a school secretary (supplemented by my father's Social Security). In a school where the guiding principles usually hung uneasily over a student body composed mainly of girls from prosperous non-Quaker families anxious to protect their offspring from the rigors of public school, my brains and (comparative) poverty made me this Quaker school's image of an ideal student. And besides, I was "different." Some people attributed my oddness to my intelligence, some to my family's Quakerism, some to the trauma of my father's death. (Nobody seemed to notice that my quirks were not replicated in any of the other students who shared one or more of these characteristics, nor by those with even more unusual demographics or life experiences.) I got away with a lot on that basis: That's just Janey. For someone so totally *other*, many rules simply did not apply. As I noted when describing how I have been adopted by another girl several times, I suspect this kind of leeway may be more available to girls than to boys—and thereby may work to keep more girls undiagnosed.

The big event of ninth grade was the sock hop, a dance in the school's Music Room. A record player was provided, and a blanket (presumably compulsory) invitation was extended to the ninth grade of a nearby boys' school. As class president, I did my best to see that everything was done properly. There were committees for decorations, music, and refreshments, and I probably micro-managed them to the utter despair of their members. The dance meant nothing at all to me, but I took my responsibilities seriously. When the night finally arrived, I was astonished to find my classmates standing around idly on one side of the room while the guests stood en masse in the opposite corner. These girls had been chattering endlessly about the hop, as if they cared for nothing else in the world, and the key ingredient in all their conversations was the boys, the boys, the boys. Now the boys were here, and the girls did nothing. After all my hard work! I even had allowed someone to put lipstick on my mouth for the occasion (everyone seemed to think it necessary), and the greasy feel and smell were a constant irritant. When the girls stubbornly refused my injunctions to move, I finally grabbed one by the arm and tried to tow her across the room. Somebody stopped me, and I gave up in disgust. I had no idea what was going on. Now, more than 35 years later, I know (intellectually) that there was plenty of communication going on in that room between that pack of girls and the cluster of boys. They knew what they were doing. But I sure didn't. Like a ship at night with no radar, I was sailing blind through a world full of gender signals invisible to my genderless self.

Perhaps I should say a few words here about physical appearance. The word *pretty* first intruded itself upon me in third or fourth grade. Although I was reading far above my grade level, my handwriting and spelling were way below par. My mother finally had to come into school to rescue me from handwriting hell. Not only was I incapable of producing the neat cursive script they required (about 40 years later I learned that AS kids often have trouble with such fine motor tasks), I was unable to restrain my contempt for the inane phrases I was required to copy out again and again and again. My mother wasn't around, unfortunately, on the day I was kept after class because the teacher refused to believe I couldn't spell *pretty*. I don't remember what happened beforehand; no doubt my spelling test was a dissector. But I distinctly remember her standing over me in that Illinois schoolroom, demanding that I write pretty 50 times. "Go on," she insisted. "Write priddy. Just write it. Priddy. Go on and write it!"

It was some years afterwards that I began to get an inkling of the fact that *pretty* was a goal to which I, as a female, was supposed to aspire. In high school I worried intermittently that my nose was too big. The cute nose of my childhood photos had grown. When the phrase "little beady eyes close together" became a standard description in my family for any shifty or undesirable character, I became concerned that my own eyes were too close together. One of my sisters assured me they weren't; it was only my nose being so big, she said, that made them look that way. I also went through a phase where I was sure my ears stuck out too much. Ears had been problematic for me ever since my first reading of Hamlet (age 9 or thereabouts); I couldn't possibly fall asleep without at least a sheet over my ears, for fear of being poisoned by the method Hamlet's uncle used on his father the king. In fact, of course, my ears were normal. It's just that my hair is so fine the ears show through.

I assume everyone goes through similar insecurities in adolescence. One difference for me was that my isolated concerns (about nose, eyes, ears) never came together into any sense of what I looked like. And I still don't know. I can give you the statistics—height, approximate weight, hair length and color—but I do not have the kind of relationship with my physical self that would allow me to participate in the female commitment to "doing the best with what you've got." As a result, there is a tremendous discontinuity when anyone tries to include my physical self in a relationship. Much of what goes on between potential romantic partners, I am told, has to do with how the two people involved react to one another's appearance. People try to present themselves to potential partners (usually, every member of one sex or the other) as attractively as possible in order to maximize the chance that a person to whom they are physically attracted will be physically attracted to them. And that is the necessary basis for every important relationship. It's also something I just don't get.

I have no desire to repel other people. At times in my life, I would have loved to attract them, at least to the extent of friendship, and I was willing to follow advice when someone (usually my mother) told me "that looks good on you," or "your hair looks nice like that." But there was no follow-through. I never developed a sense of my physical self and how it interacted with others. When interaction occurred, I was too busy with it (with the interaction, the listening, talking, thinking) to have attention left over for what my body was or wasn't doing. Nor did my body ever take the lead. I am not attracted to people physically. I used to think I was, because I'd occasionally see someone and think, "She [or he] looks nice." That's what I thought everyone meant when they talked about being attracted to people. For me, however, it meant something vague but along the lines of, "That person looks as if s/he might be interesting to talk to," and, "that person doesn't look unkind."

I never learned to see my body as a woman's body in the sense that a woman's body is an actor in socio-sexual relations. My body is the support structure for me, my intellect, my memories, my sensory experiences. If it has a gender, that gender lives on the outside, not in here where it would make a difference to how I feel or see the world (except in so far as I am shaped by how my gender causes the world to see and feel about me).

This is not to say that sexual enjoyment is beyond my experience. My body works just fine in that mode, although it's difficult to reach the necessary level of trust to experience that pleasure with another person. Invariably, it seems, the people who are interested in a deep enough friendship to support that depth of trust cannot be content there. They do not value friendship enough, not even if it includes sexual pleasure, but feel compelled to move on to a relationship based on sentiment: romantic love. I am unable to follow them there. For most people, apparently, sex remains interesting only if it is combined with romantic passion, innovation, surprise, change, sometimes even conflict and strife. They find me boring. I am always the same. I don't initiate (anything). I don't want to (in fact, I hate to) discuss the minutia behind emotional bruises that are invisible to me. I won't fight. If you're mean to me, I go away. I'm no fun at all if you're longing for passionate intensity about sex, love, or anything so far from my own special interests.

Too bad I didn't know any of this when I started out. As it was, I had no initiative but no inhibitions either. It was my good fortune to be taken under the wing of a high school classmate who shared some of my intellectual interests (or pretensions) and saw herself as an outsider of the avant-garde variety. This fit in well with both my politics (radical, anti-war) and the times (late 1960s): with her, I became a kind of hippie manqué. Actually, this first real friendship outside my family was very important to me. It allowed me to experience shared intellectual passion, to feel my life expanded by the presence in my mind of someone with whom I could share what was most vital to me: ideas. Under the influence of this passionate friendship, the whole world looked brighter; I seemed to see more acutely, to experience more fully and directly, because I was always conscious that I would be sharing what I saw, what I heard, what I thought, with someone who would care.

My friend introduced me to the lesbian and gay writers of the previous generation, and I believed I had found the source of my difference. I wasn't neurotic, as at least one friend of my mother's believed. If I wasn't following the same path as my classmates into adolescence, it was because I was a lesbian. Great!

As time went by, and particularly in the years following graduation from high school, my friend kept disappointing me. And I her, no doubt. Her assumptions about me were so often wrong. She seemed to expect me to react to people and relationships out of some standard list of cause and effect, of *if this/then that*, a list that had no point of correlation with the way I actually functioned. She was the only lesbian I knew (did I mention that I don't make friends easily?), and when she finally seemed to have settled into heterosexual relations, I decided the world at large must have been right after all. Lesbianism was only a phase. If I wanted to be normal, I'd have to find a boyfriend, too.

166

The one I found was great. As always, I found him by working on a project of interest to us both. Don't ever expect me to find a friend by socializing. Doesn't work. As Gertrude Stein (subject of my first and only adolescent crush) would say, for me "there's no there there." Socializing does not connect me. In my processor, it does not compute. I'd managed to wander aimlessly through almost a full year of college (before dropping out), living in a dorm, without making any friends other than the one assigned to me by the college as my official "big sister." (She turned out to be great, too. What she did was: she never gave up on me, never waited for me to return an initiative or play my proper part in the relationship. She was my big sister, my home away from home.) The only other people I'd spent any time with were those involved in the school's small anti-war group. One man did try to make me his girlfriend. I was happy with him (and had no objection to having sex with him) because he was good-natured and had a car. (He drove me several times to the next college town north, to see and be disappointed by my high school friend.) Before long, he became perplexed by my passivity (social and emotional as well as sexual) and, being a kind person, was relieved to find me unfazed by his decision to switch partners. I truly wished them well and felt only relief myself at no longer having to improvise (badly) the role of this nice young man's girl.

I had been out of high school for three years by the time I found the man I hoped would enable me to become normal. We met as members of a small group planning to do a "draft board action." (In the '60s and '70s, a number of draft board offices were entered by anti-war activists who destroyed the files of men in danger of being drafted and sent to kill and be killed in Indochina.) For me, this was perhaps the perfect social environment. We were intensely focused on one shared task about which we all cared deeply, and the work involved a large number of concrete tasks. Because we were under pressure both of time and the threat of detection, and because we had committed ourselves to this task wholly, all extraneous inter-personal considerations were eliminated. I didn't see or feel them, anyway. It's possible they were going on as usual in human groups but that everyone else decided to set them aside for a change. At any rate, there was an absolute minimum of socializing and an absolute maximum of attention to the substance of what we were doing. Autistic heaven—and especially so since several of the individuals in the group had senses of humor that gibed with mine. Every autistic heaven has room set aside for being silly.

I chose Frank out of that group because I really liked him. And he was available. We weren't allowed to write to one another while we were in prison, but I made sure not to lose touch. I no longer remember the details, but I retain the impression that, after we got out, for once in my life I took the initiative. Luckily, Frank accepted my overtures, and we soon became a couple. We lived together off and on for about two years before I fell apart. Almost immediately, I deeply regretted my attempt to use Frank in this way, to make me normal. He deserved far better. I am happy to say that he recovered fully from the experience and went on to a happy marriage. He even managed to forgive me, and I count him among the best friends I've had. Not that I can claim to have known him well, nor to have enabled him to know me. When I say he is among my best friends, I mean that we considered ourselves friends (within the limitations imposed by the clash between my nature and his) and that he was what my mother used to call "an elegant human being." Kind, intelligent, funny, patient. Couldn't ask for more.

So why did living with him make me fall apart? Because I couldn't stand the strain of trying to be normal every day. Now mind you, this is not a very highly normal standard of normal we're talking about. Frank didn't expect me to act like a wife, shopping, cooking, and cleaning. He assumed equality in the relationships (for the most part) and was happy with the laid back lifestyle of sub-adult lefties determined not to become clones of the consumerist middle class. He never once criticized the way I looked or behaved. It's not what he did or said. It's that he was there.

Being with someone is work for me. The presence of another person—even in another room—weighs on my attention and drains my energy. That statement probably makes me sound selfish to many people, especially to those with conventional ideas about womanliness, but it's something I have to face and deal with as a matter of fact. *Social* time (time spent with anyone) is a form of work for me, whether I'm *at* work or with a friend at home, and I always need a lot of time alone to rejuvenate. What feeds other people's mental/emotional batteries is a drain on mine (on an autistic's). When I was living with Frank, I was living in *social time* almost all day every day. Interacting with him (even pleasantly) used up a certain amount of the sensory/attention facilities I had available for that day. Talking to him, or even keeping myself in the mode that allowed me to respond adequately to him (for example, if we were settled in different rooms of the apartment but I had to expect that he might walk by me at any moment on the way to the kitchen or bathroom), fatigued me as if I were a dyslexic and had to *read* him throughout every minute of his presence. And he was almost always present.

It wore me out. Brought me to a halt. Made me feel like I was dying.

A few years later, I tried it again but with a woman this time. Maybe it was something about male/female relations, I thought, that made my attempt to live with Frank so unendurable. He was a lovely man, but maybe we both had been so deeply penetrated by the sexism of the culture around us that, despite our best efforts, we were unable to relate to one another outside the influence of the sex roles dictated by that culture. My reading in feminist analysis encouraged me to believe that the culprit must be some form or effect of sexism. Surely I would be able to handle living with a person just as nice as Frank who had the added advantage of being female.

Damn. Wrong again. It's not the sex or the sex roles. It's my brain that doesn't fit.

I find it very difficult to convey to non-autistic people how isolated I am compared to the way they live their lives. Usually they assume I'm talking about the human condition stuff again, but that's not it, although I, too, thought for most of my life that what I experienced was what the poets and novelists wrote about. Putting aside that essential loneliness of being incarnated in mortal flesh, however, people generally do make contact with one another. Contact of some kind. If they don't, they are seen as exceptional, often monstrous. The woman living stubbornly alone, not interacting normally with her neighbors, becomes known as a witch. The man who rejects human contact is suspected of perverse thoughts, if not mad bombings. I am none of the above, but I am much more isolated than those around me ever suspect. Nobody gets to me on the emotional level experienced by most people, whether in everyday socializing or grand passions of love or hate. The kinds of connections I want (and occasionally crave) are too esoteric and bloodless to interest normal people, although they would be rich and enriching for me. For the most part, I have had to do without such connections. I suspect that one of the greatest flaws, from the perspective of normal people, in the kind of relations I would like to have is that they would be non-gendered. They provide scope neither for the spice of sexualized emotional undercurrents nor for the warmth of gendered camaraderie ("just us girls," girltalk, etc.). When people perceive me as aloof, they are sensing an absence of emotional availability. It's unwomanly of me, in traditional terms, to be the way I am. In feminist terms, it's un-sisterly. I just have to accept that, for this autistic, it's normal.

© Jane Meyerding

The Boy from Bible Study

Morgan Allgood

As a teenager, I had few friends, and boys that were interested in me were fewer still. I was pretty enough, but I was always the odd one at school. Boys generally made crude gestures to me and I repelled their antics with declarations of disgust and, where I deemed appropriate, violence. It was my sophomore year of high school when I met my first boyfriend. At the time I was exploring fundamentalist Christianity as a social and spiritual pursuit, and attending Bible study in a group that met in the hour or so before school officially started. I hardly knew most of the other teens, and they hardly knew me but at least I was in a room with them with a common purpose, and this was socializing I thought.

That particular day the school bell rang and I gathered up my books, all my books—every single text for the entire school day in one gigantic disorganized pile—and walked, quick-paced, down the hall. It then sunk in that someone was following me and calling out my name. I turned around and a boy I did not recognize was standing there. He said he was from the Bible study group. He then surprised me by asking me to the Christmas formal. I did not know him or care who he was. I had been asked to the dance and I was absolutely ecstatic. I said yes, and then, realizing I did not even know his first name, turned around and asked him, "What's your name again?" "David!" he shouted down the hall.

The next day, at my parents' suggestion, I found out his last name, as well as asking him about his background—things parents want to know. But I imagine that it came off more as a census questionnaire rather than a conversation between two teens. David was a foster child who admitted he had some mental problems stemming from being different from everyone else and from the circumstances through which he had been placed in foster care. He was highly intelligent, just two days my junior, but he was in the 12th grade whereas I was in 10th. I now realize he was most likely an Aspie himself.

We dated through the rest of high school, attending every Christmas formal and prom. Ours was an extremely volatile relationship. We would break up and make up on almost a monthly basis: two control freaks addicted to one another. But on a romantic level, we were more like brother and sister. Sure we would kiss at the door because that was protocol, but I never felt anything from those kisses. And never did we neck or cuddle.

Our first sexual contact was my senior year. It was a day I regretted deeply almost from the moment it happened. David was now in college, and was being tormented by his peers for still being a virgin. And I was genuinely curious. My parents were out of town and David had come over to help me study. He and I made an awkward attempt at necking, and his sexual frustration was obvious. He'd talked a lot about how the other boys had teased him that day. I do not recall if it was my idea or his, but it was likely my doing. We were nervous as we undressed, yet we said that we were sure. But both of us knew nothing and he was ready immediately. He was also very large, and I was very nervous and very dry. The pain was intense. I asked him to stop, or at least I think I did. I cannot be certain, as I have been known to think I've said things when it only stayed a thought, albeit a very loud one. He did not stop. He was heavy lying upon me. And still he thrust. Finally he quit out of frustration, his erection still unrelieved. Both of us were shocked to see that I was bleeding. He got dressed and I went and cleaned up, packing myself with tampons as well as stuffing my underwear with toilet paper. As I was the only one of us with a driver's license, I drove him home. When I arrived home, I finished cleaning up the mess, put fresh sheets on the bed, and curled up and cried.

His reaction was quite the opposite of mine. While I was revolted, he was more convinced than ever that I was the woman he wanted to marry. Though I had since broken away from Christian dogma, he was still heavily entrenched in it and claimed we were now married in God's eyes. I wanted out and knew of no graceful way to do it. I wanted to be gentle, as he was the type to become suicidal over something as minor as getting a B on a paper.

I was going off to college in Indiana that fall, and my hope was that distance would be the cure. Unfortunately, that proved not to be the case. He called me at the dorm regularly. I tried to be aloof, but he was blind to it. Finally one day I was cornered on the phone as he said he wanted to come out to visit and go buy the engagement ring. I had to tell him it was over. He did not take it well at all, calling back with harassing frequency. The times he did catch me in he would threaten suicide. He begged to know why I wanted out, and I couldn't give him a good answer.

© Morgan Allgood

Love, Sex, and The Thing That Makes Sense

April Masilamani

Despite my interest in sex, it was very hard to make actual connections with men. I have until recently just seen them as sex objects. By that I mean I either was interested in a particular man that I would fall in love with and allow to exist in my consciousness, or they didn't exist at all and I never noticed them. I was always very nervous when approached by a boy, which I think stemmed from my mother's comment that "they are only interested in one thing." This led to some very alarmed boys being informed, soon after starting to talk to me, that "I don't want sex."

My first lover was a teacher at my high school. He was foreign, as both my husbands were. They seemed to be the only men who would ever ask me out. I have always been attracted to foreigners. It somehow makes misunderstandings easier. We are not supposed to understand each other anyway. Whereas with someone of my own culture, I'm quickly exposed as not fitting in. This first relationship didn't last very long. He was always trying to fathom me, like I was some big mystery, and I was holding out on him. I would get frustrated by this probing; it would get too intimate, and there was nothing there I could tell. Nothing that would interest him, anyway. He wanted deep meaningful eye contact, which was another burden and made me very nervous. Another partner was very romantic and was, I think, in love with love and therefore didn't mind that I didn't reciprocate. He was very social so it became the most social time of my life, but that caused a lot of stress for both of us. I was always trying to curb the socializing and got very upset if I didn't know what was going to happen. If things get spontaneous, I become very stressed, which is one of the reasons I'm so boring. I made his life hell, as I controlled everything with my rages. We lived together for four years. On my terms.

I then met a German who became my first husband. He was also social but liked to be alone at home. He was possessive, jealous and controlling, using violence to control. I was often slapped or punched for behaving badly, and once I was put in hospital. It was a very intense relationship, which for a while matched a wildness in me that was always there. However, it created very dangerous situations for me, both physically and morally, until I learned to be careful. It was only after that, after the birth of my first child, that I finally felt the strength to get out of such a stupid relationship. I was naive and had no idea what to expect in a relationship anyway, as I had no one, and no ability to talk to anyone else to compare notes. A lot of the time I'm not really present mentally, anyway, so it is hard to analyze a situation and make the best decisions about what to do.

Overall in my relationships, I was more interested in sex than intimacy. I found the beginnings of a relationship very difficult, the first awkward touching very strange, but once I get over that, sex is wonderful. In fact orgasms are one of the only things that make any sense to me; with them I feel very much like I'm connected to the universe, to why we exist at all. I remember with my first physical contact, feeling as if I had died. It was an out of body experience and I thought "This is why I was born"—which seems a little stupid. Also, it always feels like a safe physical contact, I suppose because the reason for contact is clear, whereas hugs seem a little too intimate and more of a connection on a mind or emotional level. I still act very private in terms of any other physical contact. I would never share a bathroom at the same time or get dressed in front of anyone. I dislike meaningful eye contact or intimate discussions. I very rarely care to inquire whether they love me and, if someone says it to me and I have to say it back, it sounds very false.

I develop personas to cope with the day to day contact with my partners, but when this gets too much, I can get very grumpy and distance myself a lot. In some ways, the children help keep this distance, as I'm busy with my mummy role, which helps define a lot of my time. Otherwise I would not bother with a relationship full time, and only have a lover. The wonderful thing about my present husband is, although he does not consider himself to be AS, a lot of his more personal contacts seem to be with AS types. He is practical and very much like me in terms of what we want in a relationship (I think). Also, he thinks people are illogical, overly emotional, and stupid, for the main part.

Both my husbands insisted on marrying me. It was something I never wanted to do. I wanted to go and live in a cave like Merlin, but as it seemed important to them, I went ahead. However, I have to say that the day of my marriage to my present husband really did feel like the best day of my life. He has all the qualities I like: good at sex, clever, and he likes food. I find he makes a lot of decisions for me—how I should dress, what I should do—and without his advice, normal interaction would be much harder. Although I sometimes find this controlling and it causes me to overload, I imagine it is also frustrating for him to have to accommodate someone who requires so much thought and is so useless. While I find living with someone all the time very difficult, this has been my most successful relationship. We are comfortably un-close together.

© April Masilamani

174

No Heartbreak

Sola Shelly

I have never fallen in love; I don't get the concept. I am not sure if I ever was *in* love. But I *have* known love. I ended up dating four men, and marrying the fourth one.

I met my first boyfriend at a party. I hated parties but I went to this one, because a classmate had asked me to. She and I were not really friends, and met personally (other than school and scouts) no more than three or four times during all of high school. But I felt somewhat closer to her because she, like me, wrote poems. And she probably saw my social isolation and wanted to help me. The people having the party were three years older, and I didn't know any of them. That was OK with me. She arranged someone to take us to the party and I had to stay until the guy who gave us the ride decided to leave. I was bored most of the time, but the party was not too noisy so at least I did not suffer.

When it was time to leave, the best friend of our driver asked my friend out. She said that she was busy the next evening, so he turned to me. I was kind of surprised but I did not mind going to the movies the next evening, so I said yes. From then on, we just continued. Although he was much older than I, I was his first girlfriend so he did not push for physical involvement too early. He was on the lower edge of the social scale of his group (although his best friend was very popular) and mind games did not interest him much. He was simple in many ways, and I felt comfortable with him. We spent a lot of time alone, in his home or in mine, or out of town. Gradually, we came to like each other. I found myself waiting for our dates, wanting to spend time with him. For quite a long time, I loved him. We shared many happy moments.

I broke up with him after I graduated high school and became a university student. Studying has always been a major passion of mine, and after the boring times in high school, I thrived at the university. My boyfriend could not understand my passion for studying. But there was something more about him that increasingly bothered me: He did not have intensity. Everything was just fine for him, and it did not matter to him one way or the other. There are things that I strongly care about. Sometimes, even little things can make me happy. This deep involvement throws me off emotionally, but without it I am dead. When my boyfriend started to push me to leave the university and marry him, I became very unhappy but I didn't know what to do about it. It was my mother who brought up the option of leaving him. I realized that this was what I should do, and I told him that we should stop seeing each other.

My second boyfriend was arranged for me. My roommate was keen on dating. At any given time she either had a boyfriend, or went to parties and disco clubs in order to meet one. So, one day she informed me that she had met someone who was too young to be her boyfriend (she was eight years older than me) but would be suitable for me. She arranged for him to call me, and I didn't say no.

This man *was* intense. When he got excited about something, his excitement was visible. He could talk at length about issues that interested him or that he cared about. Like me, he loved the university, and was a brilliant student. I was mesmerized by his intense essence, but also felt uncomfortable. It was not safe to be *me* around him. I also did not like his enthusiasm about the stock market and did not share his desire for making money. It looked wrong to me to make a living as a gambler.

We dated for a few weeks and I probably did not love him; I was never truly happy with him. But he did raise my interest. Breaking up came as a surprise to me. After I gave him a speech on how I viewed gender roles in relationships, he said that we should not be a couple. Our relationship was only beginning, so I was not prepared for it to end so soon, but other than that, it was OK with me to be honest and to break up if we didn't fit together. Yet I was still curious about him, and met him a couple of times after we were no longer friends. Sometimes I still wonder what became of him.

I met my third boyfriend at the computer lab. As a good student, I was known by many. He came up to me and asked me out and I didn't say no. He took me to nice places and to shows. We both liked walking, and neither of us had a car, so we used to take long walks on our way back from town. We spent many hours sitting at the old, small table at my residence, talking. He was an interesting, decent person. But...he had no *intensity*. After a few weeks, he started to talk about how special I was, and I realized that he was beginning to love me. I really liked him, and did not want to see him hurt. I told him that I liked him as a person, but was not going to love him. He decided that he would still want to remain friends with me. We met a few more times, but then, I was not used to having friends the way normal people do and the connection did not last long.

I met my fourth boyfriend at a student club. Of course, I didn't want to go to the party, but my roommate needed someone to come to the party with— she felt it was inappropriate for a woman to show up alone so after some begging I went with her. As soon as we got there she disappeared, and I spent most of the time wandering around, and occasionally dancing (or pretending to dance) with a man who would politely leave after the song was over. At some point a timid, somewhat clumsy man invited me with a slight gesture. We did the funny ritual called slow dancing. He did not try to hold me close, so we moved as my arms were stretched forward, only my hands touching his shoulders. It always seems weird to me to hug someone I had just met. He

176

tried to start a conversation, asking some trivial questions. It was too noisy to talk there, and I didn't like dancing anyway. So we went out.

We spent the rest of the evening walking, circling the club building. I don't remember what we talked about, but I do remember that it was not the usual, painfully forced smalltalk. I remember both of us making puns, and enjoying it. It was getting late, and we returned to the party hall, where I looked for my roommate, to either go back with her, or tell her that I'd got a ride so she didn't need to worry about me. I could not find her anywhere. Finally I gave up and went with the guy. Apparently, he too was not enthusiastic about going to the party, and his friends dragged him along. So I rode with him and his friends, and when they dropped me at the residence, he said something about meeting me again. It seemed natural to me that we would.

From there, things went very fast. After two dates we started to meet every evening, and spent together almost every minute when we were not in class. Two months after we met we moved in together, and at about the same time we decided to get married right after I graduated (in a few months). If someone had told me that I would marry a man I had known for only two months, it would seem crazy to me. But it did not seem crazy with this man; I felt as if I had known him all my life. Being around him had an overwhelming sense of familiarity—of finally finding my own kind. With him, things were natural. I felt comfortable telling him that I had no friends; he didn't have many friends either, and his friendships were rather loose and did not affect our relationships much. He was far from the macho stereotype as much as I was far from the image of the young female, and we joked about that. We both were deep into studying, and we liked to spend the evening together, each one of us busy with learning materials. Like me, he cared about things and did not stay indifferent. He was an intense person, he knew that I was, and we both loved each other for being that way.

There is no happy ending for this story. Marriage involved many familial problems that living together as an unmarried couple somehow did not. I found myself involved in conflicts, which I did not understand and could not deal with. I tried not to be judgmental, while he actively took sides with his parents, and dragged their issues into our relationship. Intensity and perseverance made things worse. I could understand his fixations, as I had mine. I understood how unhappy one could be when things were not in the same order as one needed them to be. But I was responsible enough to prioritize and to care for the kids and manage the household. While most of the burden fell on me, I never did enough for him. And, as perseverance goes, he could talk hours and hours about whatever made him unhappy, for which I should change entirely to accommodate him.

I can't love someone who hurts me. Facing him, I felt puzzled, frustrated, often helpless, but hardly heart-broken. Gradually I realized that I didn't want to stay with him. By then, my feelings for him were already dead. The difficult phase was merely a shift of thought; I was used to thinking in terms of *we*, and now it would be just *me*. This shift was difficult, but possible. Leaving him became a matter of logistics. Though it took me a few more years to figure out how, I finally left him.

Now I am quite sure that my ex-husband is AS. This is, of course, no excuse for his behavior, but it gives some context to a lot of puzzling things. It also explains why my parents resented him as weird, while I saw nothing weird about him. Being on the spectrum myself, I can see how we almost ran into each other, overwhelmed with the sense of familiarity after living so long in a society so alien to both of us. He still tells me that he will never find another woman like me. We still share the same language style and a world of associations. If we had known about AS back then, would it have made a difference? That depends greatly on what one does with the knowledge. Looking back, I realize how much time and effort we spent on passing for normal. It might have helped if we had both accepted being AS, learned to live with the difficulties, and understood that we sometimes needed help. Even if we did, I doubt that appropriate help would be available for people as high functioning as we are.

Is it too much for two intense people to share their lives? It's hard to tell how things could develop differently in different circumstances, but I know that I could not love someone who was not intense. I can love another person only if I get the sense that *there is someone in there*. Only then, can I share the *something* in *me*. Intensity is what I have to share with another person.

© Sola Shelly

Post-Dialogue

Sola Shelly

It's only a phone-call,
come on, how come
you drag this for weeks.
Soon it's going to be too late,
people make plans, you know.

I know, and I really try
as hard as I can, but I can't
do two things at the same time.
It takes up all my attention, all my wits
to get to the phone, and pick up and dial
and do all that talking, and listening and talking
that after I am through
I just can't move on to the next.
I must first process the exchange,
and process that it's behind me for one thing,
and I need some time-out before I can
build up enough energy to start all over again.
And time-outs are rare these days, you know.

I don't know what you are talking about,
apart from arranging that one thing for the kid
you didn't do much. I already agreed
to do things the way that suits you
and have a modest reception at my own house
while it is in fact your event. How can you say
that I don't listen to your needs?

It's true that I prefer not to have a big crowd,
but it was the kid's request, and it's his event
and I respect his wish. But you could not
take this literally, so you decided yourself
to have another reception, and invite more people
that you feel you must include
but we don't. And now it's even harder
to have to attend yet another event.

How can you say that? What is so hard
for you, when you don't have to do anything,
just to be there, while I offer to have it in my house
and prepare all the food and go into all that trouble.

I don't know how to explain, that
just being around people is so hard
and so exhausting
even when they are all well-meaning.
Days before the event I am so stressed
and after, it takes days to recover
sometimes even weeks
and all this time
I can't do anything else
barely go to work.
Life is so stressful as it is
I was going through hell at work recently
where people were using my naivete against me
and dismissing agreements we had had for years
belittling my views and values
I still have nightmares about this
and other stuff

I know, life is a constant struggle
I too had to fight hard to preserve my rights
to stand up against superiors and bureaucrats
write letters to different authorities
and I did finally win, but it was not easy

I wish I could make you understand,
what is a battle to you, is a battle
to anyone else in the same situation.
But to me,
things that are fun to everyone else,
things that help them decompress
and energize them for the next battle,
are only more draining for me,
and just make me more desperate
in the need to
disappear.
You see, I know how my mind and my senses work
and I even can put it in words
in a more or less intelligible way.

I also know myself enough, not to be surprised
that all the answers and explanations
only come to my mind
long after
the conversation with you has ended…

In Search of the Friendship Formula

Gail Pennington

Before the age of about 10 or 11, I preferred animals to people, except for my family. School was a nightmare to be endured. To have to navigate my way socially with the other students and the teachers was not something I looked forward to at all. The students taunted me and the teachers pitied me. I hated both reactions.

Every once in awhile though, there would be someone. Someone who didn't pity me, who would take the time to talk to me and not be put off by my strangeness or aloofness, who would talk to me as though I were normal, as though I were someone worth knowing. This got my attention. They would be kind. They wouldn't push me beyond my limits or punish me for my social *faux pas*.

There were not too many people like this, but enough of them for me to know that they existed. Heaven knows there were many times I wanted to completely withdraw from the noisy, confusing, hurtful world around me but people like this kept me connected. I realize this now. They would always be there, right on time, at different stages in my life, whenever I would need them, as though they had been sent by divine providence, and perhaps they were.

Slowly, but surely, I developed the desire to connect with others, despite the difficulties that presented. (It was just so much easier to live in my fantasy world.) I would watch TV shows, to study people to see how they interacted. I started asking my more social brothers questions. I learned from them the concept of slang, what different expressions meant. I hated slang, though, and it took me a while to get used to using it. I also hated using contractions. I wanted to say *do not*, not *don't*; *cannot*, not *can't*. However, if I wanted to fit in, I needed to speak as the natives did, so I forced myself to say things like *don't* and *can't*, until it became easy. I started using *expressions* and learning what they meant. I also learned to recognize when someone was using one. If it made no logical sense, it was probably an expression. All I had to do was decipher it and my brothers were good for that.

When I started going through puberty, I noticed something else. It became easier to speak. No longer did I get the feeling of my mouth being wired shut. Words flowed more freely from my lips. It almost felt like someone had pushed a button in my brain that allowed the words to come out more easily, though I still could not make smalltalk or initiate conversations.

I started learning about body language. I learned the concepts of smiling, of looking people in the eye when talking to them, something I find uncomfortable to do but have learned to tolerate. I learned that my body

183

language affected people and they would make assumptions about my motives and feelings because of it. Back to the TV I would go to observe more body language. Even though I was learning more and more how to interact with others, I was still not very good at it. I couldn't make a friend to save my life. Everyone else could, even my brothers. The things other girls did and wanted to talk about held little interest for me. My interest at that time was still animals or *guy* things.

Because of this, sometimes a boy would start being friendly with me. The friendship worked fine as long as we were doing an activity together, yet all my friendships died a quick death because I couldn't keep up my end of a conversation. The subject matter had to be something I found interesting, otherwise my brain would freeze. End of friendship.

Occasionally, a girl in school would take me under her wing. However, she would refuse to socialize with me outside of school—just as well, as I wouldn't have known what to do or say anyway. I could hang out with a group of people as long as no one started talking to me. If they did then I would be out in the middle of the ocean in a boat with no oars unless they were just asking a question I could answer or making a comment that required no response from me other than "uh-huh."

Because of this I have become known as a great listener, even though it is more about my inability to think of something to say in return than my interest in what is being said. More often than not I am bored to tears and just want to get away. But alas, I am not good at the art of making a graceful exit so I sit and endure and then get patted on the back and extolled for my listening abilities. If they only knew.

I had no boyfriends in high school. If a boy liked me I had no clue. Sometimes I would hear a rumor that one did, but he would never approach me. I remember my father and stepmother being upset that I didn't have girlfriends or boyfriends, especially boyfriends. They wondered what was wrong with me. I hated *the feeling* that I was somehow defective, and statements like that I took as meaning that I *was* defective. I wasn't chasing boys away, but neither was I doing anything to attract them. Not that I knew how! When I liked a boy I would hope that he would somehow know. I mean, other girls got guys interested in them. I just didn't know how they did it. I asked advice a few times but never could figure out the *instructions* I was given. I did have a guy friend that I went to the prom with, but he was just that, a friend.

It was probably a good thing anyway because I turned out to be very easy to seduce. When I went into the Air Force after high school I had guys chasing me and I was flattered. My very first boyfriend deflowered me within a month. Then when we were assigned to different bases I never heard from him again, after all these promises of keeping in touch, yet I wasn't particularly surprised by that. By this time I was used to people not keeping their word. I had been taken advantage of so many times in different ways that I was quite the cynic by the time I was 18. I was also used to being abused and rejected. Just another day in the life of Gail. What's new?

Before I was married at 19, I was seduced by three other guys. I must have developed a reputation for being easy. They would take me to bed and then I would never hear from them again. People have told me that I have the gift of passion, and others, that I am the type of woman who needs a man, meaning, that I have lots of hormones that make me want sex. (Boy, do I remember the first time I felt that—I was 13!)

As an adult I wasn't that much better at making friends than I had been as a child and teen, though I was better at talking and socializing. But I could never figure out the friend *formula*. What the criteria, the parameters were: whether I was giving too much or too little; whether I was doing the right thing or the wrong thing. Finally after a lot of pain and failed relationships I pretty much gave up on having friends.

I am no longer seeking after friendship with people. It is just not worth the effort I make that goes mostly unappreciated by others. I am open for friendship, but I am just not actively pursuing it anymore. I do have a very good friend in my life, and that is my present husband. He doesn't always understand me but he tries. He believes the best of me. My shortcomings and social deficits do not make him turn against me, as they have so many others in my life over the years. He tells me many times that my good qualities far outweigh my bad ones. We have been married going on nine years and this is by far the most successful relationship I have ever had.

As for having a woman friend, well, that's a challenge. So many women think that to be a friend means to be a social butterfly, to cook and make quilts or crafts with them; to engage in endless smalltalk; to chat about recipes, and how to get great deals in shopping, and other subjects that hold no interest for me. If that is what is expected of me, then I cannot be that kind of friend. I do have a woman friend who seems to appreciate my friendship. I hardly ever see her but she doesn't hold that against me, or me her. (She works a lot.) She understands my need to be alone and the days I do not return her calls because I am not up to talking. Or that in a restaurant I prefer to sit in booths or facing a certain direction. She always lets me pick out where to sit.

Like my husband, these quirks of mine do not throw her. She said I am the most loyal friend she has ever had. She went through a divorce a few years ago, and all her other friends abandoned her and chose her ex-husband's side. Or they tried to distance themselves from the situation altogether when she was no longer the upbeat bubbly person she was before the divorce. I was the only one, she said, who was there for her through thick and thin, who would listen to her vent, who would call her just to check up on her. I think that is sad. She thought she had lots of friends, people she'd known for years, who just disappeared when being around her became a downer for them. When the dust cleared, the social misfit was the only one left.

Now that she is bouncing back into the bubbly person she once was, these people are starting to come around her again. She thinks it's funny and she won't trust them anymore. Watching this whole saga with her has made me think. Why was I trying so hard? If most people are the kind of friends that she had, then I have not missed much by not having friends.

Actually, I think I have been better off!

© Gail Pennington

Madonna at Variance

My Governess

Daina Krumins

My mother also was AS, so I don't know how to figure out what was going on in our relationship. She was very strict with me, and sometimes she had these fits of irrational anger and frustration, which caused her to punish me in ways that I can never forget and which traumatized me then, and probably still now. But, on the other hand, she was excellent for me in other ways. She insisted that I would be successful and did everything—*everything*—in her power to make me successful. She was an excellent governess.

When I was about 10, I had a friend named Penny who had red hair and was not overly bright. I was amazed at the way her mother treated her—the gentleness, lovingness. I wished so much that my mom would have treated me that way. But, looking back, where would I be if my mother *had* treated me that way? I was so-o-o-o strong-minded, I doubt that a *nice* mother would have had a clue what to do with me. Who knows what the result of *that* would have been? At least with my mother, I knew that she never rejected me or thought that there was something wrong with me that should be fixed. She never failed to support my ditzy ideas and projects.

I guess my feelings about my mom are mixed. I feel enormous gratitude to her as a teacher/mentor/governess, but I feel hurt that she was not more considerate, even though I knew that her mind simply didn't understand that I had feelings.

Mommie Wyrdest

Jean Kearns Miller

How do you come to know you are peculiar? Looking back, I remember some moments when something would come home to me—Tzzt!—with such superb clarity, I'd feel an intense buzzing in my head, the sensation of knowledge being made: *I am not like others.* One such event was my sister's being down with some childhood illness with which I had already been afflicted. Maureen had been in bed for two days when my mother told me to go up and see her. I wasn't sure why I had been sent up there. People always seemed to have their reasons and perhaps I would find out when I got there.

When I arrived at her bedside, Maureen began scolding me about how terrible a person I was for neglecting her those previous two days. "How could you!" she said. "And after I came up and saw you when you were sick…twice a day!" Tzzt! Tzzt! I was supposed to have been grateful for her visits, presumably because her visits meant something to me. They did not. And if they meant nothing to me, why on earth would I ever see them as favors that needed to be returned?

Remembering the Christian mandate to visit the sick, I was able to feel guilty about it as well, but the guilt came in a form I'm still wrestling with. *Normal* religious guilt may have been to have some clue that Maureen would love to have visitors, but to allow myself to be dissuaded from visiting by the vices of sloth or selfishness. The normal moral lesson becomes a self-admonition to triumph over these completely human impulses, and do the right thing in future. My problem was that I couldn't even get to the concept of "Maureen would like visitors." I couldn't see it. And I sensed that this wouldn't be the only case in which I lacked inner appreciation of this classic good-evil dilemma. How could I have known? How might I know in the future? So guilt became an essential quality of my existence. I lacked moral capacity. And because visiting my sister would have been the loving thing to do, I lacked the capacity to love as well. I had been singled out by the God-of-the-hard-bargain to be fatally flawed. My five or six year-old thoughts weren't versed in this adult way but were present nevertheless, and horrifying.

I was lacking in the stuff that made people human and I began to size up my life in terms of this lack. Foremost among these issues was motherhood. I sensed as early as eight or nine that I would never be a mother, that it wasn't in the cards for me, and an experience eventually heightened this feeling. I was sitting on the porch of a relative's house with my sister and some others, among them an old Irish woman who claimed to read palms. She read my sister's palm and pronounced her fit to mother the large brood she eventually had. Reaching over, she grabbed my hand, took one look at it and said, "You'll not have children. You're too selfish." Tzzt! There it was. That familiar throbbing in my head affirmed the truth. As I grew up, I continued to be visited by that thought, along with the fear that, were I to have children and should one of them die, I would feel nothing. I don't believe NT girls or women are troubled by such thoughts.

Somewhere along the line, I managed to marry and actually to hope for children, despite this knowledge of my central lack. But time went by and by and by. No children. Of course. That's it. Infertility of womb is infertility of spirit as well. Nature coordinates. How perfect. How bereft I was. I divorced and remarried and finally got an explanation for my infertility, an over supply of anderosterone. Polycystic ovaries? Well, there you are, I thought. It's a done deal. The gypsy woman knew it all along. In private, I wept and wept and wept over it, even though I believed underneath that I'd be a complete failure as a mother anyway and that this was only right. But I wailed anyway. And when the wailing was done, I'd made peace with it. I let go of the hope and moved along. Then I became pregnant.

How my body managed to beat its hormonal destiny is beyond me, but there I was, plumping out nicely and on my way to an adventure. My maternal pessimism gave way to wonder and ecstasy. I struggled with my university work; I struggled with the gestational diabetes that came with the deal; I struggled to get around as what was going to be a very large baby filled my small torso. But how I marveled! How I marveled!

As I got closer and closer to term, I began to understand some things about this child in me. First, he was quite stuck. He had a very large head and was in the breach position, so, unlike most babies, for the last month or so of the pregnancy, he was unable to roll around or shift position at all. I'd feel a great pain in my ribs and look down to see the outline of his head turning as much as he could manage. Or I'd see him extend his arm, and wonder how it must feel to have so little freedom and how maybe he was losing out on the last experience of completely innocent, unmindful pleasure in his life, thanks to his cramped quarters. Because of the disproportion in our sizes, he had little in the way of amniotic fluid available to cushion the movements he did make. I wondered if he could feel frustration while still *in utero*, because surely he had reason to. "How sad for him."

The other thing that fueled my curiosity about who this being might be was his reaction to noise. Whenever there was a loud noise, he would startle. A door would slam and my belly would vibrate as his little body reacted. In general, he responded exquisitely to sounds of all kinds, as though they went straight to his core. Music activated him; conversation put him to sleep.

Adrian was born by c-section—the only possible way to liberate him—on January 29, 1985. I remember being allowed a glimpse of him before he was whisked away to be weighed and bathed, and thinking, "What a fine, big country boy that is!" I'd never thought words anything like that before. He weighed 9 lbs. 7 oz. And he'd spent the last month or so of womb time with the heel of one foot jammed into his jaw, which had caved in the side of his face. Once his facial features popped into place he was quite nice looking, without the pruny quality that makes many newborns kind of ugly. I stuffed my swollen nipple into his mouth and he sucked in the colostrum avidly.

This baby boy fascinated me. I would spend ages staring at him, sizing him up, noting the components of who he was. And I was stricken by something I'd read about Margaret Mead some years before. As I recalled, an article suggested that she could possibly be a tad too empirical about her daughter. It rubbed the journalist the wrong way that Mead took notes on her baby, studied her. I don't recall a thing that was said to indicate true dysfunction in either mother or child but it seemed inexplicably cold to the writer. And there I was doing the same thing, only without method. It would strike me at times that when I'd see mothers gaze at their babies they were invariably smiling with pleasure, which eventually became reciprocal flirtation. But my affect was, as the shrinks say, flat. The movement toward mutual seduction was not going to happen. I was lost in observation.

This boy baby was impossible for me to care for. He would feed, then start blinking, whirling his arms and legs, grimacing, then screaming his head off! The only thing that might quiet him was the breast. Otherwise, he screamed and screamed and screamed and screamed! No naps. And at night, he would sleep for two stretches of two-and-a-half hours each, separated by a feeding, then be done with sleep till the next midnight. This went on for weeks. My husband, Bernie, was very helpful but I'd heard that you must never supplement with a bottle at night during the first months of breast-feeding, so I felt unable to accept a reprieve. (As I look back, I think my milk supply would probably have adapted. I was bound by the rules in the book, to everyone's dismay.) I was also recovering from a c-section. I'm not radically against surgical birth; indeed Adrian wouldn't have been born alive any other way. But I do resent the medical community's denial of the rigors of recovery. It is major abdominal surgery and everything a mother is expected to do by way of self-care is in direct conflict with the new demands on her as a mother, especially mothers with difficult babies.

I was wild from lack of sleep. I felt barely human and completely failed. And what made matters even worse was that my sister gave me a book called *The Womanly Art of Breastfeeding* from the La Leche League [a breastfeeding support organization], as well as two or three other books on their preferred list. The books had a common thread: to be a good mother you must hold your [sic] fussy baby constantly. Madonna and child. *The Womanly Art of Breastfeeding* would say things like, a baby can never get enough of his mother's loving arms; and, don't give up! Maybe the next maneuver will be the one to do the trick. A book on baby care by a so-called distinguished pediatrician was ten times more damning. Putting your baby down and letting him *cry it out* was seen as tantamount to abandonment. How would you feel, the doctor said, if you were in tears and your husband made you go to another room because he didn't want to deal with you?

Tzzt! Tzzt! How peculiar I must be! I cannot take comfort while crying and I very much prefer to leave the room if I begin to cry. Afterwards, a firm hug may be useful and important, but not during. This was how fatal my flaw was. I was not loving. I was not loving enough. I couldn't even distinguish my baby's cries—discomfort, hunger, pain—which the books said all moms could do within a few weeks.

The day finally came, though, when Adrian and I came to an understanding. He was seven weeks old. The screaming was going on and on and on and I was raw tired and painfully alone, and my belly hurt, and I felt my body would implode from the pressure the screaming was placing on my system. I knew I had no choice but to put baby in a room by himself. If I didn't, I would harm him. So I took him to the crib, angrily pushed his face down in it, and my mouth said, "If you're going to take a nap, you'll just have to do it yourself!" I returned to the living room and wailed and screamed and sobbed and pounded couch pillows as hard as I could with a much-weakened fist. And after some minutes of this, I noticed something. I stopped crying and I heard it. Silence. Silence! Adrian was taking a nap! Though I couldn't sleep. (I found it excruciatingly painful to nod off only to be shocked awake by screaming, and my sleep deprivation allowed no small fixes), I regained my composure. And I sat quietly with myself on the couch, aware that the sun was shining, ecstatic with gratitude for it. When Adrian woke up, after a full hour, I brought him into the living room and held him in my arms. He met my gaze and suddenly his blank little face swelled into his first, golden, radiant, magnificent social smile! I smiled back, feeling my face plump up and stretch out. "We just might make it," I said.

There are a number of morals to this story. It turned out that Adrian needed long, long stretches of time on his belly in the crib, in a dark, quiet room to get himself settled, as much as three hours some nights. That's three hours of screaming. At the three-hour mark I'd feed him and change him, but he seemed mostly indifferent to those maneuvers, resuming crying immediately after, but settling down in due course. In about three weeks on this new plan, he began sleeping all night and taking at least one nap a day. I didn't know anything about Asperger Syndrome back then, his or mine, but I'd stumbled upon a reason for all his screaming: *over-stimulation*. Picking Adrian up and holding him in a way that would soothe most babies would feel to him like being jostled. Indeed, most of the normal soothing behaviors were downright painful to him and it wasn't until I stopped doing them that he began to get happy about being alive.

In Adrian's case, the books were wrong. Any baby care book that doesn't include the topic of over-stimulation is not credible. The exception to those dismal books was one by T. Berry Brazelton, who introduced me to the concept and at whose shrine I will worship forever! He didn't go far enough for Asperger's but at least I had a meaningful way of seeing my son. Once I knew about over-stimulation, I could make good decisions and, perhaps more important, know why I made them. For example, Adrian would often have a severe startle reaction to being laid flat on his back. It felt like falling to him. So I was able to use a practical suggestion from Doctor Spock, the changing pillow. We didn't have baby furniture anyway, so the idea of covering a nice, plump pillow with plastic, then a soft pillowcase, and doing diaper changes on it worked brilliantly. I also knew to put Adrian to bed on his stomach to sleep, something frowned on now by those concerned with SIDS, but a necessary strategy for babies with intense startling.

Good decisions based on sound theory and information doesn't exactly have a motherly ring to it but the practice mothered Adrian well. In living an AS life, I have collected abundant personal examples of using alternative means to good result. It's still very difficult, though, for me to override the cultural belief in a socially sentimental and intuitive form of loving as the single, legitimate source of parenting. My mother-love is deep and passionate, but it's really quite useless!

Adrian thrived and so did I. Twenty months after he was born, I gave birth to Cassie, who has also thrived beautifully. I call Cassie my seeing eye kid, because she helps me function, and she also waves her hand in front of my eyes to get my attention when I'm off in my world. I still feel pangs of sheer inadequacy. My peculiarity will smash me in the face time and again and I think, "What in the hell am I doing raising kids? I'm no mother at all!" I certainly don't mother the way most women mother. My affect may still be flat as a pancake on too many occasions (though I've taught myself to smile more and laugh more and touch more), but I know something now. I think I do. Maybe I do. It appears likely that I'm a good mother, a loving mother. How very peculiar!

On Being an Aspie Mother

Morgan Allgood

Being a mother has been the most challenging part of being an Aspie. Trying to figure out what the needs are of my kids from the minute they were born has been difficult since, as Aspies themselves as well as teenagers, they often expect me to be a mind reader and a need anticipator.

But there are other things that I didn't expect, social things. Sometimes I'm not sure if my kids have so few friends because of their social problems or mine. I know my son tends to be a little afraid to bring friends home because he tends to be easily embarrassed. My daughter never had many friends, none that came over at least. Except for one time that a friend stayed the night and I about had a nervous breakdown listening to the laughing and happy teenage noise. The whole disruption of having a strange person in my house is always very difficult for me, even with my own friends.

I've also had trouble with anger management. I've worked hard on it, but there's always the guilt. I know the lack of control and the rages come from being an Aspie, but that's no excuse. I'm sure this reality of never knowing what mood I'll be in, and my lack of housekeeping skills have been a source of embarrassment for my children. I never did the whole PTA thing. I am thinking of it this year and my kids are afraid because I'm very vocal about my opinions and my opinions are rarely mainstream. I'm not afraid to discuss anything, so my children and I have had some very frank discussions on sex and drugs and drinking that just don't seem to take place in normal households.

And because I don't drive, they've missed out on a lot of cultural things such as special lessons, and activities. My kids never had a piano, martial arts, dance, or gymnastics lesson. They never had play dates. And until last year when they decided to walk to after school activities, they never participated in those either because I couldn't get them there and back.

I've taken driving lessons, but that still doesn't relieve the fear of a collision because I am threatened by the proximity of the cars whether they are beside, behind, or in front of the car. I have difficulty anticipating hazards and tend to panic if I see a child in a yard while I am driving. I can't judge distance. And it's all too scary and too much input to deal with all at once.

I also often need my children's help, and often they are the ones in the nurturing role, the children parenting the mother. But somehow they understand this and do so willingly.

Still, my children love me and are turning into loving human beings, in some ways more caring than most children their age. They seem to be more responsible than their peers in that they don't use drugs or drink or engage in sexual exploits. Is this because they were raised by a mother with AS? I guess I'll never know. But what I do know is that I am proud of the beautiful young people they have become.

Solitary, Solo Motherhood

Coa

I've been a solo parent throughout my children's lives. That I am on my own arises, I believe, from not having my AC idiosyncrasies understood or tolerated, even within what I had thought to be a committed, caring relationship, but perhaps it is understandable that a partner would misinterpret my ways. The outcome is that I am unquestionably on my own with my children, from start to finish. Really alone. Even the support that more socially able solo mothers usually have, from extended families or friends, isn't there for me. Although at times I would have liked some help, I can't blame others for not knowing when and how help was needed, or for thinking that I didn't want or need or deserve help. What I do know is that this being alone has been an ever-present reality for me. (I should qualify this by adding that I am very grateful that my mother looked after my children in the early years during my working hours, which gave me the benefits of part-time work, but made it all the more difficult to get help any time other than when I was at work.) The real issues I have faced alone.

There is a stigma associated with being a solo, unmarried pregnant woman, in a family and profession where this is virtually unheard of. Yet, for me, it was merely one of the many, many ways in which I never have fitted society's norms or expectations. It did help me to stop hiding my oddness. After all, it's not easy to hide a pregnancy or a baby. Although I had as a child assumed I would one day be a mother, and had looked forward to it and even planned some things about it, as a young adult I had begun to have misgivings due to the rigidity of some of my habits, and what I assumed (from the feedback of others and my own attempts to explain why my life differed from my peers') to be my underlying selfishness and stubbornness. Also I felt very awkward around children and wondered if I would know how to relate to them.

But once it was clear motherhood would be a reality, and once I had dealt with the letters from well-wishers advising me to terminate it, I took it on wholeheartedly, like I take on anything else I make a commitment to. That, I think, is one of my strengths as a mother, and what I hope helps redeem my shortcomings. Once I had made that commitment there has never been a moment, not even a fleeting one, that I have wished I wasn't a mother, or that these two particular young people who have grown up from and with me were not my children and were not here center-stage in my life. I hope that, when I don't show my love for them in the more traditional ways that other parents do (it has been pointed out to me, for instance that I seem to hug and interact with them less), they still recognize my love for them in qualities like the determination with which I stand behind them through thick and thin, like the fierce mother animal defending her young.

How do I manage? My parenting instincts are alive and well, despite my lack of know-how in social situations. It seems like these come from different sources. Breast-feeding was easy and a pleasure. I actually still remember the delight of breastfeeding when I was a baby myself, even though I have no such memories about other early sensory experience. Maybe breastfeeding, too, comes from some more instinctual place than most sensory experience does? Or maybe sensory problems are caused by particular social uses or styles of touch.

In the early stages of motherhood, I was carried through by the combination of instincts and my own childlikeness, which made it very easy to relate to the worlds, of both my NT daughter and my AS son. Strangely, I hadn't noted anything odd about my son's social lacks until he started kindergarten, when very soon I was being asked why he wasn't making eye contact and why he played in a world of his own. At home with me, there wasn't a communication problem, though I had noticed his sensory problems and some strange fears. Maybe I knew the way into his world without having to think. Maybe, since relating to children at all was something quite new to me, I just learnt how to relate to him because I didn't have any preconceptions of how it ought to be done.

We spent a lot of time out in nature when they were little. Their playgrounds were the nearby river rocks and the elfin forests. The winds shook and the rains lashed our little house that stood on its stilts in the middle of nowhere, while the river lulled us to sleep. I sang good-morning songs, tidying songs, Easter-egg-searching songs, and we developed our own funny language from the words we loved to invent together. But it wasn't all so easy.

What I did realize very early on, as I'd feared, was that I would have to adapt some of my habits. How to cater for my single-mindedness, my obsessive interests, my processing difficulties that meant everything needed to be arranged in order in time and space and that I couldn't be interrupted in the middle of certain things? Babies wouldn't respect these needs. Well, after a certain amount of trial and error, my own ways of coping, my own style of parenting, emerged.

One of the first obsessions in my early days of parenting was my garden. While other mothers were off at their mother-and-baby meetings, comparing their darlings, and brands of baby food, there was I, out establishing our garden. It was important for mothers and babies to eat good food wasn't it? And there was all this good earth around us. But I couldn't have a garden at all if it weren't perfect, which meant it had to have every vegetable that would grow in that climate, and it had to be done by good organic principles, with a very sophisticated plan incorporating every kind of companion planting that had ever been written about. This meant studying lots of books, making pages of notes and plans drawn to scale, and incorporating compass bearings, shelter belts, likely wind patterns and so on. Later, when to my horror the opossums came up out of the nearby forest and discovered this new source of food, I had to study and build electric fences as well. And then when those failed despite a succession of sophisticated wiring designs and nights hiding in the bushes with my baby, trying to discover how those darned possums were bypassing my latest defenses, after the failure also of both natural repellents and a meditative approach (asking the king of the possums to intervene and ask his subjects to live in harmony with us), then I enrolled in night-classes to gain a firearms license.

There we sat at school in the evenings, my baby and I, along with all those male hunter types, learning the rules and regulations of firearm, I gained my license but never a firearm, and never my dream-garden, either. I just couldn't bring myself to shoot one of those creatures. Anyway, it was getting increasingly difficult to create the perfect garden with a baby. He was getting too heavy and awkward to wear in the gray shawl while digging. So I tried to garden during his daytime sleep, which meant him sleeping in a tent the garden so I could hear him. This seemed OK until I discovered he had one of those awful phobias of tents (along with similar shape-changing items like umbrellas and balloons). So in my true all-or-nothing style, I simply gave up gardening completely and utterly and forever—accepting that there were indeed sensible reasons for buying food from shops.

A similar approach was applied to several other passions in succession. I gradually learnt to make the most of the hours my children were asleep for whatever most needed uninterrupted focus, and made sure I stayed within earshot of where they slept. That helped me keep my sanity, because there was a bit of the day *for me*, for however I needed most to use my solitude, and I could cope with and even enjoy all the unpredictability of young children as long as I knew this time would come. I learnt to be very organized about this, to have my books arranged, ready to dive into the moment the children dropped off to sleep. I also adapted my own biological rhythms to going to bed at the same time as they did, so that I could make the most of those inspiring early hours of the morning when I was most alert and the rest of the world (especially babies and phones and potential visitors) was most predictably silent. This is a rhythm I have maintained ever since. But heaven forbid if they wouldn't sleep or woke too soon, and heaven help any outsider who should intrude at such times! My children soon learnt, perhaps from the determined look on my face, that they *must* sleep at these times, and that they *must not* get up before a set time in the morning (quiet books in bed was OK). Of course this would be relinquished if they were sick or something, but fortunately such times were rare.

Over the years, as the work I bring home has become more complex, I have had to devise a more complicated system for what gets done when.

Looked at from the outside, you might say this is just a person whose OCD, or rigid personality, is getting more severe and systematized. But, without a system that reduces the overload, I simply can't think clearly enough to put words together into sentences, at least not newly composed sentences. (I could still parrot something automatic or intervene in an emergency.) There are some tasks I can do amid the full chaos of family life, such as filling out a form involving copying words or simple housework. Other tasks can be done while noise is going on providing no complex input is required from me: single sentences (such as some forms require), simple calculations, or a phone call requiring a simple question or answer, as long as no interpretation or weighing of significance is needed.

Anything more requires a period of silence, and the various durations of silence available have to be carefully matched to the various complexities of silence-requiring tasks. Short reports, letters, ordinary phone calls, or the process of wordlessly *thinking* my ideas about the meaning of a conversation can be done when there is an hour or so (the length of time a child might be at a music lesson). More complicated activities, such as putting a series of complex issues into words and into context for a specific purpose, might need hours or days or weeks of largely uninterrupted time. Writing this account is such an example. I write now because I am off work for a fortnight recovering from surgery, and my children are away at school most of the day. When the normal working week begins again next week, the space to organize and translate my experience and thoughts into words will be gone. Is it any wonder then, that if a child comes home unexpectedly early, my immediate response is an indignant "What are you doing here now?" An apology and explanation are hastily added, as I resign myself to the reality of another mode-shift: "Yes, of course it's your home too, you have as much right as I to be here. It's certainly not that I don't love or want you. It's just those silly old processing problems again. I was in the middle of a 90-minute task. Now it's interrupted after 60 minutes, and I'll have to stop and begin again at the beginning, goodness know when."

If the children come home when expected, I have had time to change back out of thinking-writing mode into welcoming-mother mode before they arrive. Welcoming-mother-mode was somewhere in my system all the time, of course; I just need a little time to re-locate and put it back into operation. But it is unquestioningly clear in my hierarchy of different roles and modes that mothering is a basic one: it will never be deleted, it runs un-opposed for a part of every day, it is always there somewhere even when invisible, and it always has priority if there is a serious conflict of interests.

My children have been much more accepting of my oddities than any NT adult I know. I guess that is because they have grown up with me and knew me long before they realized that other people's parents were different. They don't altogether like that I am how I am, but at the same time we don't seem to have serious hate or rejection issues.

Some of the things they have had to put up with because of my differences are:

- A mother who rarely goes to social events, even those associated with their school.
- A mother with annoying and unpredictable processing delays and requirements, who may tell them to speak up or quiet down or not disturb under any circumstances, or utter an eloquent answer long after they have forgotten what they asked.
- A mother with extra-embarrassing habits, such as lack of makeup, hairy legs, and who is liable to appear in public still in bedroom slippers with pen in mouth.
- A mother who cannot model social skills (beyond her level, which they've surpassed). The rest they have to learn elsewhere, wherever it can be picked up, from TV, from school, from other people's parents. Our conversation is mostly limited to major issues affecting one or all of us directly, or things to do with the running of the household. Yet watching my NT daughter with a friend one day (one of the rare times she had someone home), I could see what a range of subtle fluid social and emotional nuances played between the two of them and thought, "You have it all in spite of me."
- For my son, a mother with anger issues (the clash of two strong wills, with little lubrication for the clashes). Occasionally, with combination of mutually high stress levels, and the suddenness with which I can be driven beyond my coping limit, I have physically hurt him. I never hit him, but sometimes grabbed him roughly to "make him attend and see sense", and even bit him slightly once, an incident that filled me with shame and a sense of failure I still haven't fully dispelled. It happened so unexpectedly, like an animal instinct, so great was the tension in me. It wasn't him or *anyone* I was attacking. My jaw would have closed on any object that approached my mouth at that moment.
- A mother who provides a largely asocial home environment, with rarely anyone here besides us, because that's how I need it to cope. This actually suits my AS son well too, but my NT daughter has to mostly go out for the social life suited to her.
- No other adult who takes a close interest in them. I worry what would happen if I suddenly dropped dead, although it is less of a worry now they approach adulthood themselves.
- A mother who requires them to take on adult roles beyond their years. This has happened more in recent years as my life has become more

complex. I find my home-keeping falling apart due to my increasing need for simplicity and isolation. I've more or less given up cooking because it is all just too much on top of everything else, so my children cook the meals. They also engage with the world for me (deal with my phone calls, run errands, get help). I usually collapse in bed before they do, or my daughter will tell me to go to bed and come tuck me in. To quote a Christmas card from my 12-year-old: "Thanks for helping us with moving house (well, at least my room), and I really appreciated it (the help)!—x x x x o o o o—p.s., Thanks again for helping me and I hope that you have a good Christmas/New Year!"

It sounds pretty odd and harsh and indeed I often feel despondent about my parenting. If you were to ask people who know us about my parenting, I think their response would depend on the perspective they took. Those who look into the windows of our lives at isolated incidents or interactions might use words like *harsh*, *controlling*, or *unfeeling*. On the other hand, people who look at what emerges from our home, those who know my children, comment on how balanced and mature they seem—even my AS son, whose difficulties, like mine, already are not very obvious to other people. I was further heartened last week, when my daughter confided some personal difficulties in me, and then added, "I'm surprised I'm telling you all this—none of my friends tell their mothers this kind of stuff."

When I try inwardly to justify the difficulties my children have had to put up with, I think back on two bits of wisdom that have helped stave off that despondency about my weird parenting. One was from a TV program I happened to overhear one day. Someone talking about the effect of stress on children said it wasn't the stress itself that's so bad, it's how children see the adults around them handling it that's important. In the heat of the moment, my children see me dealing apparently very poorly with stresses. They see me weep regularly, and pace up and down at the end of most days muttering "Oh how embarrassing! How stupid!" as I mentally go over all my blunders of the day and work them out of my system. But they also see me, day after day, rise full of determination and optimism to tackle another day. And they see that I never ever give up and always find some solution or other. Perhaps these are not such bad things to be exposed to and to learn from. Perhaps it's not so bad to have challenges so pervasive that one simply has to find solutions other than the traditional ones.

The other thought that has helped, from one of my esteemed teachers in life, is that children learn more from the struggles of those adults around them who are striving towards their goals than from those who have already reached their goals. They learn more from the invisible forces at work in someone's journey and its challenges than from someone sitting smugly at their destination. If that's the case, I guess my children will have learnt something valuable from me.

Mother at Odds

Sola Shelly

I have two sons. I love them. I think that I am a fairly good mother. Looking back, this is a big surprise for me. One of the things that being a woman involves is the role of caregiver: the one who responds to needs, who nurtures, who extends affection and acceptance. Even a woman who does not have a husband or a partner and who does not take on the role of a parent, is at least expected to naturally relate to children of her neighbors or of her extended family. Behind this expectation is the basic premise that, to women, kids are lovable—all kids—solely because they are young. Women who do not click with kids are portrayed in the literature and cinema as cold and uncaring, or even downright selfish or cruel.

I am a caring person, and I don't think that I am cold (although at times I have been told so). I am aware of the expectation that I relate to kids, but I don't know what to do about it. Most kids, like most adults, are like black boxes to me: I have no idea of their feelings and wants. I am mostly indifferent to adults; kids intimidate me. They always have. From a very young age, whoever was younger than me, intimidated me. Being older than someone implies being wiser, knowing better, and being able to support the younger child. But being around kids usually makes me feel stupid.

Girls know, from a very young age, their future role as caregivers. Do they learn this role by imitating their mothers, or from playing with peers? They play with dolls, taking the role of a mother: "The doll is crying. Maybe she is hungry. I am going to give her food, I am going to hug her." I don't get to spend time around little girls very much. I remember once when I attended a meeting with a few parents of my son's class. The parents who hosted the meeting had a little girl, who was only beginning to speak. At some point in the meeting, the toddler appeared, hugging her rag doll. She came up to one of the women who sat around the table, looked at her, and handed her the doll. I don't remember whether she said anything or not; The woman somehow understood that she was expected to relate to the doll, and she took the doll and hugged it. Then she gave the doll back to the toddler, and the toddler was told to go to another room so that the adults could proceed with the meeting. As she left, people were making comments about how adorable the girl was. She was indeed adorable. For one thing, she was really beautiful, and her behavior was very sweet. So I joined the others' admiration of the girl. But I was also amazed at how easily and naturally this whole event went for the woman and the girl who participated; how this little girl, at such a young age, already knew so much about human relationships and about being a female.

And I was relieved that she did not come up to me. I would not know what to do with the doll. I might just say that it was a nice doll, or ask her if she loved the doll, or what the doll's name was. Even if it occurred to me that I was expected to hug the doll, it would feel odd to me to do that.

When I was growing up, I had a few dolls but I don't know how I got them. I remember my mother once actually giving me a new doll that she had just bought for me. But I never asked for dolls as presents. Playing with the dolls was more a technical thing for me. I liked to make things, so I made dolls clothes and Purim costumes. My grandfather who was a carpenter made a small doll's bed with bars around it. It had a little mattress which I could wrap with a small sheet, and a little pillow and blanket which had covers that I could change. I liked to play with all these things; but it never occurred to me to treat the dolls as if they were creatures who had feelings and needs. I never hugged them or pretended to feed them or put them to bed, other than literally just put them in the small doll's bed. And since I had a few dolls and the bed was made for one doll, often there was a pile of dolls in the bed.

Kids, especially girls, are also expected to care for other kids who are younger than they. I never knew what to do with them. Maybe I did not know how to relate to kids of my own age, but then I still had the option of following them, to the best of my understanding. With younger kids, I felt that I had to be a leader in some sense, or at least to respond to them on their own terms. Simply imitating them, or trying to join in their games, made me feel silly. What they were doing did not make much sense to me. Obviously, I tried to avoid situations where I was expected to accompany younger kids; but that didn't always work out, because I was expected to Interact with children of my parents' friends and in the broader family. I remember once when I went with my parents to the Beach. Usually, I used to play on my own at the Beach, or have my parents do something with me. This time, I went for a walk with my father, and he saw a friend. As we approached the man, I was told to join his son, who was bathing near by in the shallow water. The boy was much younger than I, but he seemed to expect me to play with him. So I just did my best at following whatever he was doing, or whatever he asked me to do. All of this time I was thinking, "Why am I doing this?," and wishing it to end as soon as possible. But I was also kind of pleased that I was a good person who unselfishly *did the right thing*.

Some of my difficulty with younger kids was because I connected on intellectual level, or based on well-structured activities. The only game that I felt comfortable playing was "Teacher and pupils," and I started to participate in this game when the other children asked me to be the Teacher. I took the game seriously, and I really tried to teach them things. From the age of twelve I started to give private lessons to younger kids, and I was pretty good at that, judging from the Achievements of the kids and from the referrals they made to me to other kids. But in unstructured or nonintellectual settings, I was not that good. Once a neighbor asked me to watch her two children, a two year old toddler and a six year old girl, while she went on errands. I said OK, because I did believe that I was a responsible person who could keep both kids safe. As soon as the mother left, the toddler hurried to the kitchen window, where he saw his mother on the street. He started to cry and call to his mother. I didn't know what to do. I tried to talk softly and tell him that his mother would come back soon, but of course this meant very little to him. It did not occur to me to pick him up and hold him. After a couple of minutes, his sister started to make funny faces and talk silly to him, and he stopped crying and started to laugh. Then I understood that I needed to distract him by keeping him busy. I asked his sister to show me what he liked to play with, and we managed to pass the time till their mother came back.

Other girls of my age actually *liked* to care for babies and toddlers. As a teenager I didn't have a close girlfriend, but I knew that having friends was important; so I made some efforts to occasionally meet with other girls after school. I remember one time, when I set up with a classmate who lived near by to visit her in the afternoon. When I came, she said that she was going upstairs to her neighbor to take her little daughter to the garden. She said that having the girl with us was going to be fun. It was not fun for me; I was bored. Occasionally my classmate turned to me and said "isn't she cute," but I didn't understand why she enjoyed the activity.

It is obvious, then, that I could not envision myself having children. It was not a decision that I made not to have children at all; I did not make any decision, neither to have nor not to have. It was just one of the many things that fit everyone else, but not me. I was rather boyish, and did better with boys' games. Getting easily anxious and stressed out, I did not seem to have the patience and compassion needed for motherhood. At times I was referred to as emotionally or socially immature and this does not make a good mother.

Even physical maturation did not change my feelings about babies in general. Babies are supposed to get everyone's admiration. Even now that I have the experience of caring from birth for my two sons, I still can't force myself to be excited when a new baby is born in the family. Everyone rushes to the baby's crib to look at the little one and I pretend to be interested, but honestly, this is a person whom I never met and know very little about. The only interest I have in him or her is, that I know the parents, and would like them to be happy, and therefore I wish them to have a healthy and happy baby.

It was not until I had been married for a few years, that I really wanted a baby of my own. I sometimes hear about people's dreams for their children: how they will enjoy doing with the child things that they had enjoyed doing with their own parents; how proud they will be when the child reaches milestones like learning to walk, or graduating school, or even getting married and having his or her own kids. When I was carrying my baby, I didn't think of any of these. I didn't expect the baby to be this way or the other. All I wished for the baby was, to be healthy enough to grow and reach adulthood.

The first feeling that I had for Ron was not really love, but an overwhelming sense of responsibility. This little creature depended on me, totally and at all times. I did not have any instincts or intuition to guide me. Other than medical advice, I did not rely on books, nor did I have friends to share experience with. I didn't look up to my mother or anyone else in the family. I just learned to know my baby, and found—much by trial and error—what worked for him. Surprisingly, I did have patience for Ron. I am not perfect, so I could sometimes become frustrated or lose my patience, but at least I knew that needing me was not his fault. With time and a lot of interaction, I came to know Ron, to share moments of joy and despair. I came to love him.

The very few times when I lost my patience with my children or did not attend to their needs, were when I felt obliged to social norms, or how I perceived them. When my sons were small, this happened mainly when we attended family events. The only reason for coming was a sense of responsibility, trying to keep in touch with my family and provide familial experiences for my children. Trying to be polite and involved with the others often conflicted with the needs of my children (and myself), and induced stress in me, and between me and my children. Once we went to my niece's birthday party, and all the guests were sitting at the living room, the kids being entertained by someone who was hired for that. Ron, a toddler a few years younger than the niece and most of the other kids, was not interested in their Activity, and kept trying to get my attention. That irritated me, because I thought my obligation was to socialize with the other adults rather than to pay attention to Ron, and that Ron should somehow connect with the other children rather than hang on to me. Finally my mother saw how uncomfortable Ron was, and pointed out that another child about his age was calmly playing with toys in the niece's room. The possibility of letting Ron leave the party and enter someone's room to play with her toys while she was not even there did not even occur to me, and even if it would have, I would view it as bad manners. Once I understood from my mother's comment that it would not be viewed as offensive to my brother's family, I was pleased to find a quiet corner for me and Ron to play together.

I guess that my love for my sons shows, but in rather subtle ways. I never did the silly-talk that many adults use for young children. Our interaction was more matter of fact, and included a lot of teaching on my part, and asking questions on their part. Although I told them how I felt or what I thought about things they did, I very rarely told them I loved them. I wanted them to feel confident in my support for them, and be comfortable enough to share with me whatever they wanted to. But I did not expect that being my sons would automatically mean intimacy and emotional closeness between us.

My younger son had a rough time as a baby. Eventually, Ami got the diagnosis of autism. However, caring for him was not different to me than caring for his elder brother. Obviously Ami was much different than Ron, but my approach to caring for a baby did not assume anything about the baby being this way or another. Just as I learned what worked for his older brother, so did I for him. Early on I found out that he got tired of interaction very quickly, and would calm down and fall asleep, if left alone. So after feeding him and changing his diaper, when I was holding him, the moment that I saw that he was uncomfortable I would put him back to bed and leave. When he started to play with objects, his fixations became apparent. It did not seem weird to me, and I didn't try to stop him; it was his way of playing and exploring. I was very annoyed when the psychologist pointed out Ami's "lack of imaginative play" as an evidence for something "being wrong with him." To me, the numerous ways he found for playing with clothes pegs (his fixation at the time) were highly imaginative, much more so than the standard ways other children played with conventional toys. I now understand that his fixations and way of playing were typical of autism. But the message conveyed by the psychologist was more than that, it implied that the very fact that this symptom pointed at the direction of autism meant that this was something to be corrected. When I tried to argue that there was nothing wrong with some of the *symptoms*, I was treated as a mother in denial. Indeed, I *was* probably in denial then, unaware of the way society judges AS life experience. Getting Ami's diagnosis involved a lot of battles with the system, in order to get him good education and services, but this was no crisis in my life, or shattering of my dreams for him. There are many things that most people usually achieve in their lives that he most probably won't achieve; But I never envisioned him doing those things, just because most people do them. His brother is not handicapped, so he has more possibilities opened for him; I don't expect anything specific of him either. I wish both of them to choose their own ways and I would support them both.

Facing the demands of parenting finally led me to realize that I am on the spectrum. Before, I survived by keeping the amount of contact with people to minimum; in case of conflict, giving in was my strategy. I could not do that with my children's needs—I had to fight for them. Dealing with the school system—staff and parents—hit me, again, how different (and sometimes deficient) I was.

Discovering my AS-ness did not make social interaction easier for me, but at least I no longer feel bad about not knowing what to do. I don't feel inferior any more. Now that I am aware of social differences, I look at NT kids with the eyes of an anthropologist. I am amazed at their social skills—from so early in life. I watch how a baby in the stroller tries to make eye contact with everyone—every human, and I think, this baby immediately knows who is human, and where their eyes are, and how important it is to get them to look at you. They know all this without having to learn it. I see how teenage girls from the scouts group that includes Ami express their gender, and I realize how different it is for them than it was for me. I know that it is OK for them to be who they are, and for me to be who I am. I know that Ami is not like the teenage guys in the group, and that only those who do not buy into stereotypes can be his true friends. Not many people are free of social norms, but then there is always the hope to find a true friend among his AS peers.

Is it good or harmful for my sons to have an AS mother? My lack of social life has denied them the opportunity to be around people and to experience a sense of belonging with kids in various groups—neighbors, family friends, and the extended family. I see how mothers take their children to the park, where the mothers chat and their children play together. I see how a woman goes to her next door neighbor for a cup of coffee, laying the basis for relationships between the families—a relationship that may be a foundation for friendships between the children in both families. I see women (and couples) having friends who have children themselves. The children of both families can play together. I saw this at my parents' home, and I can't provide this environment for my sons.

For Ron, it might be bad to have a mother who is socially clumsy, and who can not teach him subtle social skills. It feels even stranger for me to hear social criticism from my son. He notices my poor *face recognition*, and reacts impatiently when I mistake one person for another. Ron probably notices that I am overly trying to be nice to people when I don't know what to do; so I sound "phony" and hypocritical around others, while I never need to put on an act when I relate to him. Maybe Ron would be more social if I were more normal and led a normal life. Maybe if I were more affectionate, my sons would be more outgoing. But, at the end of the day, these questions are really hypothetical ones. For Ami it is extremely important to be accepted and understood. I never felt alienated from him. I never felt this abyss that many NT parents of autistic kids say they feel between them and their autistic child. Keeping emotional boundaries from a very young age made it easier to let my sons find their own way as they experience adolescence. There is some advantage in having a mother who does not project her own needs and wants on her children, and who just accepts them for who they are.

Getting through, (around, under, over, inside) the Day

Domestic Bliss?

Susan Golubock

Housekeeping has always confounded me. I either become hyperfocused on one small aspect of a task and accomplish nothing else, or I scream in torment as I realize that I have gone in circles starting multiple tasks and finishing none. I told my husband shortly after we were married that the first dollars that I earned working were to go for someone to clean the house. We also agreed early on that he would do the grocery shopping, which I could not handle due to the sensory overload, and I would do the laundry, which he hated. I rarely go to a store to shop for clothes. The fragmented way in which specific pieces of clothing are displayed defeats me. I shop catalogs because at least this way I can see them put together as a whole. I also don't need to deal with the lights, and the movement of people, that are inherent in a shopping mall. All clothes that I purchase have to be cotton and comfortable. Labels go immediately because the light touch against my skin is irritating. Trying to follow a recipe is a major ordeal because as soon as I start to *do* what I just read I forget what I just read, and the cycle repeats itself. My husband has learned to not talk to me if he wants dinner because I can not do anything and listen at the same time. I often echo what he says just to buy myself that 3 seconds that it takes for the words that I heard to make sense to me. If he doesn't give me that time before going on, I either miss the next thing said or skip processing what already was said. I simply did what I had to do. I often marveled at these women that I knew who would go out in the evenings to shop or socialize or attend events with their children. I crashed.

Scenes from the Rubble

Jean Kearns Miller

Psst!

It's me!

Over here in this rubble. If you look with

exquisite care you might see an eye peeking out as though

from a cracked shell.

I live in here

in laughable misery

an egg cup upside down, a tipped over bottle of vitamins, a sheaf of papers that need marking, piles of bills and junk mail, labeled folders empty as though their contents had been evacuated to safety, a dish towel, a box that an inkjet cartridge came in, a tupperware lid with no box, a music CD without a case, a pill splitter, three clothespins, a day old juice glass, the shoulder strap of an unknown suitcase, a Christmas doily, a gel heal shoe insert without a mate, a spindle with cash register tapes folded ever so neatly before their impaling in my ritual of object permanence...

and this is only the floor.

Every surface is covered in a peculiar kinship of inanimate entities.

My daughter and husband gossip about me.

Me, too.

I'm despicable.

How can I live like this?

Where is order?

The way it looks in my debris pit is I

Might like it here, prefer it this way.

Or maybe I don't see it

Which can be true when I actually move through it in my mind to focus

somewhere.

But truth is

I crave order!

And craving order creates the disorder.

A world class epistemic dilemma, wrath of god proportions.

I start to organize

straighten

neaten

arrange,

and someone, something interrupts me,

moves something,

217

throws something out,
adds junk of their choosing
appropriates my shelf or container
pulls me away
and this wonderful
spectacular whole my heart yearns for and my mind and hands work madly for
is dashed to pieces.
My brain cannot pick up where it left off.
So I must start over
But the despair's too great
And when I look at it now,
My idea gone
It's a whirl of incomprehensible
Tornado matter
Morbid incoherence
And I shut down
Senses numbed.
Heart broken,
Spirit crushed like
waste paper.

© Jean Kearns Miller

'Cause Its Friday

Kimberly Tucker

Colin asked me if love even existed. "Yes." I told him, without hesitation, in my e-mail reply. I decided to give him reasons because knowing him, he'd want validations to back up my reasoning. (Ever the cynic, Colin.) I realized that love is indefinable in mere words, and told him this. It can't be described with language. How do we define love when mere words seem not to suffice? This is why in the best of poems a metaphor comes close. And when relationships with people or with nature or with pets begin to feel like poetry, that is love. I know that love exists.

I told Colin this. Even though he does not like poetry. So I sent him a Walt Whitman poem to whet his toes:

> *O you and I! What is it to us what the rest do or think?*
> *What is all else to us? Only that we enjoy each other and*
> *exhaust each other if it must be so…*
> *From sex, from the warp and from the woof,…*
> *From the soft sliding of hands over me and thrusting of*
> *fingers through my hair and beard,*
> *From the long sustained kiss upon the mouth or bosom,*
> *From the close pressure that makes me or any man drunk,*
> *fainting with excess.*

It's not filled with metaphor and has more lust than love but if your intention's to get a guy interested in poetry; you've got to start somewhere. Colin's always polite enough to read what I have to say, listen to what I have to tell him when he phones me up, both before and after my husband, Howie, got his diagnosis.

The diagnosis of ALS (Lou Gehrig's Disease) dumped an arctic slush on us, my husband and me, who, after hearing it, were thrust into a crisp autumn day, complete with a view of rolling hills surrounding this hospital marked "M.D." What right have you? I thought, to seduce us with your splendor. With your oranges and siennas. Such haughty exhibitionism on this day of days, a day gone as flat as a New England postcard. And as my husband blew warm smoke into the air and fumbled for car keys; he said aloud, "I'm only 37."

We are all together and that in itself is a rare thing. Our 19 year-old son sits between his siblings in the backseat. Since his girlfriend traded his heart for that kid who sells hot dogs, we see our son more. Kerry, our bright kindergartner; lover of classical music, kitties, and motorcycles, sits on one side of her big brother, and ten year old Jeremy, our artist/poet/sensitive soul, sits on the other. The younger two have pestered all week about Burger King. "How come we don't go out to eat anymore on Fridays? We want to go to Burger King on Friday!" They want it to be like before.

The kids have never known a time when I drove, because I've never driven. Well, there was the time I tried. It was in the school parking lot and Jeff was not yet a teenager. The little ones weren't born yet. He sat in the backseat, frantic, pulling on his ears. "We're gonna die! Mommy's driving! We're gonna die!"

I'm literal. I remember when my husband told me to turn the corner that time. He had said, "Cut it sharp!" What does cut it sharp mean? I hit the snow bank.

Oh, there are lots of HFAs, or for want of a more accurate label, people with Asperger Syndrome, who do drive cars, but as of this writing, I do not. There are lots of things my children have not seen, nor have they heard me do. I don't swear, for instance. Well, not often. Not very well. You cannot miss the things that communication impairment takes away if you have never had them, and such is the way with me. My children would not blink twice if I danced with the family cat Sweet Pea. Or if snipped fringe from our sofa set (named Giddy Moonbeam) to sew onto an elf. Throw pillows, buttons from old clothing, and just about any old toy or cast-off thing is fair game when I've got an inkling to make an elf. Aren't all mothers elf-makers? Dancers with cats? Namers of couches? Writers? Poets? Painters?

Nuts? My eyes are aptly hazel. You know—like the nuts.

And so I had married, Howie, my first boyfriend. We met when I was 14. He was16. Today we find ourselves, like we used to every Friday, just 'cause it was Friday, but some of us are a little taller now—crammed into the little Hyundai. He'd been getting worse. We stopped going inside. He had this idea everyone was staring at him when I had to cut his sausage or if he couldn't tear open his sugar packet.

Not going inside was fine with someone like me. My like-minded friend with Asperger's, Colin, likes to say, "Avoidance is not cowardly! It's a form of self-preservation." He also likes to say, "I'm a pretty unsafe pedestrian. I'm sure I'd be an unsafe driver!" I'm not advocating avoidance, but for people like my friend and me, sometimes it sounds supreme! And if my husband wanted to eat in the car instead of going inside, that meant no fluorescent lights to hit me in the eyes laser-like when I walk into restaurants. No waitresses I didn't understand. No eye contact. No surprises.

Of course the drive-through window posed its own unique problems for my husband. His left arm was limp. Some fingers on it were bent and kind of stuck that way. The muscle goes away and does not come back. It was gone in some places. There was tremor. He had to over-reach with the right arm to

220

grab the bag at the window, and he had to keep his arms steady. Heck, lighting his cigarettes was a two-handed effort. He was especially miserable that Friday.

He was even snappy to the dog, who always meant well in his too friendly, in-your-face-with-the-squeaky-toy way. Pralphdog, the beagle, didn't even beg at the door to come with us after my husband told him to "Git and lay down and take your stupid toy with you and don't chew anything up while we're gone, for Christ's sake, ya piggy chow hound!" (Some days are better than others.)

I pretend I'm like that woman on TV sometimes when there's a mess in the kitchen. I cross my arms, put my hair in a genie-like ponytail, and wiggle my nose and blink my eyes once and twice. But predictably, this bit does not make little problems or big problems go away. Sometimes though, like when I pretend there's magic in the world, or when I dance with Sweet Pea, the people around me laugh or start to believe, or seem to believe there might be magic. A little twinge, a minute one, a little chink occurs like a healing. At least that's what laughter feels like to me when I hear it.

Sometimes my husband and I are allowed moments to be mundane! Ruts are the basis for roads, you know. back before any pavement was set down, the ruts were there, are there, beneath. Sometimes, Howie and I are so far in our rut; it that we forget, momentarily that doctor who said, "…two to six years." I don't want to trudge ahead. I want to be stuck *right here*.

Well I had to say to that doctor, "How sure are you its ALS?" (This after a year of ruling out every other ailment the kind doctor with the wet eyes could think of.)

"96%…"

"Oh, well then we have 4%! Good!" I said.

And that day we went out into the parking lot with the news and we were slapped with the beauty of the perfect autumn day. That building was high on a hill. That hospital was put there in a place so picturesque I thought, "My meager attempts at pointillism do not surpass this display." But it could've been a piece of paper, that valley view laid out before us, filling me, inspiring me to dash home and paint one more matte page of a fall scene. But maybe the trees knew more than we did. And I have since forgiven them.

Some days we are consumed by the stark reality of the 96th percentile. Other days, like when we watch the MDA telethon, or learn about chromosome 21, the marvelous research, like the unraveling of the DNA genome, we live in the ever-hopeful 4th percentile. When we are blessed enough to be *in a rut*, to be *mundane*, like any couple with three kids and a dog and two cats, and a past and a present; we are simply living.

We say, "Shall we pick up crushed gravel to put in around the back of the tree?" This is a plan. A project. He can still drive and at the store the discussion turns, mundanely, to mulch. Yes! How lovely to have these topics in our minds. We will plant bulbs. We will watch shoots rise and break ground in the spring like anyone else. We are only 36 and 38 after all, and like many couples, we have three kids and a dog and two cats, and a past and a present. We are simply living.

That Friday was not mundane, I regretfully say. He'd been let go at work. After 20 years of saying, "Roofing's backbreaking work. I do quality work. I don't drink on the job. Hell, I don't drink. I see these doofuses who break OSHA rules and throw houses together like cardboard...I gotta change my line of work. I got guys working on the crew who don't care about the product they put out. I care what kind of job I do. But what thanks do I get? A bad back? We don't even have *our* house yet. I gotta get out of this line of work. But it's all I know. And I'm good at it."

He wanted to quit the business, but not because of a disability. Retiring at 38 wasn't in his plans. Before we left for the fast food place, he'd kicked the dog's rawhide toy. It hit the wall. He slammed the bathroom door so hard we all looked at each other funny. Since I have a hard time reading people's moods and looks, I was confused. He came out of the bathroom after some time and said, "Let's get this over with. You only want to go to Burger King because you like the toys and you two damn well know it." We all weren't sure we wanted to get in the car with him after that but we did.

He sputtered all the way to Burger King. "They always forget to put my fry in the bag. They put on cheese when I tell 'em leave it off. And so help me, if yous two act up back there..."

And what kind of threat is that, I thought...he's never laid a hand on them, this gentle man...

We had to pull up behind a long line of cars in the drive through lane. It was dinner rush hour on a Friday. He thumped his left knee against the car door. *THUMP. THUMP.* It got attention but none of us said anything. back and forth went his knee between the steering wheel and the car door. I glanced into the backseat at our six-foot-one son. Limbs, hot breath, a weird twister game...we were all together! It wasn't even our car. It was my parents' car. We couldn't afford one, and had to borrow this one on a permanent basis. That was bothering him too. It was really small for this family of ours.

I caught the penetrating gaze of my husband's eyes and didn't recognize him. He was tight-lipped and his stare went through my eyes, cold and hard. I copied his knee thumping, and started in to knocking my own knee against my car door, really hard. *THWACK.* He slowed his thwacking down to a steady impatient roll. He gave me a disinterested sidelong glance but I thought he was interested in what my noise was about. I was only just starting. I wasn't angry. Far from it. I wanted a chink out of him. He looked like a coil on a catapult about ready to fling into space. I wouldn't get him back if he flung into space. If he climbed into a black hole, there was a temptation to climb in with him. If I went in I wasn't coming out. If he'd unwind the coil, a little...he was the sweetest nicest guy I'd ever known.

Having Asperger's means relearning for every situation what I need to know. It means copying. It means acting sometimes. It means studying what people do so as to better fit (as much as I detest conformity) because sometimes it is necessary to be in social situations where I am required to play a role I do not feel cut out for. I started into acting. I punched my thigh. I was a lunatic I'd seen on TV, a hyperactive, angry, tense person thwack-thwack-thwacking my knee. But I needed more.

The cars hadn't moved much. We were about two cars behind the ordering window now. My voice, being naturally soft, lent humor to my novice's attempt at cussing, and my results were achieved easily. I added tight lips and a cold hard stare for good measure! *THWACK* went my leg against the door. There were bruises later on the side of my knee!

"Those fuckin' whoremongers!"

"Mom!" said Jeremy. "Did everyone hear Mom? What's wrong with Mom?"

Jeff snickered.

"Bastards making us wait for stinking food—I don't care how good it smells—they're gonna' screw up the order anyhow—always do!"

I couldn't help but glance at poor Jeremy who was searching his older brother's face for clues as to why I'd flipped. "Jeff, do you hear Mom?"

I swallowed hard and tried not to laugh and started in again. As for my husband, I saw his body go slack. His leg went quiet. Mine didn't. I started it going locomotive speed and then decided flailing my arms would be a nice touch. He turned his head to look away from me; and rolled his window all the way up.

"Dirty sons of bitches!"

"Mom!" Jeremy was practically spitting like Sylvester the cat now, the way he does when he's really frustrated. "I don't believe this!"

"Let me tell you," I went on, flailing and thwacking, "if they don't get our order right I'll personally go in there and open a can o whoop ass all over their sorry burger flippin' asses! Sons of bitches! Move this fuckin' line! We're important people! Son of a bitch!"

Chink.

I heard an escape sound come out of my husband's face. Maybe out of his nose. Like he was blowing it. But I looked and he wasn't. Then another blowing nose sound.

"Mom you're nuts. Dad, you're laughing."

He was laughing. Then talking. "I'm not that bad, am I? Now shut up, will you? We're at the window! Mom *is* crazy, guys!"

He pulled over near the big dumpster so Kerry might get a chance to see a train go by. The track ran right behind the dumpster, handy to throw our food bags in when we were through eating. The oversized hamburger shook and squirted nasty stuff when he tried to grasp it. No small feat for the *non*disabled!

I unwrapped the tacos I had brought with me. (I did not eat hamburgers or fast food chicken or French fries.) He saw me looking.

"I'm *fine*."

I did not like the way he said fine.

A train rumbled by and Kerry leaned into the front seat to see. I figured she wasn't too damaged by my swearing. After all, it isn't as if she'd never heard the words before. Her father wasn't a habitual cusser but he sometimes slipped up.

"What's this extra bag?"

"Did we order this many fries?"

"Mommy, am I 'posed to get seven chicken nuggets in my meal?"

"They left off the cheese. I still don't believe they got it right."

"What's with the extra chicken sandwich? We did not order this many sandwiches. Who wants this? Its even plain!"

"Oh, gosh! You don't suppose they heard all my swearing?"

He was laughing then; they all were. I had a view of his hand, the lettuce, the fixings in his lap. I laughed. I wanted to be in a rut. I damned myself for all the years I'd wasted complaining what a rut we'd been in. Because what a road we now had ahead. I had no idea if that road had working street lamps on it for us to see. If it did, surely we were turning each one on individually as we went along. One by one. What's more, neither of us had any knowledge of street lamps, how they worked, or of what was around each bend in the road. We climbed each lamp; by chance got it glowing, shimmied down, and happened along again. That was our future. Occasionally we hit ruts. For that we gave thanks. We lingered in each rut as long as we could flounder but eventually we had to trudge ahead.

I was glad to hear us all together. I was glad it was dark in the car, what with my tears falling down. We try to go out to eat every Friday, just 'cause its Friday. Lately we've been ordering pizza in. That's just fine with me.

On Valentine's Day, some people appeared at our door with some boxes. They were papered with cutout hearts. I sat down on the floor with the boxes of food and gifts, and valentines, and I cried. Then I carefully removed every paper heart from the boxes with a kitchen knife to save in my keepsake box.

"We care about your family!" the messages said in crayon and in glitter and colored pencils. (Thank you, Girl Scouts and Brownies.) "We love you! God bless your family!" were the messages I read in little girls' writing. There must've been a hundred hearts.

It's these things that get us through. It's not always easy. Before the diagnosis, there was a time for our family when we didn't have insurance. Because of this, we ended up with some medical bills. You might be surprised to know that there is a bill being voted on in the state House of Representatives which would prevent banks from taking out the first $1,000 of funds when a bank account is executed on.

Unfortunately, we speak from experience, because last month a creditor tried to collect an old debt on an unpaid medical bill when they knew full well the only money coming in was social security/disability. They put an execution on our checking, freezing ALL funds. We had no access to money and six unfilled prescriptions with a twenty dollar co-pay each for our son who has a condition which requires him to have steroids on hand at all times. We had to go to court to have the execution lifted on money that it was unlawful for them to take! This bill must be passed.

My husband faces ALS with swords raised. He is courageous, beautiful. When I paint him, I find I cannot paint him in the realistic style I once painted in. My paintings of him are now done in bold rich color, the patterns surreal. Certainly our lives have become such. I was lucky enough to marry a poem. If a cynic ever asks you if love exists you can take my word for it.

© Kimberly Tucker

Originally appeared in *Kaleidoscope*.

Birth from the Other Side

(Or Alone Doesn't Always Equal Lonely)

Coa

My waters broke while I was sitting on the bucket (my makeshift toilet), as I was about to go to bed in my tiny caravan. It had been raining hard all weekend, and, having just been down to check the river condition, I knew that crossing it to get to hospital would be impossible. It would be sensible to get some sleep, before the labor really set in, and, considerate to the family in the house on the hill (the only other people on this side of the now impassable river) to let them sleep, too, rather than walking over just yet to tell them my baby was coming. A home birth with no midwife? Well, I wasn't afraid of that. Birth is a natural biological process women have managed for countless generations, before modern interventions were devised, and so would I. So this being my last chance for many years to savor my aloneness, I snuggled into bed and drifted off to sleep to the reassuring roar of the river.

Once it was a decent hour to disturb other people, I set off across the fields, a somewhat lurching gait, clutching the nearest fence post during the height of each contraction then scuttling as far as I could before the next one set in. Somewhat to my disappointment, I found the river had gone down, so hospital it would be after all.

Labor in the hospital was OK, apart from the extra stresses of needing to concurrently communicate and labor. For example when my sister, who had been rubbing my back had to leave the room in the height of the labor, I cried out desperately, "Oh, someone rub my back!" And the midwife responded, "Say please!"—causing me to feel thereafter very guilty at being so rude, and to divert energy from labor into struggling with the questions of correct etiquette.

And then when I said I was ready to push, she said, "Don't be silly, it'll be hours away at your age"—which set off another inner conflict between a biological being following my instincts, and the good little girl following instructions, till my instincts soon proved themselves to be irresistible and indeed correct:

And there he was! I had known this would be a glorious arrival! Early in pregnancy, I had meditated on the question of whether or not it was right for me to continue this pregnancy knowing my baby would be fatherless, as well as realizing my personal peculiarities that might make me a poor parent, and into the meditation had flooded the music from *Messiah*, "For unto us a child is born…and his name shall be called Wonderful…the Prince of Peace." I knew then, he would be a very special child, and would have a very special effect on my life.

In the early hours after the birth, we were the whole world, my prince and I, getting to know each other. I was dimly aware of the peace rosebush blooming outside our window, but little else. Until, that is, they moved us into *the ward*. In the ward were other women and their babies and along with them came things like husbands and flowers and pink or blue booties and other color-coded baby paraphernalia. And kisses. And fussing. And descriptions of their purpose built nurseries. And that was when I felt…lonely.

It's not that I especially wanted those things, but maybe just a touch of them? Maybe just the choice to accept or reject? It brought me wistfully tantalizingly close to that world from which I seem forever excluded. One which I had many years sought and aspired to, but which had repeatedly rejected me because I simply didn't fit however hard I tried…

One by one, the husbands proudly bundled up their darlings, placed them in their comfortable car seats, and off set the pink-and-blue-bootied babies to commence their training as good NT citizens.

I bundled up my little prince into a long gray cloth, which wrapped us together, chrysalis-like and we two ACs, set off on our rugged journey. The river was back to half-flood, waist-deep, too deep for a vehicle to ford, too deep for gum boots, but passable for barefoot wayfarers willing to risk the wobbly river-rocks and swirling currents. Well, that's life isn't it? Give me raw nature any day. I don't need frills to find fulfillment in life.

We went on living there, on the edge of the wilderness, reveling in the ever-changing elements, skies, river, forest, with no other house in sight, for seven years, gradually expanding our family, with the arrival of my daughter, and our accommodation, from the 11 foot-caravan to a half-house (a house that was up for demolition, one half of which was towed there by truck). It was never lonely there, with or without my children. One day I'll go back there to retire.

I enjoy my meetings with other travelers in life, but don't find it necessary to live with them. It's not that I wouldn't or couldn't live with others, just that dispelling loneliness would not be the motivation. We are each alone in our journey through life, though living together in an intensive social way may give the illusion of togetherness. But facing death is frightening for those who haven't come to terms with their aloneness and that is something that doesn't frighten me at all, just like birth.

© Coa Jonassen

Scenes from a Car Wash

Jean Kearns Miller

A week ago: It's me,
standing in the bay of a self-serve car wash up to
mid-calf in soap suds,
with a soap suds wand tucked under my arm
rummaging frantically in my purse for quarters.
In my head at that moment is an idea
out of the blue sky or was it gray as they mostly all are
that if the car wash ends
it's buzzing to say it's on my last quarter
someone driving up will believe I am ready to leave
and I'm not done yet.
This means I have to get at the quarters
to put them in the slot to keep the water and soap
from stopping so I can hold my spot
and not mislead the other and fail
to communicate again.

I've observed it countless times.
Someone drives in,
gets out of the car,
puts the money in,
washes their car,
and when it's done
(always by the end of the quarters),
they hang the spray or soap wand
back on the wall brace
where they got it,
get back in the car and drive off.
So I cling to this protocol
until faced with the mud and salt the sprayers missed
that didn't turn up till the buzzer started going,
and my realization that I'd spent too much of the
allotted time soaping and not enough
rinsing.
Everything is in pieces in my head.

It's in my field of consciousness

229

—like peripheral vision—
the idea won't come clear that I might possibly
shut off the soap suds
but I have absolutely no cognition of steps in the sequence
of doing just that.
The idea dodges my mind's eye and hides from view
the more I try to conjure it.

It's just me
and car
and soapy shoes and tights
and those damn quarters
and the buzzing,
and the big streaks of road salt and mud
that haven't been washed off yet
and the increasing traffic of SUVs
cruising for their turn.

Analysis,
given maybe a minute of pause would have helped me
clarify and sort this experience
so I could've strategized,
but the way I experienced the event
is broken up
in pieces already.
That it occurred to me all at once in a bombardment,
doesn't make the experience integrated and whole for me
and it never will. After the fact
I can piece it together and maybe
create some sort of makeshift template
for future encounters, as long as the encounters are car washes.
Waiting in line at the grocery and realizing I've forgotten something
is an event that will benefit little from the car wash knowledge.

What analysis never does for me is make meaning.
I don't grow any through it, I don't really learn from it.
I can't move from the knowledge to new discoveries.
So if Aristotle says there are five types of souls
(1.2.3.4.5),
that concept only ever means that to me.
I might pass the exam but I'm ad-libbing and hoping
my writing ability
will obscure my emptiness.

I find a kind of stim in analysis,
and can be sort of fond of the ideas because of the symmetry,
but that's all.
I truly don't know what the hell Aristotle got
out of classifying and analyzing every damn thing.
All I know is I know what Aristotle's five types of souls are.
That and 94 cents will buy you coffee at McDonalds.

Synthesis for me is a coming together of
memory,
imagination,
cognition,
recognition,
direct experience,
ideas, so that
things become meaningful to me.
It often appears with apparent suddenness but when it does,
I've usually been struggling to work it out for some time
and it finally all came together.
Often it comes to completeness when a final
event,
image,
bit of data
comes along.

And even if others may benefit from my sharing my insight
the insight is
alwaysalwaysalways
personal.

I'm driven to sort and reconfigure
but I now know
exactly what doing that will do for me
and what its limitations are.

Turning points for me are always synthetical.
Discovering modernism, contemporary art and poetry, were big
breakthroughs.
Dylan Thomas. Yippee!
I'm on to something!
He's on to something!

The force that through the green fuse

drives the flower, drives my green age;
that blasts the roots of trees is my destroyer.
And I am dumb
to tell the crooked rose
My youth is bent by the same wintry fever.

You could say it was a poem about
The Ironic Juxtaposition of Youth and Death
and pass the quiz, but what was so
stunning was how you really couldn't take it apart
without destroying it.

And nonrepresentational art—well, there it was:
Utter synthesis!
Not about anything, not about nothing,
no topic, no parts, all parts.
"Kandinsky was on to something, too!"
I brighten as I get in my soapy car and go.

© Jean Kearns Miller

Bus Routes and Lifting Machines

A Life of Obsessions and Routines

Marla Comm

According to my records, I was diagnosed as having autism at age three. My parents took me for evaluation because I had no speech other than echolalia and isolated words, had numerous fears, rejected cuddling, and rejected human contact. When I did start speaking by the age of four, my parents thought that whatever I had was gone or that the doctors had been wrong, so they chose to bring me up as a normal kid. They expected me to function like my NT sister and grow up to be a completely independent adult with husband, kids, nice house and lofty career. I was even punished for not making friends, for obsessing with weird things, and for the Tourette's tics that started at age seven.

I was sent to a regular school and enrolled as a regular pupil. That meant doing the same work as the others with no aide and being expected to function socially and behave maturely. Thanks to my math ability and a school system that counted only multiple choice or short answer tests based on material learned by rote, I got through school with no real problems. I behaved immaturely (crying when I didn't get my way) and had odd mannerisms, but I never made enough trouble to draw serious attention.

When I was 13, the high school guidance counselor found me disturbed and referred me for psychiatric help. I always suspected something was wrong with me. Even at age five, in kindergarten, I sensed I was different from the others, that I perceived the world differently. I had my own made-up words for everything (still have them) and experienced everything through those words. Even at five, I knew the other kids didn't have their own language to the extent I did. I also realized that I couldn't play games or move as well as the other kids.

I started having number obsessions as soon as I was old enough to understand numbers. When I was six and seven, I inappropriately asked people how much they weighed and how old they were. Those were also the years when I made up most of my private words and associations. My interest in buses started at age seven when I began to beg to go to the street where the number 7 bus ran. Something in me wanted to associate myself with a bus, and I didn't know why. Until my mid teens, when I was old enough to take buses on my own, my obsession centered around watching buses and finding out whether a given number had a bus route. Along with the obsessions, I had a set of rules to determine when it was appropriate to indulge my obsession and when it wasn't. The rule said, for example, I had to justify in particular ways using the bus whose number I liked at the time.

Although obsessions come and go, they never disappear completely. I no longer get pleasure from the old ones after new ones come along, but I do retain memories of the things I did to indulge the old ones and the odd thinking that went with them. When an obsession loses its power, I start finding the things I did and thought ludicrous.

My childhood obsession with needles and medicine had me thinking I wanted to be a lab technician, and I enrolled in a three-year program after finishing high school. After the first semester, I switched to general sciences because I didn't feel up to the social demands of dealing with patients. I also realized that my lack of manual dexterity would hinder my performance as a lab tech. Like all three-year programs, this one was intense and high-pressure, which I found very hard to handle.

I had no intention of going to university after I finished the three-year program, because I had become obsessed with the machine I used as a nurse's aid to move heavy patients. Under the grip of that obsession, I thought I wanted to remain a nurse's aid forever.

A few years later, I applied for a nursing assistant course because I didn't like being told what to do by nurses. Nursing assistants can do the same work as nurses in my workplace, which means they can be team leaders and have more say in what they do. My dream was to have the freedom to work alone and choose patients who needed the use of the lifting machine. My science grades impressed the nursing-assistant teachers so much they accepted me on the spot. Classes got off to a bad start, however, with a major panic attack after my bike was demolished by a car on the very first day. The whole school called me a mental case. After a week of classes, the teacher had me removed from the program because she noticed my odd mannerisms and symptoms of anxiety.

When my lifting-mechanism obsession ended in the early 1980s and I started getting fed up with my nursing aid work, I decided to go to university part time to do math. My aim was to teach math to adult classes. In the beginning, I loved school and did really well. As time went on, I felt increasingly unsure about my ability to stand up in front of a class as a teacher, but I finished the BSc. Honours math program because I was doing so well and found the work interesting.

The only things I found hard in my undergraduate days were exams held in the evening, which interrupted my supper routine. I always needed and still need that routine to give me something pleasurable enough at the end of the day to keep me going through the rest of the day. I used to try to get out of night exams by feigning illness, but that only worked twice. I developed anxiety attacks when graded exams or assignments were returned, because my whole self-image hinged on how well I did. Teasing was still an issue, though not as bad as in earlier years of schooling. The only classes where I had no teasing were the few graduate-level courses I took, where some of the students were adults.

I didn't like graduate school at all, though. The work was too difficult, less straightforward and more confusing. The sheer volume of math concepts overwhelmed me. Also, classes were held in the evening, which was never my best time.

I ended up lucky to have my current job created for me after I was fired as a nursing aid for my rigidity and other behavior problems. All along, I knew I'd never be able to handle any career that required social skills or flexibility. The thought of sudden requests to travel or attend evening meetings daunted me. I couldn't see myself as a teacher, a real nurse, or anything else professional. Nor could I stomach spending my life doing menial jobs, which not only bored me but drove me nuts because of my lack of physical (especially manual) dexterity. My job is just right: an interesting but routine position as a medical library/records assistant. Things can still upset me about work, but I can't ask for more in a job.

© Marla Comm

Going Public

Social Dyslexia

Jane Meyerding

Somebody asked me recently if there might not be some way in which I could enjoy doing social things. How about, he said, if we removed the pressure of expectations (to react, to talk) and kept the number of people to two or three and didn't get noisy, etc., etc. Well, I answered, if you took away all the things that make me not like socializing, I guess the answer is, yes, I might like that kind of social activity.

My answer didn't satisfy me, though, because it leaves out something major. To wit: I can enjoy (I am able to enjoy) only those things in which I have an interest. The list of those things is long, it seems to me, but it does not include idle chitchat, trading personal information with acquaintances, or discussing clothes, hair, weight, relationships, etc. (Lack of interest in such things tends to have a snowball effect with people whom one sees regularly. If you can't remember, because you can't be interested, whether they have kids, want to lose weight, follow a particular sports team, or the like, you get further and further *behind* in terms of establishing a *normal* social relationship with them.)

Over the course of my adult life, I have learned how to redefine many topics in order to make them interesting to me. I did this partly by nature (I notice/home in on the little flakes of interesting-to-me material buried within what everyone else considers a different subject altogether) and partly on purpose. There are times when I *need* to have an interest in what is before me. School/university was a prime example. I needed to be interested in the courses I took or else I would fail them. (I cannot *apply myself* sufficiently when I lack interest.) So I would delve into the material presented until I could dig out the interesting-to-me elements. Either that or I would re-invent the material, interpreting it into something I could use to hold my interest.

This process worked well for me, for the most part, thanks to my ability to impress teachers with my writing. Even if I took their subject off into some unexpected byway, they gave me points for how I presented my ideas.

Outside the classroom (and even occasionally inside the classroom, depending on the professor), the process has some drawbacks. People who notice what I am doing, who realize that I am distorting everything so that it fits my own interests/needs, see me as self-centered and stubborn—they don't know the word *perseveration*.

(And isn't that an example of how a survival mechanism, a skill an AS person—me, in this case—has learned in order to negotiate her way more successfully through the NT word, becomes a *symptom* of a *disorder?*)

239

I think this is what was missing from my response to the man who thought I would be able to enjoy being social if only being social were cleansed of its AS-unfriendly elements. For me, my social deficits are not all a matter of what I need to avoid (crowds, noise, sensory overload); they also include the inability to focus sufficiently on anything but what interests me. My brain has to work overtime at manufacturing reasons for interest or else I float away like a helium-filled balloon without a string. Social occasions do not provide enough raw material for my poor stressed brain to work with.

A while ago, Kay wrote: *I liken our low tolerance for social contact with a dyslexic's easy fatigability with reading. It's hard for us to interact, and our neural machinery is lacking in this area. It's easy to overtax what we have. To put it simply: I just ain't wired for the social stuff.*

Kay's original analogy assumes a person whose dyslexia can be overcome by sheer dogged effort. Reading remains difficult and tiring, but it does become possible. Sometimes, though, I suspect my autism (or at least some aspects of it) is like a dyslexia that cannot be overcome. I know I often appear to be performing social functions (more or less well or badly, depending on what they are and what my energy level is at the time). But often what I actually am doing is analogous to the way a totally dyslexic adult might hold a book in front of her eyes to simulate reading and thus prevent other people from guessing her secret. I have learned to act out certain rituals of socializing, just as a 100% dyslexic (non-reading) adult might have learned to appear to consult a bus schedule, read the label on a can of beans, or while away a bus ride by reading the sports page of the newspaper. NT (non-dyslexic) observers would assume that the dyslexic person was having the same kind of experience as they would have if they were consulting the bus schedule, etc., and that she was obtaining the same kind and amount of information as they would extract from the print material. In fact, however, the totally dyslexic person would be under a lot of stress, hoping her pantomime would pass as the real thing. She would obtain nothing useful from the schedule/label/newspaper and would be struggling to pick up clues from those around her that might clue her in to the kind of comments she ought to be making herself in order to appear normal. Quite often she would have the experience of being found lacking in information she was supposed (by those around her) to have gotten from the *reading* they thought they saw her do.

That description of a total-dyslexia experience fits me pretty well with regard to many social experiences. Although I may look as if I am participating, I actually do not get anything out of it, neither enjoyment nor information. People are likely to assume that I know more than I do about them and about others (e.g., at work) because they have seen me engage in what they thought was successful socializing, the kind of situations from which they themselves glean an enormous amount of information.

Another aspect of the analogy is the way the two conditions (dyslexia and autism) close part of the world to those who are affected. The world of print (not only books and newspapers but also street signs, clothing labels, etc.) excludes the totally dyslexic. The world of social interaction excludes autistics.

Rape

Coa

One of the paradoxes of my life is my experience of what is and what isn't stressful, compared to what other people apparently experience. This is also one of the reasons I seem to be seen by other people as such a "poor coper." If someone as educated, talented and mature as I bursts into tears over such seemingly trivial matters, then I must be really very weak, hysterical, self-centered, or maybe using tears to manipulate.

Once I was raped. But this actually ranks very low in my list of stressful life events (so much so, that I've never bothered to mention it in any of my counseling sessions over the years). After all, it is clear why it happened, I dealt with it sensibly at the time, it's over and unlikely to happen again, and didn't impair subsequent relationships, so what's the big deal? It happened because of my social naivete. During my tropical island adventures, I had sought out a certain waterfall in the jungle where there was reputed to be an impressive natural sliding rock. So there I was, biologically an attractive young white lady in my 20s, but socially the level of a pre-school kid. And there were the local youths. And there was the rock, in this stunning steaming jungle setting, offering an exhilarating natural slide down the waterfall into the crystal-clear pool at the foot of the falls. Over and over I went, a delighted kid on the physical level, an awe-inspired nature-lover on the spiritual level, but socially totally blind to any hidden nuances. We were all just kids playing in a God's playground, weren't we? It was on my way home along the jungle track that it happened. I screamed and struggled but to no avail, as he was very strong. When I realized that rape was inevitable, I shifted goal to simply staying alive. Thus it was with a sense of relief rather than trauma that I survived this incident. Finally, a shot of penicillin in the backside, in case of VD, and that was the end of that.

On the other hand, a type of incident high up on my stress list, involves the difficulties of communicating with co-workers. I am still as helpless as ever at dealing with this sort of thing. For example, one of the places I used to work in, would seem to most people a pleasantly friendly informal place to work. Meetings were held irregularly. But a lot more decisions than people realized, were made by words exchanged during the gaps of everyday working life. I used to watch in awe how others did this. A work of art, this weaving in and out of the spaces of social life. It was something that seemed to flow seamlessly, these people could switch without a breath between doing something for a client and discussing the politics of the workplace and back again. If one of them asked me something in this way, I would blurt out an answer as best I could so as not to be rude and at the same time not lose track of whatever I was actually trying to do myself at the time. But try as I could, I could never do what they did. It seems one would need to find compelling words and quite a direct eye contact and something sort of friendly but irresistible in the tone of voice and facial expression, all in a precisely timed split second. Whereas the best I could manage was a polite but somewhat stiff and formal "Can I ask you something please?" which was usually answered by a "Not now!" (even if I'd said something small/brief/simple). And if I then said "When then?" they would say something like "3.20 tomorrow" and I would have to drop whatever I was doing at 3.20 the next day, and likely enough that time would be no longer convenient and another time would have to be scheduled for my question. This is not a criticism of any particular person because they were all like that, and they were all very "nice," easy-going, well-meaning people. So clearly it was my problem. Or was it? Even when I explained why I had these sorts of difficulties, they listened very nicely but never remembered the relevance when it came to these apparently trivial incidents. (Maybe I was too timid? Maybe I was too stubborn and inflexible to try a new approach? And of course too self-centered. And simply not trying. Or on the other hand perhaps trying too hard, you just have to relax. you know! The usual tedious string of criticisms).

But look here! I've been to a lot of personal growth stuff over the years, and I've learnt a lot of things rather quickly. I've learnt to value myself, I've learnt to communicate well one-to-one. I've learnt to be assertive, resolve crises, and overcome fears. I've slept on the crater-rim of an erupting volcano. I've spoken up about a moral issue when none of you had the guts to do so to his face (even though you were happy to mutter privately behind his back). But I simply can't weave my way into your conversations. I lack the speed and coordination and style, and as for the spaces, well, I can't even see them till you're filling them in.

Of course by the time I had carried such a question around for a week trying to slip it in somewhere, it had become a much bigger question, and then unable to bear the burden and the uncertainty and embarrassment it caused any longer I would suddenly burst into floods of tears. Bingo! The final proof that I'm such a poor coper, to get so upset over something so tiny! Well, that kind of incident is like a rape of my whole person, my whole way of being. And it's repeated over and over again, year after year, place after place.

Now do you see why that's so much more traumatic than the incident in the jungle?

© Coa Janessen

The Personas

April Masilamani

This was the most stressful thing to write. Everything else seemed a bit boring on rereading, as it is just based on my memories and I have not lived a very exciting life. But I put it all in, because it was hard to work out what might be useful. This, however, is more to do with who or *what* I might be, and it is something I have not analyzed before. I was not sure where it would take me, especially as, when I try to get to the essence of things, there is a strong pull to go there and never come back. This could be regarded as a form of madness, I suppose, and dangerous, given my present level of responsibility.

My personas developed over the years, usually forced into creation mostly as the result of shock, not something I deliberately set out to do. Shock is my way of describing what happens when the NT world forces itself into my fantasy—or my real world, depending on how you look at it. The personas are usually based on nothing one could call a personality, but on a mimicked personality developed by careful observation of what was required by the NTs. However, there is a common theme running through all of them that may be my link to who I really am, (I have trouble with the word *who*—*what* might be a better choice). This theme is slightly manic, humorous, a bit larger than life or larger than what is required, and, even when I'm aware of having to watch my Ps and Qs, it is still inappropriate. Humor plays a big part, as everything seems slightly odd and things are often funny, even when tragic, although I'm not sure that they mean to be. In looking at my personas, it's a bit like looking in the wardrobe for a specific outfit that I've just remembered I've got, instead of putting on the usual blue or gray clothing.

Using my new AS perspective, I've almost convinced myself that I'm not AS because, if the common theme of my personas is a funny, social, nutty person, that's not very Aspie. However, most of the time, without the personas, I'm actually nervous, neurotic, worried, grumpy, and stressed. So which part is real? I then thought that maybe when I'm drunk, that would be the real me; there is diminished control then, and I'm very aware of always being in control. However, once again, I'm a happy drunk, although extremely inappropriate, according to those who will still speak to me the next day. But, as I don't consider myself happy, then once again I come back to the question "What is real?" Because the neurotic *me* is like a computer, always analyzing and sifting through the data input, always studying and thinking about the object in front of it (usually human, as they represent the most challenging data-processing), trying to make sense of everything that comes in. Once the data are processed, an appropriate persona is activated and goes out to deal with the situation. This persona is only a front forced into being by the world trying to get in. Behind all this is nothing in particular that I can work out, and I'm really trying. It's more of a trance state, a state of nothingness, that would be perfect if everyone would go away and leave it alone. I am wondering if this is the normal core center for everyone. Perhaps it is. I should ask people. In fact I will. It might be useful for this book. (Attempts to do so, so far, have not proved very enlightening. The NTs asked were hostile. Most felt that they had a strong sense of self and didn't feel comfortable with me trying to question whether there was a basis for their feeling, or asking for proof—it was apparently supposed to be self evident. Also I did make it clear that I was not talking about a soul concept, as that was even more debatable.) If everyone has this core center of nothingness, then maybe I'm not AS, or is this one of the things that makes ASers different? I can enter this state if left alone playing with water or looking at clouds. Obsessions come close to it as well, as they are so consuming that they become almost all that you are, although I don't allow myself any, as they are like a drug. Obsessed, I cannot deal with the real world or engage personas, and feel I could kill if anyone tries to interfere, so I leave the obsessions alone, especially while bringing up children. I cannot seem to get a connection between this core, and its interests that keep it contented, and what I would call a personality, or a *me*, if you like, an Interactive connection with the outside world.

My anger is another issue that is not connected to other bits of me, in a way that I can understand. If people are not particularly nice, I don't mind too much any more. I can't be pushed around, though, and use an aggressive persona to deal with the problem, usually in the nicest possible way. If I overload or am pushed into a corner, I have no control. In fact, I often lose my vision, or am not aware of processing it, and just howl like an animal or bang my head on walls and smash things. (This does not happen often now—nobody would push me there twice). The physical pain that is sometimes created by hitting myself seems to match the confusion and mental pain I am experiencing.

Maybe my overload anger represents the real me, as it represents very little control at all. It is my easiest emotional state because it requires very meager thought processes or decisions to engage. It just seems to happen. Although it is the least deliberate or controlled of any of my actions, it is the most exhausting, and I'm trying to move away from it.

People often say, when coming in contact with my personas, that they have never met anyone who understands them as well as I do. They say things like, "You think or feel exactly like me," and seemed quite pleased. I always felt like a fraud and a bit guilty, because I wasn't aware of a connection between us at all, although obviously some people are more engaging or interesting for me and this is usually when it happens. (It's as though the challenge of quickly creating a new persona to deal with them is very interesting to me: can I do it or not?) I could now say to them that, actually, far from being understood, they have never been imitated so well. Sometimes the imitation becomes almost a parody, which makes people feel uncomfortable instead. I very rarely meet an NT that I have trouble understanding if I study them long enough. By understanding I mean predicting or anticipating their most likely response, though why they do what they do is often still a mystery.

In some ways, as men's behavior is far easier to predict than women's, NTs are far less complex than ACs. One of the things I enjoy about AC contacts is that they follow their own agendas a lot. I find it more relaxing as they are not looking for a lot of reflection of themselves in the person they are with. Connecting with fellow ACs makes a lot less work for me. I find I can be myself and not have to adopt personas.

People often say I should make time for my self, or do I have any interests, or do I have mental health days and give myself little hugs (*yuuuaarrrggg!*) as they do. I have always found this a strange concept. Again, this elusive sense of self. I guess these suggestions might work, and there is some logical sense in not stressing out. But it is a hard concept to grasp when you don't seem to be able to define or even create an awareness of a sense of self in the first place. To tell the truth it's only since I've had this AS concept to deal with that I've started thinking I might have a sense of self, which is a bit tiring because I now feel obliged to work out where or what it is.

I feel like I used to exist a long time ago, possibly when I was born. I was a little transparent egg filled with liquid of some sort (mercury perhaps, my most favorite). Then the outside world tried and kept on trying to get in, forcing the egg to be aware of its own existence and the existence of the world around it. This forced invasion was very painful and the egg had to build up layers to withstand the onslaught, layers of different shapes to cope with this outside attack. All these layers covered up the egg with so much stuff that it ceased to exist, or forgot its existence. I am now trying to remember or get back to being the egg or core center and yet am obliged to remain also as something that could be called human.

To remember and experience the egg state and exist as human: maybe that is not possible. Maybe it comes down to a choice between the two. Maybe I've already made the choice and exiled myself. Maybe the two can never co exist and can never meet, or maybe that's what death is. I was always comforted as a child with the thought of lying in a grave, ceasing to be, joining nothingness again. Rebirth or heaven sounded scary; this contact with people would never end. So maybe that's what it is, in my half remembered concept of my beginning is also a concept of my end.

While I observe that I exist and am aware that this constitutes existence, the same as for everyone else, the comfort and certainty this seems to afford most people isn't there for me. This existence is just imposed on me, or was at the beginning. It is partially created by me, based on choices I have made. I am forced to acknowledge this (and in many ways am very grateful for it), but it's not what I had as an expectation for existing. That lies, for me, more in a state of non-existence as a core truth for being.

© April Masilamani

Public Recognition

Mary Margaret Britton Yearwood

I have always jumped from job to job to stay kind of anonymous. Something about being recognized means more interface with other humans than I can tolerate and so whenever I show signs of success I jump.

Starting tomorrow night I have volunteered to go back behind the scenes to go on night duty at the children's hospital as the chaplain for the next seven Tuesdays nights. This will put me in a better spot to do more of the same for pay. In the mean time my work with Alzheimer's patients is yet again putting me in the public eye. All this recognition has led to my being on Zoloft and Zyprexa to keep me from panicking about all the gaze on me.

Sometimes I wish somebody, anybody understood how hard it is for me to shift into becoming more and more in the public eye. The cool psychiatrist I see encourages me to stay as hidden as possible. But this past Friday I met with the representative of the people who are providing my fellowship to continue to do research and to write as an autistic chaplain who has special insight into Alzheimer's. Also in the meeting was the VP of the big hospital complex in which I work and my boss.

These events put me into total overload come Saturday night to the point that I wanted to tear off my skin:

- At the urging of my possible publisher, I had sent some of my writing to Oliver Sacks since he and I had met in the fall, and I had just received a letter with Sacks's praise for my writing.
- One of the big bishop bosses of the Methodist system had sent word through the fellowship rep. that he thinks my work is some of the most valuable work with Alzheimer's.
- The big VP at the meeting began to cry in the middle of one of my stories about an encounter with one of my patients.
- My boss was talking about all the national and international level work he envisioned for me since I had done so well at the International Alzheimer's Congress this past July.

All of this was going on Friday. By Saturday night I felt like I was going to crack inside. I wanted to run and hide under the bed just as I did as a child over and over again. I don't have a fear of success, as so many have told me I have all these years. It isn't the success that I fear. It is the interfacing with too many humans and the trappings and noise that come with their mouths and souls.

So why don't I run like I always have in the past? Well, all that running in the past has meant low level jobs and barely scraping by. I am hoping that this new success will mean some bucks that will mean savings to buy a place where it is quiet. It's probably a childish dream, naive and all of that.

I hate NTs sometimes because they think I am flirting when I say I am afraid of fame. They think I am like them. That I am lying and saying the opposite from what I mean. But I really do fear fame. I already have a lot of local fame and it is so hard to have people come up to me and say they know who I am when I don't know who they are.

I fear these words:

"So you are Mary Margaret. I've heard so much about you and your work!"

When I saw Sacks lecture at Emory this fall I wondered if he was on the spectrum. I sat in the back of the crowd as usual. I had written him to ask him some questions about my Asperger's. I watched as all these people were flocking to him and I saw him flinching from their touch and their words of praise. I waited until the crowd was gone and walked up to the podium next to him. He was dropping his books like an absented minded professor. I said, "I am Mary Margaret. I have Asperger's and I am a chaplain to persons with Alzheimer's."

As he dropped more books and both he and I were picking them up he said, "Yes, I read your letter. You are an interesting case."

I asked my question then, "Do you know anybody who can help me with my sensory overload and do you know if there are any more theories of how my brain is functioning?"

"Actually, I'm doing more on Alzheimer's than your area. But others are working on it. Just give it time."

I said, "Oh" and walked off.

I remember his voice calling after me, "It was nice meeting you Mary Margaret."

I was too disappointed to say anything else. I guess I was hoping for a magic pill. Instead he had no answers for me and I got sensory overload for sitting in the back of the crowd that had come to hear him lecture. Mostly I contemplated how he didn't seem to be handling the crowd any better than I was. In his lecture that night, he said the first time he was asked to lecture he climbed out a back window and ran away and that he had thought of doing that again this night.

I fear not having the means to be as hidden as my flesh requires.

Fame

Jane Meyerding

For years in my youth I was active in peace, anti-war, social justice work. I assumed everyone involved was like me, acting out of conviction. I didn't know I was autistic. I didn't know that for most NTs, every thing they do, even if they do it with real conviction, is also social in very basic ways and therefore they act/react with one another according to NT social cues/patterns even when engaged in activism for social change. Only occasionally did a window open and force me to glimpse a bit of the NT content that was there all the time for the others.

One thing that confused me was the way people kept track. They boasted about what they had done, where they had been (which demonstrations they had been to, for example). This made no sense to me. My motivation was interior, too, but it was *self-less* in what seems to me now a particularly AS/autistic way. People say we are self-centered, but I think that when we are engaged in something that we believe in (which often is a "special interest"/perseveration, and which may be related to a savant attribute—an island of superior ability in the midst of autistic disability), we often are acting much more *purely* (disinterestedly) than the vast majority of NTs do (or can do).

They seem automatically to incorporate everything they do into NT ways of experiencing the world. That's not surprising, I guess. But the NT way is intrinsically social, which means it is intrinsically comparative and thus all too readily becomes a covert (when not overt) competition. "I'm holier than thou." "I'm more radical than thou."

I got really, really sick of people admiring me ("You're so brave!") at a certain point, for two main reasons:

- It was so beside the point (and showed that they didn't have any idea what I was about).
- It was a kind of fame. They thought they knew me, and I couldn't stand it.

I had lived all my life east of the Mississippi. I moved to Seattle to get away from fame.

Subsequently, I had a couple other brushes with fame. There were a few stray people who contacted me here in Seattle because they *knew* me either from my past activism or from my political writing. A couple of times, I could not get out of having to meet these people in person. What happens is that they are very disappointed in me when they interact with me face-to-face. I assumed for a long time that this was my fault: I'm just much less impressive in person than I am in writing, I said to myself.

But then a co-worker of mine (on a volunteer project of mutual interest) got fame, and I had a chance to see the process from the outside. Being famous (she had a non-fiction book published about her work in Nicaragua and then went around doing readings) had a definite effect on her. It changed her. I'm not good at reading NT non-verbal signals/communication, but I felt the change. If I were a dog, I would say she developed a different smell.

Here's my theory: I think NT people not only read and respond to each other's signals in a way we ACs cannot, I think NT *signaling* actually effects changes in other NTs. NTs *adjust* each other in subtle ways by the way they interact with one another. When a whole bunch of them start bombarding one person with *you are famous* signals, that person is changed in ways that satisfy something in the mass of NTs (and possibly offers some measure of shielding or other form of protection to the *famous* one).

The trouble for us, when we inadvertently acquire fame, is that we lack the NT mechanisms that would cause us to make that automatic adjustment when we are bombarded with the non-verbal (and verbal) *you are famous* signals. We definitely can feel bombarded, but we do not change. We remain the way we were and are and will be, which is confusing to the NTs and may cause them to bombard even harder, subconsciously looking for the expected (NT) reaction in and from us.

That's my theory.

© Jane Meyerding

On Being a Woman

Gail Pennington

I never could relate to other females, as a child or a teen. As an adult I can relate to them better than I used to, but I still feel like such a different creature from them. So much of what they say and do is so foreign to me. I am not into clothes, makeup, hair, shopping, decorating, cooking, all the things that seem so very important to most of them.

Yet I am every inch a female. I love my femaleness very much. I don't wish to be anything other than female, and never have. I remember as a child being very happy being a girl. I guess one thing I had in common with some other girls is that I have always desired to be a wife and mother. My two big ambitions in life. They still are. It has never changed despite the many opportunities that exist these days for women to have careers. I was just never interested. I tried to be, but it was a no go. Just couldn't muster the ambition.

However, I was never interested in playing house, or with dolls. I was a tomboy in that I loved to climb trees and do other boy things, like playing with snakes and frogs. I was not afraid of getting dirty or ruining my clothes. My hygiene was not the best growing up. Unless prompted, I would not take a bath, mostly because I never thought of it! Or I was too busy doing things I enjoyed to take the time out to do it. (Thank God for showers! Very quick.) I never realized that the grunge look made me stand out in any way until teachers at school started pulling me aside to mention it. I also went through many years of school believing that if I weren't looking at other people, they were not looking at or noticing me. I discovered the incorrectness of this assumption in about the 9th grade, again, courtesy of a kind teacher.

Although a tomboy, I didn't fit in with the boys either except for my brothers. The boys thought I was strange and they let me know it. They would call me "retard" and "tartar." The only time they didn't was when I was with my older brother who would stand up for me. They would play with me and treat me decently when he was around.

When I was in home economics class I really felt like the odd one out. I knew nothing. I didn't want to know it either. I didn't care about learning how to sew or cook. It was boring to me. I really didn't like having to interact with the other girls when I would be sewing or cooking something either. The other girls helped each other out. I just wanted to be left alone to do it myself. Their presence only confused me if they tried to help me. I found it intrusive.

To this day I cannot do what I shall call the Kitchen Ritual, when after a party or before it, all the women are in the kitchen cooking, cleaning, and talking up a storm with each other. They seem to enjoy it but it is a nightmare for me to have to participate. I hate people watching me do things, for one thing. I cannot cook or clean and talk at the same time, for another. It can be too noisy, for a third. I also feel totally uncomfortable using another woman's things in her home. The only way I can participate in the kitchen ritual is if I am either allowed to clean or cut something up without being distracted by someone trying to engage me in conversation, or talking to them without having to do one of those other things.

Even in this I have to be told very specifically what to do. If someone just shoves a knife or a cloth in my hand I am at a total loss until they tell me what it is they would have me do with it. Other women just seem to know. They grab the knife or cloth and just go for it. I, of course, feel very stupid not knowing how to do that. I just stand there feeling like a dunce until either I work up the nerve to ask what is expected of me, which gets me a "huh?" look (which I dread), or they figure out that they need to tell me. Sometimes I just end up walking away.

© Gail Pennington

Epilogue:

I Am Me

Toni Sano

At its heart, being Aspie means seeing the world differently.

For me, it means I'm a poor judge of people. I can't/don't/won't judge others by their exteriors. I expect the best of everyone. I don't/can't/won't play games.

I meet the world differently. I startle to touch, sound, sights, even when expected. The need to conform and the unspoken social rules with which to conform are seemingly random.

Changes to routine, settings, clothing, meals are all traumatic.

I'm empathic, intuitive and sensitive. Words distort. Non-verbal people and I get along very well together.

In the outside world, I had a successful career as a programmer/systems analyst, before becoming a stay-at-home parent. I'm an excellent mother; my success can be seen in my four children. As a volunteer advocate for children and families in the education and social services system, I am known to be knowledgeable, articulate and successful.

In my world, there is non-stop sensory bombardment (touch, sound, light, taste). Every social encounter requires constant decoding and then selection of an appropriate response. I have preprogrammed/learned behaviors for church, meals, restaurants, casual, semi-casual, formal situations.

With these programs as a cover-up, I am able to accomplish much that is considered normal, successful, desirable. But this is a shell, and within it I'm bombarded and puzzled. Knowing I'm Aspie has encouraged me to choose a shell that is more selective and also harder.

Being an Aspie woman is both wonderful and disheartening. Now I know why I was never part of the gossip vine in my work environments. I always heard the gossip later, and by accident.

My university degree is in computer science. Computer programming used to be and still is a male dominated profession. As a young adult I had little understanding of the common social differences between men and women. I love to tinker with my computer parts and software settings.

I try to read women's magazines but they have so much fashion, cooking, beauty. Clothes are something I wear to be warm and socially correct. Food is for eating. I could and do eat the same meals for days. As for makeup, it feels horrible. Why would anyone choose to wear it? To look better. I can't get my head around why people are considered better if they look nicer.

I enjoy interesting conversations, but have little ability for smalltalk. Many women's get-togethers have a lot of smalltalk. It is my understanding that this oils the machinery of connectedness in women, but it does nothing for me (even my metaphors are not woman-like).

Now that I am 50 and looking at the second half of my life, things are looking up. I like being Aspie. My encounters with the world fit a model I understand. For years, I tried desperately to conform and fit in and be one of the gang. Now I know I can't and I know I don't want to. I am me and I am proud of me and I like me.

© Toni Sano

Glossary

AC (n., adj.). Autistics and Cousins. An inclusive term used by autistic adults to designate those with autistic disorders and others (*cousins*) with one or more autistic traits, or related neurological disorders, such as Tourette's Syndrome, ADD/ADHD, and bipolar disorder.

Asperger Syndrome (AS). The syndrome of traits identified by Hans Asperger to include a number of information processing challenges or just differences: social, cognitive, affective, and others.

Aspergic. An adjective form used in a number of English speaking areas.

Aspie (n., adj.). Shorthand for someone with Asperger Syndrome; best when used by ACs and trusted others.

Autie (n., adj.) Similar to *Aspie*, used occasionally to distinguish autistic s with Kanner traits.

Autism. See introduction. (Hate to send you back to the front but we Aspies hate duplication of effort.)

Autism Spectrum (AS) (n., adj.). A description of autism as an array of variants, rather than something unitary and highly specific.

Autistic (n., adj.) Denotation of *autistic* is obvious, but mentioned here to note that, in general, *persons with autism* eschew "people first" language (*persons with autism*), preferring to be called *autistics*, in recognition of the pervasive nature of our conditions and the inseparability of autism from the essence of who we are.

Autistic Culture. Autism seen as a culture, which autistics can participate in, contribute to, and be nurtured by, despite our asocial functioning.

Cultural Hegemony. The imperialistic standardization of a particular set of the cultural traits of the majority and/or a particular powerful, influential, or wealthy population within the larger culture.

Echolalia. A fascination with sounds separate from meaning, and often expressed in repetition.

Executive Function. A range of abilities necessary to keeping one's life together, including task sequencing, inference making, *sizing* a variety of things *up*. Many autistics have poor executive function, as do people with a variety of cousin disorders.

High Functioning Autism (HFA). This term is commonly used but perhaps lacking precision. It has been used to designate autistics who are not intellectually impaired (retarded); autistics whose communication level has improved as sensory sensitivities have been addressed; people with Asperger Syndrome.

Mindblindness. An inability in ASers to anticipate the thinking of NTs as to motivation, prior knowledge, and contextual information, which powers, by contrast, NTs are presumed to have. Concept fleshed out by Simon Baron-Cohen.

NeuroAtypical (NAT) (n., adj.) Anyone whose neurological makeup is in any way atypical, to include those on the autism spectrum, along with others, including those with Tourette's syndrome, ADD/ADHD, bipolar disorder, schizophrenia, et al., such that it has significant consequences for the person's life and function.

Neurological Hegemony. The notion that neurological configuration is an element in a culture's definition of preferred cultural values, such that certain configurations are affirmed by the culture at the expense of others, which may be disparaged. The NT configuration is dominant and therefor able to determine the standard, thereby marginalizing the various NAT configurations.

Neurotypical (NT) (n., adj.) The neurological configuration that is predominant within the culture and is therefore typical. The vast majority of people is NT. Neurotypical traits are often regarded in the culture as qualitatively superior, mandated, or absolute as a result of their substantial proportion. To NATs, neurotypicals lack recognition of the neurological diversity that exists in their midst.

Normie (n., adj.), Normal (n.). Somewhat like NT, but used by any disability community to identify those without the disability. To autistics, NTs are *normies* or *normals*; to the wheelchair bound, ambulatory people are *normies* or *normals*. Normies/normals tend toward hegemonic self-generalization apparent in blindness to the existence of other variations, or lack of awareness of the significance of difference. Normies frequently offer sympathy when recognition of the impact of the disorder and outrage about social injustice to those with it, leading to support and allegiance, are what is appropriate.

Perseveration/perseverative (n/adj.) A tendency toward repetition manifest in special interests over which the AS person has mastery, to the exclusion of other interests. Many AS persons develop careers out of perseverative interests. Aspies have difficulty mastering topics on which they lack such formidable focus.

Pervasive Developmental Disorder (PDD). As the name suggests, a label for disorders to the normal development process that affect multiple information systems.

Prosopagnosia. An inability to perceive faces in an integrated way, resulting in difficulty recognizing people by their faces, even those seen frequently. Prosopagnosia is often comorbid with autism and may be another manifestation of autism in some persons.

Social Delusion (SD). Clinically significantly impairing neuro-typicality (NT) in view of its pathology, specifically, NT hyperfocus on social information to the exclusion of facts, reason, and any direct experience other than the social; and the conviction arising from this social imbalance that others' assertions can be known without having been uttered. SD has been shown to have detrimental consequences for individual(s), family, community, and society, reports AC Laura Tisoncik.

Stim (n., vi.). Shorthand for self-stimulation, a repetitive process ASers use to settle themselves, including but not limited to finger flipping, spinning, rocking, hand flapping.

Theory of Mind (ToM). A capacity NTs have to distinguish between their own minds and those of others, which enables NTs to make more or less accurate conjectures about others' thinking as different from their own.

Bibliography: References & Suggested Reading

Adamec, Christine. (2000). *Moms with ADD: A self help manual.* Lanham, MD: Taylor Trade Publishing.

Attwood, Tony (1998) *Asperger's Syndrome: A guide for parents and professionals.* London: Jessica Kingsley.

Baron-Cohen, Simon. (1999). *Mindblindness: An essay on autism and theory of mind.* Cambridge, MA: Bradford.

Bashe, Patricia Romanowski & Kirby, Barbara L. (2001). *The OASIS guide to Asperger Syndrome: Advice, support, insight, and inspiration.* New York: Crown Publishers.

Birch, Jen. (2003). *Congratulations! It's Asperger Syndrome.* London: Jessica Kingsley.

Blackman, Lucy. (2001) *Lucy's story: Autism and other adventures.* London: Jessica Kingsley.

Blakemore-Brown, Lisa. (2001). *Reweaving the autistic tapestry: Autism, Asperger Syndrome, and ADHD.* London: Jessica Kingsley.

Brazelton, T. Berry. (1994) *Infants and mothers: Differences in development.* New York: Delacorte.

Conlan, Roberta (Editor). (2001). *States of mind: New discoveries about how our brains make us who we are.* New York: Wiley.

Davis, Lennard J. (1995). *Enforcing normalcy: disability, deafness, and the body* London & New York: Verso.

Downey, Martha Kate & Downey Kate Noelle. (2002). *The people in a girl's life: How to find them, better understand them, and keep them (dear daughter).* London: Jessica Kingsley.

Downey, Martha Kate. *Tap-dancing in the night.* Stratham, NH: Phatart 4.

Gerland, Gunilla (1998). *A real person: Life on the outside.* London: Souvenir Press.

Grandin, Temple with Scariano, Margaret (1996) *Emergence Labeled autistic.* New York: Warner Books.

Holliday-Willey, Liane. (1999). *Pretending to be normal: Living with AS.* London: Jessica Kingsley.

Jackson, Luke & Attwood, Tony. (2002). *Freaks, geeks, and Asperger Syndrome.* London: Jessica Kingsley.

James, Muriel & Jongeward, Dorothy. (1996). *Born to win: Transactional analysis with Gestalt experiments.* Reading, MA: Addison-Wesley.

Keith, Lois (Editor). (1996). *What happened to you?: Writing by disabled women.* New York: The New Press.

Kennedy, Diane M. (2002) *The ADHD-autism connection: a step toward more accurate diagnoses and effective treatments.* Colorado Springs, CO: Waterbrook.

Lawson, Wendy. (2000*). Life behind glass: A personal account of autism spectrum disorder.* London: Jessica Kingsley.

Lerner, Michael. (2002). *Spirit matters.* Charlottesville, VA: Hampton Roads.

Lowen, Alexander. (1975). *Pleasure.* New York: Viking.

Mooney, Jonathan, & Cole, David. (2000). *Learning outside the lines.* New York, NY: Fireside.

Morris, Jenny. (1993). *Pride against prejudice: A personal politics of disability.* London: The Women's Press.

Oliver, Mike. (1990). *The politics of disablement.* London: Macmillan.

Oliver, Mike. (1996). *Understanding disability: From theory to practice.* London: Macmillan.

Prince-Hughes, Dawn. (2002). *Aquamarine blue 5: Personal stories of college students with autism.* Athens OH: Swallow/Ohio University Press.

Ratay, John J. & Johnson, Catherine. (1998). *Shadow syndromes: The mild forms of mental disorders that sabotage us.* New York: Bantam.

Ratay, John J. (2001). *Users guide to the brain: Perception, attention, and the four theaters of the brain.* New York: Knopf.

Sacks, Oliver. (1995). *An anthropologist on Mars.* New York: Knopf.

Sainsbury, Clare. (2000). *Martian in the playground: understanding the schoolchild with Asperger Syndrome.* Bristol, UK: Lucky Duck.

Saxton, Martha & Howe, Florence (Editors). (1987). *With wings: An anthology of literature by and about women with disabilities.* New York: The Feminist Press/CUNY.

Schneider, Edgar. (1999). *Discovering my autism: Apologia pro vita sua.* London: Jessica Kingsley.

Shearer, April. (1981). *Disability: Whose handicap?* Oxford: Basil Blackwell,.

Solden, Sari. (1995). *Women with attention deficit disorder.* Grass Valley, CA: Underwood Books.

Stone, Karen. (1997). *Awakening to disability: Nothing about us without us.* Volcano, CA: Volcano Press.

Tannen, Deborah. (2001). *You just don't understand: Men and women in conversation.* New York: HarperCollins.

Tito (Mukhopadhyay, Tito Rajarshi). (2000). *Beyond the silence: My life, the world, and autism.* London: The National Autism Society.

Upham, Dayle & Trumbull, Virginia H. (1997). *Making the grade: Reflections on being learning disabled.* Portsmouth, NH: Heinemann.

Waterhouse, Stella. (2000). *A positive approach to autism.* London: Jessica Kingsley.

Wendell, Susan. (1996). *The rejected body: Feminist philosophical reflections on disability.* New York: Routledge.

West, Thomas G. (1997). *In the Mind's Eye: Visual Thinkers, Gifted People with Dyslexia and Other Learning Difficulties, Computer Images and the Ironies of Creativity.* Amherst, NY: Prometheus Books.

Williams, Donna. (1992) *Nobody nowhere.* (1995) New York: Avon Books.
Williams, Donna. (1996). *Like Color to the Blind.* New York: Times Books.
Williams, Donna. (1995). *Somebody somewhere.* New York: Times Books.
Yearwood, Mary Margaret Britton. (2003). *In their hearts: inspirational Alzheimer's stories.* Victoria, BC: Trafford.

About the Contributors

Morgan Allgood was born in Alexandria, Virginia on November 14, 1959. She has been married twice and lives in Indianapolis with her husband and two children from her first marriage, Tamara, 20, and Robert, 17. She never was able to complete college. Morgan is a stay-at-home housewife due to her Asperger Syndrome.

Ava Ruth Baker. Ava Ruth's knowledge of autism is both personal and professional. A gifted but odd child, she was obsessed with other cultures and languages, resolved early in life to be an interpreter, but trained in mental health. Eventually, she found her niche as a medical practitioner interpreting between insider and outsider perspectives of autism, and between orthodox and alternative approaches to health. Many of the paradoxes in her own life were explained by the diagnosis of residual Asperger Syndrome made when she was in her 40s. She is co-founder of ASK, a charitable trust providing support to New Zealand adults on the autism spectrum, and is a resource for insider viewpoints.

C. J.'s regular name is Candy but she writes under C. J. She describes herself as "progressing within," taking on daily challenges in the NT world anew. She attributes this "enormous step" forward to meeting with, working alongside, and befriending other women on the autism spectrum during the last three years. With the knowledge that she will not be judged in this supportive milieu, Candy has been able to see herself as OK in who she is and to look forward with confidence.

Marla Comm lives and works in Montreal, a city she finds decidedly AS unfriendly. She's an avid rollerblader and a dedicated vegetarian who hates it when she can't get the fresh produce she depends on. Marla was diagnosed autistic at age three, but was not able to seek supports until adulthood because of family denial.

Patricia Clark was diagnosed with autism about 1950, but was not told about it. In those days autism was supposedly caused by bad mothering, so her mother covered up the diagnosis. Patricia has two adult children by a past marriage. She has worked for 25 years, about 15 of them as a writer, but is now retired on disability. She lives in Atlanta, Georgia with her significant other, who is also on the autism spectrum. She is a board member of Greater Georgia Chapter of the Autism Society of America and speaks occasionally on the subject of what it is like to be an adult autistic and what preparation should be made for life as an adult autistic.

Susan Golubock. Susan Jean Golubock gravitated into the field of occupational therapy, sensory integration, and working with autistic children because of her own sensory differences as a child and a strong need to understand how peoples' brains worked. She self-diagnosed at age 50, and was diagnosed PDD-NOS, then AS several years later. Susan is grateful to have a very supportive husband, understanding family and friends, as well as support from others like herself through Autism Network International (ANI) and a local Asperger support group.

Coa Jonassen is a solo parent, and a solo traveler through life in general. She was recently diagnosed, in middle age, as being on the autism spectrum.

Daina Krumins is an artist/filmmaker who makes avant-garde films and more recently, digital still images. She lives in New Jersey with her teenage son.

April Masilamani has been hiding under the guise of wife and mother, along with lots of other personas, for the last 17 years. They help make her bearable to those around her and meet their demands that everything present as normal. The diagnosis of a close relative and subsequent information from AS adults opened the possibility that she wasn't the only one on the planet with a non-mainstream consciousness. Her diagnosis compels her to redefine how she wants to live her life in a meaningful way.

Jane Meyerding was born to a loving Quaker family in 1950 and spent the first decades of her life benefiting from the presence of Friendly adults (and two big sisters) in her life. "All autistics should be so lucky," she writes. She has lived in Seattle since 1972, works part-time in a not-for-profit office, and shares her home with two cats and several hundred teddy bears, many of the latter homemade. Her 1996 autistic self-diagnosis was confirmed officially in 1999.

Jean Kearns Miller was born in Lancashire, England to Irish parents March 13, 1949, emigrating to the U. S. eight years later. A driven writer and emerging neuroAtypical advocate, she teaches (something she once swore you'd have to drag her kicking and screaming to do) full time at a community college in Ann Arbor, Michigan. She's married with two children and calls the four of them and at least one of the cats the "DSM IV poster family." She is currently officially diagnosed with ADD with Asperger traits, and recurrent major depression.

Kim Motola, single mother of a teenage son, discovered her own AS when her son was diagnosed at age 10. It explained her life difficulties, which she had attributed to abuse. Giving up her childhood dream of becoming a mathematician, she focused on the power of film and earned a BA. She currently works in a law firm in Los Angeles, California and thrives on her loving relationship with her extraordinary child.

Wendy Peabody is an adult with Asperger Syndrome, and was diagnosed in 1998. Her forte is art, dragons, and JRR Tolkien's works. Wendy lived most of her childhood in Spain, the daughter of an Air Force fighter pilot. She has two older brothers, one who has an autistic son. She is currently writing a fantasy novel many years in the making, and creating fantasy art, seen at www.dragonytes.com.

Gail Pennington lives in upstate New York with her husband, dog, and cat. She has two grown sons and twin grandsons. She is very spiritual and loves to express herself through singing. She discovered she was on the autism spectrum a few years ago after researching online for an explanation to the many relational difficulties she has had all her life.

Schuyler has a doctorate in her chosen field, and is an active advocate in both the disability and queer communities. She has multiple disabilities, both visible and invisible, and because of her significant language and social deficits, was labeled retarded both as a child and as an adult. Schuyler enjoys people but has to limit social activities because of the exhaustion caused by monitoring people's social behaviors. Schuyler is a think-aholic!

Sola Shelly lives in Israel with her sons. She was diagnosed with Asperger Syndrome in her 40's.

Judy Singer is the fourth of five generations of women in her family who are somewhere on the autistic spectrum. She has some AS traits, and identifies as being "on the cusp," with one foot in both AS and NT worlds. She is a sociologist with a special interest in disability politics and the social construction of autism/autistic identity. She has published in several anthologies, given conference papers and seminars on this topic, and runs a support group for children of autistic parents.

Kimberly Tucker is a prolific and accomplished artist/photographer and poet/short fiction writer. Her writing has appeared in a number of little literary magazines, including *Curbside Review* and *Planet Vermont Quarterly*. Her work is featured in the forthcoming anthology, *Clay Palm Review*, and *Chicken Soup for the Mother Daughter Soul*. Kimberly's visual art shows a passion for texture. She is also deeply immersed in the study of anthropology.

Mary Margaret Britton Yearwood lives in Atlanta, Georgia with her family. According to the Emory Autism Research Center, she has Asperger Syndrome. Mary Margaret is a hospital chaplain who relates well to persons with Alzheimer's. She is the author of *In their hearts: Inspirational Alzheimer's stories*, which can be purchased at http://www.trafford.com. Mary Margaret is in the process of writing a book about her childhood with high-functioning autism.

2297006

Made in the USA